Hub City
Music Makers

One Southern Town's Popular Music Legacy

by Peter Cooper
portraits by Mark Olencki
foreword by Frye Gaillard

 Holocene 1997

ISBN 0-9638731-9-9
First edition, June 1997

Hub City editors, John Lane and Betsy Teter
cover photography by Olencki Graphics, inc.
cover/book design by Mark Olencki
        *The cover guitar is a 1979 Martin D-37K owned by George McCorkle of the original
        Marshall Tucker Band. It was hand picked by George directly from the Martin factory.
        The guitar would often be played by Toy Caldwell, as well as many Capricorn studio
        musicians. Two notable features are the exceptional mother-of-pearl inlay and the
        beautiful Hawaiian Koa wood construction.*
collage photography by Allen McDavid Stoddard, Ace Rickenbacker, Larry Turner,
        the estate of George McCorkle, Mark Olencki, Dorothy Chapman, Alfred Willis,
        Matthews Knights, and the Spartanburg *Herald-Journal*
darkroom technician, Karen Huff
studio technician, Christina Smith
family support, Diana and Weston
printed and bound by Thomson-Shore, Inc. in Dexter, Michigan

Holocene Publishing
Post Office Box 8421
Spartanburg, South Carolina 29305
(864) 597-0740 • fax (864) 597-4549
e-mail laneje@wofford.edu

To John and Louise Cooper and Ray and Ruth Hughes

TABLE OF CONTENTS

Foreword by Frye Gaillard

FOREWORD
by Frye Gaillard

Peter Cooper has performed a great service. With meticulous historical and journalistic research and a writing style that is clear and to the point, he has produced the story of one city's music—a heritage, of course, that connects with the stories of many other places. There are some respected musicians who trace their roots to the city of Spartanburg, South Carolina—performers like The Marshall Tucker Band, whose Southern rock sound in the 1970s made them one of the hottest bands in the world. Country singer David Ball, who surged to stardom with his quirky hit, "Thinkin' Problem," also happens to be a Hub City native.

But Cooper has produced more than a simple Who's Who, a catalogue of the musically-renowned. On the contrary, he demonstrates in the course of this book that lesser-known artists, whose talents were far more impressive than their fame, played a critical role in the Spartanburg story. The whole thing began with classical music—with Spartanburg's emergence in the 1880s as a place where the best musicians in the nation might play. Spartanburg was a hub for the railroad lines, which made it accessible, and there was a concert hall at Converse College where the acoustics were superb.

Over the years, guest conductors from Leopold Stokowski to John Philip Sousa made stops in the city, and the classical tradition became an important part of the landscape. But there was more. Pink Anderson, the great blues artist, was a Spartanburg resident, and his music became a major influence on performers ranging from Johnny Cash to Pink Floyd, a group of rock and rollers who took a part of his name as their own. Spartanburg's Ira Tucker, lead singer for The Dixie Hummingbirds, was a musical tutor for the R&B pioneer Bobby Bland and a major influence on rock and rollers Clyde McPhatter and Jackie Wilson. Guitarist Hank Garland became one of the greatest session men in Nashville, and bluegrass legends Don Reno and Arthur Smith got their radio start in Spartanburg.

Peter Cooper documents all of these stories and more, and he brings impressive credentials to the task. A musician and songwriter as well as a journalist, Cooper approaches his subjects as a peer, bringing a level of musical empathy and understanding that a more academic writer might lack. He can hear in the music of The Marshall Tucker Band the intermingled sounds of country and jazz that band member George McCorkle had absorbed. He can hear the ghost of Elvis Presley in the rock and roll beat of Marshall Chapman and the jazzy folk ballads of Daryle Ryce—and it comes as no surprise to Cooper that a country artist like David Ball once played bass in the Spartanburg symphony.

Cooper, like many of the people about whom he writes, understands that walls and categories are almost never the creation of artists. They certainly meant nothing to Walter Hyatt, who was one of Cooper's favorites. Hyatt was the force behind Uncle Walt's Band, whose repertoire ranged from bluegrass to swing, and whose influences included a little of everything. There was a player piano in the family living room, programmed with songs like "St. James Infirmary," and there was Arthur Smith on WSPA and John R. beaming down from Tennessee, playing Bobby Blue Bland and Solomon Burke. The first song Hyatt learned was a Vernon Dalhardt standard, "Wreck of the Old '97," the first country record to sell a million copies.

It was no surprise, given all of that, that Hyatt's music never quite fit the programmer's niche, and he was more admired in the course of his career by other musicians than the casual consumers of Top 40 music. Cooper tells his story with sensitivity and grace, searching for the qualities of character and heart that made the music come alive. It is one of the strengths of *Hub City Music Makers* that Cooper writes about the people as well as their songs, and there is often a sadness at the heart of these stories—an off-stage poignance keeping pace with the talent.

All in all, it's a fascinating story, told with honesty and a sense of respect. There are probably other cities with artistic histories as rich as Spartanburg's. If so, they should write them, assuming, of course, that they can find somebody like Cooper for the job. MM

Frye Gaillard, former editor of the Southern section of the *Charlotte Observer*, is the author of numerous books about the South including *The Heart of Dixie*; *Southern Voices*; *Race, Rock and Religion*; and *Watermelon Wine: The Spirit of Country Music*.

Mark Olencki

PROLOGUE

Twenty-year-old photographs line the walls of Paul Riddle's office at Smith Music. The pictures are almost exclusively of a long-haired musical sextet for whom Paul used to play drums: a group called The Marshall Tucker Band. At present, Riddle is walking excitedly around the room, waving his arms, and talking about how easy it's going to be for a group of young Spartanburg rockers called Albert Hill to record a hit record when they go into the studio in a few weeks. Paul has parlayed his quarter-century of acquired musical knowledge into a position as Albert Hill's manager, producer, and, as he likes to put it, "head cheerleader."

"They're going to have a great time. We're really looking forward to it," he says. "The only thing I'm worried about is that these guys, bless their hearts, have never been inside a real studio: they've never recorded tracks in a nice room. They're used to

making records in their bedroom and garage. I don't know how they're going to react now that they'll be able to hear each other."

Albert Hill is an alternative rock band named after a dead Baptist (courtesy of the obituary pages of the Spartanburg *Herald-Journal*) and led by Aaron Whisnant, the twenty-two-year-old son of a Wofford College professor.

Paul Riddle, Albert Hill's manager

Mark Olencki

None of the group's members were born by the time that Riddle's Marshall Tucker Band began to stake its claim in the annals of Southern Rock history, and the original members of the Tucker band broke up before any of the future Albert Hill kids were teenagers.

Not yet fifty years old himself,

Mark Olencki

Albert Hill plays to a Halloween midnight group at Magnolia's Pub, Spartanburg (1996)

Paul Riddle is the discoverer, advisor, and tutor for Albert Hill (drummer Kenny Hogan still takes lessons from Riddle at Smith Music). The band trusts Riddle completely, in large part because they know that he has been where they would like to go. If musical success is measured by record sales, and it almost always is, then The Marshall Tucker Band is by far the most successful act to spring from Spartanburg. The group sold millions of records and packed venues from hometown clubs to Madison Square Garden. Led by lead guitarist Toy Caldwell and his brother, bassist Tommy Caldwell, the Tucker band

fused rock, country, and jazz influences into something that became known as Southern Rock. Whisnant and his bandmates are much closer in sound to 1990s favorites like Pearl Jam, R.E.M., and The Dave Matthews Band. Riddle, however, sees some parallels between the two groups.

"I sit back and watch what's happening here, and it's like watching a movie that I've already seen. One of Marshall Tucker's producers, Stewart Levine, said, 'I have never seen music pour out of one person like it flows from Toy.' Now, Stewart played in Count Basie's band and also played with Miles Davis. I've told Aaron

Whisnant that he reminds me of Toy. They have the same sort of musical personalities.

"Toy was a compulsive song-writer, and Aaron is that way. Toy would go into the bathroom and come back with a song like 'Can't You See.' It was ridiculous. I swear, one time Toy said, 'Paul, go get me a cheese sandwich.' I said, 'Okay, man.' I went flying out and came back and Toy had written 'Searchin' For A Rainbow.' I'm serious.

"There's a song that Aaron and Joel wrote that's going to be on the Albert Hill record. The song is called 'Better Steak.' Aaron doesn't talk about being influenced by Marshall Tucker, but there's a rhythmic thing that he and Kenny do in that song that is straight out of a Tucker song called 'Take The Highway.' I about cried when I heard them do that for the first time. They played it and looked at me and just smiled."

"Better Steak" is, at this early stage, the song that Riddle sees as Albert Hill's ticket to stardom. It's a mid-tempo pop song with enough bite to please rock fans and a melody that sticks in listeners' heads. "We could take some bets," says Riddle. "I think you'll be hearing that song a lot. Everyone from my eleven-year-old to people my age love 'Better Steak.' Even if people don't like the band they still like that song. It's catchy enough to where after you hear it you sing it in your sleep."

Several nights of melody-impeded slumber prove that analysis to be spot-on. "Better Steak" is a maddeningly catchy song. The chorus is jazzy, almost scat-sung, and it takes a few listens to make out Whisnant's words: "The deal is that if I could find a better way to live I would/ So shut him up." A slacker message built on a boomer melody. How on earth could it fail?

But people have failed, you know. The gutters alongside the main thru-way of popular music are lined with the trashed remnants of songs far greater than "Better Steak." Likewise, dream homes and muscle cars all across America have been built with the proceeds from songs half as accomplished as the one that Riddle and his young protégés are hoping will carry them onward and upward.

"If they market us right, I think we could do well," says drummer Kenny Hogan. "But timing's a lot, too. I've got so many records at home that I love that just barely went gold."

Barely went *gold*? MM

Alfred Willis

THE LEGACY

A 1973 press release for the album that would become Spartanburg's first gold record, *The Marshall Tucker Band*, started out like this: "When asked about the musical history of Spartanburg, South Carolina, Tom Caldwell, bassist for The Marshall Tucker Band, said, 'Man, there isn't any.'" In truth, the commercial success of Caldwell's Marshall Tucker Band in the 1970s was preceded by almost a century of groundbreaking artists. And, while the names of too many of Caldwell's predecessors have fallen from popular memory, the album for which the ill-considered press release was intended is shaded by the blues influence of Pink Anderson, the guitar of Hank Garland, the gospel of the Dixie Hummingbirds, and the jazz sounds of the numerous musicians who spent time at the old Sanitary Cafe in downtown Spartanburg. There are ghosts in the music of the Tuckers, as surely as a sleeper's dreams are colored by the whine of a 3:00 a.m. train whistle.

"Highbrow Music"

For years, it was not popular music but classical music and opera that gave Spartanburg its artistic reputation. Spartanburg's classi-

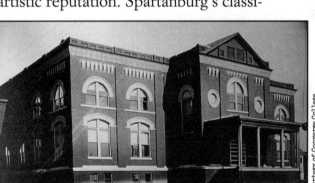
Converse College's Concert Hall (1899)

cal prominence was from the beginning due almost entirely to the presence of Converse College and Twichell Auditorium. The auditorium, first called Concert Hall, was proposed in 1899 by the Converse College Choral Society, a group headed by Albert H. Twichell, in order to meet the growing needs of a

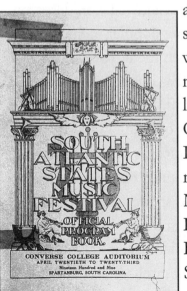

Concert Hall interior view

Courtesy of Converse College

concert series called "May Festival," a yearly four-day stint of programs that would soon earn Spartanburg a regional reputation as an arts center. May Festival was renamed The South Atlantic States Music Festival in 1898, and the auditorium was completed and opened to the public in 1899.

Spartanburg was then known as the "Hub City" and was a center for the convergence and departures of trains. A city promotional brochure in the late nineteenth century remarked that "there are about twenty passenger trains arriving and departing daily, which makes things very lively at the depots, especially with about thirty-five freight trains thrown in . . . Spartanburg is emphatically the gateway to the Western World."

The South Atlantic States Music Festival took full advantage of the town's standing as a railway center, selling hundreds of tickets each year to wealthy Northerners with winter residences in Florida. Many of these boomerang carpetbaggers would time their Northern returns to coincide with the festival, and hotels and tourist homes would fill to capacity each year at festival time. To meet ticket de-

mand, Concert Hall was remodeled in 1908 and expanded to hold approximately 1,600 people. The acoustics were, from the hall's first opening, exquisite, and visiting conductors such as Leopold Stokowski remarked on the sonic beauty of the room. In 1915, the festival was renamed the Spartanburg Music Festival, and it ran every year through 1930 (with a two-year respite caused by World War I). Dr. Ernst Bacon revived the Festival in 1938.

THE SOUTH-ATLANTIC STATES
Music Festival
(SIXTH YEAR)
Under the Auspices of The Converse College Choral Society.
WEDNESDAY
THURSDAY
FRIDAY
May 2d, 3d & 4th, 1900
Grieg's "Olaf Trygvasson" and
Mendelssohn's "Elijah."
Chorus, Artists.
Grand Organ and Full Orchestra

ARTISTS

Miss FLORA PROVAN, Soprano.
Miss ISABELLE BOUTON, Contralto.
Miss GERTRUDE MAY STEIN, Contralto.
Mr. EVAN WILLIAMS, Tenor.
Mr. GEO. W. JENKINS, Tenor.
Mr. GWILYM MILES, Baritone.
Mr. ARTHUR D. HADLEY, Solo Violoncello   SIGNOR CAMPANARI, Baritone
SECOND APPEARANCE AT THIS FESTIVAL

The Boston Festival Orchestra,   Converse College Choral Society.
45 PERFORMERS 45   PIANIST ORGANIST
Mr. EMIL MOLLENHAUER, Conductor,   MISS MAY BELL LOW, MUS. BAC. MRS. WALTER DUPRE.
DR. R. R. PETERS, Conductor

2 Afternoon Concerts at 4; 3 Night Concerts at 8:30
Special Railroad Rates from all Points—One Fare for the Round Trip.
Season Tickets to Admit to Five Concerts, Price $4.00.
On sale from March 20th to April 14th. After that date all tickets
will be $1.00 for Each Concert.
Write at once to Mr. Warren DuPré, Spartanburg, S. C., and
enclose Money Order for Reserved Seat Tickets.

Courtesy of Converse College

The Spartanburg festival drew a number of major artists, including Mme. Schuman-Heinck, John Philip Sousa, and Walter Damrosch with the New York Symphony Orchestra. Even after the festival years were over, musicians like Van Cliburn, Itzhak Perlman, Birgit Nilsen, Jan Peerce, Beverly Sills, the

SOUTH ATLANTIC STATES MUSIC FESTIVAL
OFFICIAL PROGRAM BOOK

CONVERSE COLLEGE AUDITORIUM
APRIL TWENTIETH TO TWENTY-THIRD
Nineteen Hundred and Nine
SPARTANBURG, SOUTH CAROLINA

Courtesy of Converse College

Leipzig Gewandhaus (Kurt Masur), and the Philadelphia Orchestra gave concerts at the hall, which by 1940 was renamed Twichell Auditorium.

Twichell Hall was, and is still today, also used as a place where hundreds of young people take music lessons, and the auditorium has been utilized continually for local concerts. The Spartanburg Symphony Orchestra, founded in 1933 by Dr. Guy Hutchings, was until 1995 the oldest and largest volunteer municipal symphony orchestra in America.

The presence of a major performance hall in town was often the im-

Courtesy of Converse College

Twichell Auditorium (1996)

petus for school children to begin playing classical music. "I played string bass in the Spartanburg Symphony that rehearsed over there," says former Uncle Walt's Band member and current country star David Ball. "You know the reason I did it? I liked playing music at Twichell. I loved that hall. That's a big part of wanting to play music: you see these places that are so nice. Uncle Walt's Band finally got to do a big show at Twichell in 1973."

The success of the hall over the

years may be credited in large part to the expertise, music industry connections, and general good taste of Dr. Henry Janiec. Oberlin graduate and conductor of the Spartanburg Symphony from 1952 to 1994, Dr. Janiec was dean of the Converse School of Music from 1967 to 1994. Janiec booked performances and provided artistic direction for the college. Twichell Auditorium was Spartanburg's main connection to the classical music world, and events that took place in the hall would have a lasting effect on Spartanburg's classical and popular music scene. Walter Hyatt of Uncle Walt's Band remembered his mother taking him to a number of Twichell concerts. "My mother was very big into highbrow music," he said. "It was sort of a required thing: to go hear those symphonies."

Another of Spartanburg's schools, Wofford College, is known for its long tradition of glee clubs and choral music. Many conductors, including Wilson Price, Sam R. Moyer, Roland Smith, and Victor Bilanchone have offered a music alternative on the

Courtesy of Wofford College

Wofford College Glee Club (early 1900s)

north side of town, training thousands of singers over the college's one hundred-plus-year history.

Wofford also provided a childhood stomping ground for Carlos Moseley, who served many years as president of the New York Philharmonic. Moseley's grandfather, Daniel DuPre, the first president of the Spartanburg Music Foundation, was a dean at Wofford, and Carlos grew up on campus. In 1955 Moseley joined the New York Philharmonic as director of press and public relations. The year 1961 brought a promotion to managing director, and Moseley became the orchestra's first president in 1970. Moseley was instrumental in the Philharmonic's move to Lincoln Center, the creation of a free Central Park concert series that greatly enhanced the orchestra's visibility, and the formation of the Philharmonic Radio Network.

Called "The New York Philharmonic's greatest friend . . . over the last thirty years" by the *New York Times* in 1985, Moseley has maintained close ties with Spartanburg throughout his life, keeping a residence in the

Mark Olencki

Carlos Moseley

city's Converse Heights neighborhood, founding Converse College's Friends of the School of Music organization, and serving on Converse's Board of Trustees.

Spartanburg has also spawned three well-known opera singers: Gianna Rolandi, David Daniels, and Alexander Bernard Smalls. Rolandi, one of the most prominent sopranos in the world, is the daughter of a former professor of voice at Converse College. After leaving South Carolina to attend school at the Curtis Institute of Music in Philadelphia, Rolandi made her Metropolitan Opera

Courtesy of Rolandi family

Gianna Rolandi

debut in 1979, and has since performed with Placido Domingo and Lucianno Pavarotti. She is married to British conductor Andrew Davis.

Daniels, another child of a Converse voice teacher, is a thirty-year-old opera singer who is considered one of

Courtesy of Daniels family

David Daniels

the genre's rising stars. His high countertenor voice is heard regularly at New York's Lincoln Center. Smalls, a baritone whose early talents were recognized and bolstered by public school music teachers Beatrice Cleveland and John Mabry, attended both Converse and Wofford. He has performed at Carnegie Hall and other national and international venues.

A final Spartanburg-New York connection exists on Broadway. Converse graduate Jennings Thompson, Jr., born in Spartanburg in 1928, co-wrote *Once Upon A Mattress*, a Broadway musical that recently has been revived with Sarah Jessica Parker playing the "princess" role made famous by Carol Burnett. That play debuted in 1960. In 1967, Julie Andrews sang "Jimmy," another Thompson composition, in the movie musical *Thoroughly Modern Millie*. Thompson's father, Jennings "Jinx" Thompson, was once Spartanburg's mayor.

"Singin' Billy and Southern Harmony"

Long before Converse College played host to classical concerts, two Spartanburg men developed religious song-books that remain influential today. Spartanburg's first commercial musical success was a man named William Walker. "Singin' Billy" Walker's *Southern Harmony and*

THE
SOUTHERN HARMONY, AND MUSICAL COMPANION:
CONTAINING A CHOICE COLLECTION OF
TUNES, HYMNS, PSALMS, ODES AND ANTHEMS:
SELECTED FROM THE MOST EMINENT AUTHORS IN THE UNITED STATES.
TOGETHER WITH NEARLY ONE HUNDRED NEW TUNES, WHICH HAVE NEVER BEFORE BEEN PUBLISHED; SUITED TO MOST
OF THE METRES CONTAINED IN
WATTS' HYMNS AND PSALMS, MERCER'S CLUSTER, DOSSEY'S CHOICE, DOVER SELECTION, METHODIST
HYMN BOOK AND BAPTIST HARMONY;
AND WELL ADAPTED TO
CHRISTIAN CHURCHES OF EVERY DENOMINATION, SINGING SCHOOLS AND PRIVATE SOCIETIES.
ALSO, AN EASY
Introduction to the grounds of Music, the rudiments of Music, and plain rules for beginners.
BY WILLIAM WALKER.

SPARTANBURG, S. C.
Sold by the AUTHOR, at Spartanburg, S. C.; Rev. S. S. BURDETT, Pleasant Hill; MATTHEW LYON, Cheraw;
ROBERTS AND WADDLE, Union; WILLIAM RILEY, Charleston; J. R. and W. CUNNINGHAM,
Columbia; and by MERCHANTS generally in the Southern States.
1835

Courtesy of Sptbg. Historical Society

Musical Companion sold over one million copies and helped teach people in rural areas to recognize "shaped notes," simple musical notations that could be understood by people without formal musical education. Before *Southern Harmony*, which was released to the public in 1835, most Southern church hymnals had words but no music, and people were expected to learn and teach melodies from memory. Walker's work preserved hundreds of popular religious songs, such as "Promised Land" and "Wondrous Love," that may otherwise have been lost. *Southern Harmony* was the first book in the world to print together the words of "Amazing Grace" and the now-familiar tune known as "New Britain."

Walker's wife, Eliza Golightly, had a sister, Thurza, who had married Walker's

Courtesy of Wofford College

William Walker

partner, Benjamin Franklin White. After publication of *Southern Harmony* in 1835, White moved from Spartanburg to Georgia where he published the *Sacred Harp* (1844) also using shaped notes.

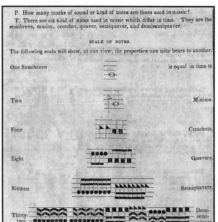

White used *Sacred Harp* in his singing schools in Georgia, and the book became competitive with *Southern Harmony*, eventually overtaking "Singin' Billy's" hymnal in popularity. The *Sacred Harp* was adopted as the official song-book for all singings and conventions, and *Southern Harmony* lost its popularity, although *Southern Harmony* has seen a revival in popular interest in the late twentieth century.

Today, both B.F. White's and "Singin' Billy" Walker's books are revered by folklorists and utilized by (mostly elderly) parishioners in Southern Christian churches of several denominations. The influence of *Sacred Harp*, particularly, goes far

beyond the church, however. Reverberations of B.F. White's work are still being felt in the world of popular music. The music of Emmylou Harris, Gram Parsons, and The Everly Brothers, for instance, is firmly rooted in the sibling harmony sound of The Louvin Brothers, one of the great traditional country duos in history. In Charles Wolfe's *In Close Harmony*, Charlie Louvin says, "If anyone really wants to hear where Louvin Brothers harmony came from, all they have to do is listen to a session of *Sacred Harp* singing."

"Trottin' Sally, Pink and Simmie, and the Blues"

By the 1920s, classical music was bringing acclaim and recognition to Spartanburg, but the best-known musician in town played fiddle, not violin. If Trottin' Sally was not the best fiddle player in the region, he was certainly the fastest. Sally would run all over town, playing bits of fiddle songs but never finishing a piece, often making strange barking noises. The Spartanburg *Herald Journal* reports that, "Regional folklore has it that Trottin' Sally used to hand his hat to the engineer of the Carolina Special, which

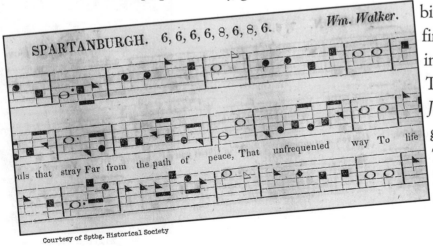

ran from Charleston to Cincinnati, when it stopped in Spartanburg. Trottin' Sally would run ahead, reach Chesnee first and wait there for his hat." (A run from the Spartanburg train station to Chesnee is approximately twelve miles).

The Roaring Twenties also marked the first recordings of Spartans Pinkney "Pink" Anderson and "Blind Simmie" Dooley, who cut four sides together for the Columbia Record Company in 1928. Anderson, a medicine show performer throughout most of his life, went on to record several albums' worth of material, including three 1960s recordings that were taped in Spartanburg by blues historian Samuel Charters. Anderson's first name was borrowed by fan Syd Barrett when he put together a rock and roll band that became known as Pink Floyd (the "Floyd" part was from North Carolina bluesman Floyd "Dipper Boy" Council).

Other Spartanburg bluesmen who made recordings through the decades included multi-instrumentalist Carl "Fiddlin'" Martin, harmonica player Arthur Jackson (also known as Peg Leg Sam or Peg Pete), and guitarist Charles Henry "Baby" Tate. In addition, blues guitar legend Rev. Gary Davis learned to read Braille at Spartanburg's South Carolina Institution for the Education of the Deaf and Blind, though he left after six months, citing bad food as the prime reason for his exodus from Spartanburg. Today, the once fertile "Piedmont Blues" scene in Spartanburg is practically barren, though Pink Anderson's son, Alvin, has reemerged after a long hiatus as a fine electric guitarist.

"Johnny Blowers and other Hepcats"

The most famous and influential jazz musician in Spartanburg's history is drummer Johnny Blowers, who was born in 1911 on Brown Avenue. As a teenager, Blowers played locally with his parents and with the Bill Davenport Band, then left Spartanburg to further his musical studies. He eventually made it up to New York City in 1937, where he began working with musicians Bobby Hackett, Eddie Condon, Pee Wee Russell, and Bud Freeman. Soon he was playing drums for Frank Sinatra, appearing with Ole Blue Eyes in Sinatra's famous 1947 Paramount

Drummer Johnny Blowers with The Harlem Blues and Jazz Band

Theater engagement.

The latter half of the century found Blowers recording with Louis Armstrong, Billie Holiday, Ella Fitzgerald, Maxine Sullivan, and other jazz and Dixieland greats. His life is the subject of the biography *Back Beats and Rim Shots: The Johnny Blowers Story*, written by Warren Vache.

Spartanburg's Sanitary Cafe was the rowdy center of the town's jazz community in the 1930s. Situated next to the Palmetto Theater, the Cafe was attractive to musicians for a number of reasons, not the least of which was that it was the only place in town where you could buy 3.2 beer. The Sanitary Cafe was a prime hangout, but the Piedmont area's nicer hotels were the musicians' bread and butter. One of the top dance bands on the pre-World War II Piedmont hotel circuit was the Fielden Cantrell Band. Cantrell was a drummer who had spent time with Paul Whiteman's band in New York City, and a number of musicians passed through Cantrell's group on their way to bigger and better things.

Those bigger and better things, unfortunately for Spartanburg, were often found well out of town. A few musicians, like trumpet player Ross Holmes and saxophonists Lewis and Paul Clayton, stayed. Trumpet-player Howard "Dad" Gaffney, pianist Alvin Jolly, multi-instrumentalist George Ed Thompson, and tenor sax man Russ Fike left Spartanburg for places like New York, Atlantic City, Detroit, and Baltimore. Likewise, Henry Letman, a black jazz banjo player, left Spartanburg for Kansas City in the late 1920s and joined Benny Moten and the Kansas City Stompers.

Also passing through Spartanburg in those days were Arthur Prysock, a jazz/blues singer, and his brother, saxophonist Red Prysock. Born in a rural area outside the city, they spent some time taking in the downtown jazz scene and sitting in with local musicians before moving to make their marks in the music business as residents of New York state. Red became a popular instrumentalist, in the Rev. Billy C. Wirtz' words, "a founding father of the honkin', hard-drivin' school of tenor saxophone," who had some jukebox success on Mercury Records in the mid-1950s, while Arthur's deep baritone is featured on many records from the mid-forties through the

Alfred E. Willis

Popular in Spartanburg during the World War II era was The Duke Chaney Band.

1980s and was at times imitated by a young, impressionable Elvis Presley.

Clara Smith, a prominent African-American blues singer of the Roaring Twenties, was born in Spartanburg in 1894. Smith, who left town while still a child to perform on the Southern vaudeville theater circuits, recorded for Columbia Records between 1923 and 1932. Billed as "The Queen of the Moaners" and "The World's Champion Moaner," Smith was a contemporary, but not a relation, of Tennessee-born Bessie Smith.

"Gospel Greats"

"It's the music of the black church that underpins so much of what we value in American pop music," says Jerry Zolton, biographer of the Dixie Hummingbirds, probably the most famous of all gospel quartets. Spartanburg's Ira Tucker led the Hummingbirds, and his soaring voice and energetic performing style proved influential to many rhythm and blues acts. Another Spartanburg-bred gospel performer, June Cheeks, was a direct inspiration to Sam Cooke and James Brown. Tucker and Cheeks altered the face of popular music, helping to develop the "hard gospel" performing style that became secularized (and popularized) first as doo-wop, then as rhythm and blues and rock and roll.

Founded by James Davis in Greenville, South Carolina, in 1928, the Dixie Hummingbirds invited Ira Tucker to join the group as a baritone singer in 1939. Tucker, who was only

The Dixie Hummingbirds with Ira Tucker

Lloyd Yearwood

thirteen years old and delivering groceries by bicycle when he joined the 'Birds, had been raised by his widowed mother and musically influenced by his grandfather, Ed Moore, who sang and played accordion. As a child, Ira formed his own gospel quartet, the Gospel Carriers, in Spartanburg. The Carriers looked to the most famous Spartanburg quartet, the Heavenly Gospel Singers, for inspiration. The bass vocalist for the Singers, native Spartan William Bobo, would later become a member of the Dixie Hummingbirds.

Bob Beatty, who grew up with Ira Tucker, was a member of the Heavenly Gospel Singers (and, later on, a member of June Cheeks' Sensational Nightingales). When the Dixie Hummingbirds made it plain that they needed a new singer, Beatty referred them to Tucker. "I'd heard him sing because he was friends with my brother," says Beatty. "At the time, he was the most qualified person I knew of. He had a lot of talent, and he could imitate any voice you'd ever heard." Soon after Tucker joined the 'Birds, William Bobo was asked to move from the Heavenly Gospel Singers to the Hummingbirds. The vocal interplay in the 'Birds between Tucker and Bobo was echoed in the doo-wop sounds that emanated from Philadelphia and New York in the late 1940s and early 1950s. Through the early 1940s, Tucker began to assert his

presence as lead vocalist, and the Hummingbirds evolved from a rather sedate performing style to the energy and vocal gymnastics that would later prove so influential to rhythm and blues musicians.

"When the 'Birds first started, they were very low-key and spiritual," says Jerry Zolton. "When you hear their first recordings, there's nothing fiery or cathartic about the performances at all. They discovered, though, that there was a new, growing taste for something that had an emotional impact to it. It was no coincidence that the hard gospel style caught on right after World War II, when African-Americans were becoming passionate about civil rights. The 'Birds' career parallels that whole period of growth: it begins with staid, spiritual performances, shifts to the later acapella recordings that move a little differently, and then evolves into the Peacock Records sides with guitars and shouting and screaming."

The Hummingbirds moved from South Carolina to Philadelphia in 1942, and it was working from their Pennsylvania base that they reached the top of the gospel quartet field. The 'Birds toured throughout the country beginning in the 1940s, giving performances and participating in competitions in which two quartets would face off to see which group could draw the biggest response from the audience. While the audiences were comprised mostly of members of black Christian churches, there were others studying the recordings. "Elvis Presley and other young white folks who became early rock and rollers were terribly cognizant of black gospel music," says Zolton. "Other people, too, who grew up in the forties, talk about tuning into gospel shows on the radio or visiting black churches to hear the music. Most white people were not aware, but enough knew about it for groups like the 'Birds to provide a model for all kinds of singers."

Some of the rock or R&B singers who came to be influenced by Tucker and the Hummingbirds are Jackie Wilson ("Lonely Teardrops"), Hank Ballard, Clyde McPhatter of the Drifters, and David Ruffin of the Temptations. B.B. King has also acknowledged Tucker's influence. Tucker also became a tutor for blues shouter Bobby "Blue" Bland, and earned further praise as a songwriter (his "Jesus Children" appeared on Stevie Wonder's *Innervisions* album). The Hummingbirds broke through to mainstream audiences during the folk music boom of the 1960s, performing to rapturous applause at the Newport Folk Festival. Millions of pop fans were introduced to the 'Birds when the quartet lent their harmonies to Paul Simon's 1973 hit, "Loves Me Like A Rock."

"Paul Simon listened to black radio in New York City when he was a kid, and he tuned into those gospel shows," Zolton says. "He knew the Hummingbirds, and he loved their harmonies. The 'Birds' involvement in that record wasn't due to a couple of managers trying to work out some deal: Paul Simon was a fan from his kid days, and that's the sound he wanted on his record."

The Simon record established the 'Birds as the most recognized gospel quartet in the nation, and it opened the doors for quartets such as the Fairfield Four to get work singing on pop records. Though "Loves Me Like A Rock" was the first example of the group's work to penetrate the ears of casual listeners, the Hummingbirds' legacy and importance was solidified years earlier. Today, almost sixty years after he joined the Dixie Hummingbirds, Ira Tucker still leads the quartet in concerts around the world.

The Rev. Julius "June" Cheeks' roaring vocals not only were the defining ingredient in the sound of the popular quartet, The Sensational Nightingales, they were instrumental in the creation of the performing style that would characterize the work of Wilson Pickett and James Brown. Cheeks was, if you will,

Godfather to the Godfather of Soul. Rev. Cheeks was also a prime influence on Sam Cooke, one of the most popular singers of the twentieth century. Known as a "shouter," grinding out expressive leads that were, especially in the 1950s, astonishing in their intensity, Cheeks left the Nightingales in 1954 and joined Cooke's Soul Stirrers briefly before returning to the 'Gales. In Daniel Wolff's *You Send Me: The Life and Times of Sam Cooke*, Wolff writes of a recording session for a song called "I'm So Glad," in which "at the end, in a lesson learned from June Cheeks . . . Sam turns the first-person-singular pronoun into 'I-uh-I-uh.' It's a rasp that would soon be called soul singing. Here, it's a gospel cry."

Born in Union County in 1929, Cheeks grew up idolizing Ira Tucker, who was only four years older than June but who made his mark in gospel music while Cheeks was still listening to the radio and working at a Spartanburg filling station. While working at that station in 1946, he met Barney Parks, manager of the Nightingales, who had heard Cheeks sing with a local quartet. Parks asked Cheeks to join the 'Gales, and June soon became

well known as a fireball on stage who could "wreck the house" most nights. Bob Beatty sang with Cheeks in the Nightingales (as did Spartans Providence Thomas and Bill Woodruff):

The Sensational Nightingales

"The Nightingales had a great variety, and we did things no other gospel groups were doing. It was a new kind of showmanship; the rock and roll bands that came later adopted our style of performing."

If Cheeks was one of Spartanburg's greatest exports, he was not the town's best public relations man. In his *How Sweet The Sound: The Golden Age of Gospel*, author Horace Clarence Boyer reports that Cheeks hated the overt racism that he had known as a child and thus left instructions upon his death that his body be buried no further south than the Fourteenth Street Bridge in Baltimore, Maryland.

A Spartanburg-based white gospel group, The Blue Ridge Quartet, was not an influence on early rock and

The Blue Ridge Quartet: Beryl Striebel, Elmo Fagg, Bill Crowe, and Fred Daniels (pianist Kenny Gates)

roll, but they recorded over one hundred albums from 1950 until the late seventies. The Quartet broadcast live over WSPA Radio beginning in 1946, and they crossed over to television in the 1960s, syndicating shows from Spartanburg to such cities as Baltimore, Hattiesburg, Cincinnati, and Miami. The members toured the Southeast in a 1948 Buick convertible, playing for audiences of up to 10,000 people, and had a number one gospel hit ("I Know") in 1975. "People around Spartanburg, all they knew was we were a Sunday morning television show," says Kenny Gates, the Quartet's keyboard player. "Very few people knew how big we were, other than our families, our banker, and our accountant. Wherever we went,

though, we were always sure to mention Spartanburg, South Carolina." In a bizarre, aurally unsettling postscript, lead singer Elmo Fagg and the Quartet were mentioned in the rock band R.E.M.'s song, "Voice of Harold" on the Athens, Georgia, quartet's *Dead Letter Office* album. "To Elmo Fagg," the spoken-word piece begins, "founder and leader of The Blue Ridge Quartet."

"The Boys From the Radio"

Spartanburg was both a magnet and a launching pad for major talent in the 1940s and 1950s because of WSPA, which went on the air in 1930 as the first radio station in South Carolina. The station's willingness to broadcast live music along with its far-reaching signal resulted in a bevy of musicians vying for on-air slots. A few of these musicians, including Arthur Smith and Don Reno, went on to lifelong careers in music in the years after they left Spartanburg.

Arthur Smith, who achieved his greatest fame by co-authoring "Feudin' Banjos," was a native of Clinton, South Carolina, and began performing live on Spartanburg's WSPA radio as a member of "Baby Ray and His Country Cousins" in 1939. In 1940, as an eighteen-year-old, he was given his own show on WSPA and began fronting his own Dixieland band, Arthur Smith and the Crackerjacks. Smith's show was very popular

WSPA owner Walter Brown and Arthur Smith (1975)

in Spartanburg, and was listened to by, among others, future legends Hank Garland and Don Reno.

After a brief stay in Charlotte, North Carolina, Smith joined the Navy in 1944 and played in the Navy band. While playing in his Naval quarters in Washington, D.C., in the mid-forties, he developed an idea for a song called "Guitar Boogie." He and his Rambler Trio then recorded the

song in a D.C. studio and released "Guitar Boogie" on New York's Super Disc label. MGM bought the song from Super Disc and re-released it in 1947 to a receptive public. The song became a hit (it made the Top 10 on the U.S. country chart) and was highly influential with early rock and roll and rockabilly guitarists. As a result of Smith's growing instrumental reputation, the Fender company began producing his "Broadcaster" model. The Broadcaster was soon changed by the company to the Telecaster, and it is now among the two most popular guitars for country and rockabilly guitar players.

Smith used the royalty checks from "Guitar Boogie" to open his own Arthur Smith Recording Studios in Charlotte, and he parlayed his new-found fame into a long-lived syndicated television program. In 1955, Smith and Union County native Don Reno wrote and recorded "Feudin' Banjos," a song that would reappear in the 1973 movie *Deliverance* as "Dueling Banjos" (Smith and Reno had to sue Warner Brothers to collect royalties for the pilfered song). Arthur Smith, with his Crackerjacks, spent over twenty years on television, and by the mid-seventies his show was networked all over the United States.

One of the greatest banjo players in the history of bluegrass music, Don Reno, cut his professional teeth as a youngster on WSPA Radio.

Courtesy of WSPA-TV

Don Reno and company playing outside of
J.M. Fields in Greenville, S.C.

Reno (1927-1984) was raised in Buffalo, South Carolina, a small town in Union County, just a twenty-minute drive from Spartanburg. He began playing on WSPA in 1940, appearing on Arthur Smith's program. After performing regularly at the station in his teen years, Reno became one of Arthur Smith's Crackerjacks. One of Reno's early fans was a Shelby, North Carolina, teenager who played in Spartanburg's Morris Brothers band: Earl Scruggs. Scruggs came to national attention as a member of Bill Monroe's Bluegrass Boys in 1944, playing in a new style that became the basis for bluegrass banjo from that point forward. Scruggs' three-finger method allowed greater speed and versatility than was possible in the "frailed" (the banjo equivalent of a guitar strum) or "double-thumbed"

(the thumb plays most of the melody while a single finger picks along) style.

The visibility that came with a place in Monroe's band brought attention to Scruggs, and his method of playing became known as "Scruggs-style," though Don Reno was actually using that style before Scruggs. "Earl came on and Don Reno got moved into the background," says banjo virtuoso, author, and Rounder recording artist Tony Trischka. "Don was not as smooth as Scruggs, but he was already playing in the three-finger style before Earl did. Scruggs used to come and shyly hang back in the corner of the radio studio during Reno's shows. Reno was actually supposed to play with Bill Monroe in 1943, but he wanted to go into the Army. They accepted him and gave him a 1-A, and he went to Burma for a few years. Reno came back and found that Scruggs had joined Monroe. Don would play and people would say, 'Hey, you sound just like Earl.'"

To keep from being constantly compared to Scruggs, Reno set about redeveloping his style. When Earl Scruggs left Monroe's band in 1948 to start a group with Lester Flatt, Monroe enlisted Reno as Scruggs' replacement. Following his stint with Monroe, Reno hooked up with guitarist/vocalist Red Smiley and the two formed Reno and Smiley and The Tennessee Cut-Ups. In their mid-1950s heyday, Reno and Smiley were among the four most popular blue-grass acts, along with Bill Monroe, Flatt and Scruggs, and The Stanley Brothers. The group recorded two top-10 country hits for King Records in the 1950s: "I Wouldn't Change You If I Could" and "Don't Let Your Sweet Love Die." Reno continued to work with Smiley until 1964, and he led his own groups for years afterward, playing regularly at bluegrass festivals and other acoustic music events until his death in 1984.

"A whole new way to play"

Two Spartanburg County musicians, Bobby Thompson and Buck Trent, found audiences on national television in the 1960s and 1970s after redefining the way that the banjo could be played and heard. While Trent's flashy gold electric banjo and country humor helped him to become a recognized personality, Thompson's reclusive temperament and lack of self-promotion have kept him from receiving proper credit for the development of the "melodic-style" of banjo playing that has influenced such modern masters of the instrument as Bela Fleck and Tony Trischka.

"Bobby should be seen as a towering figure, but most people don't know who he is," says Trischka, who wrote about Thompson in *The Melodic Banjo Book*. "He just re-thought the instrument."

In bluegrass history books, Thompson is usually a footnote, a name mentioned in passing when the text details the contributions of Bill Keith. Through a sequence of events similar to the one that resulted in Earl Scruggs receiving the credit for the three-finger style while Don Reno was pushed to the background, Bill Keith is today given credit for the development of a technique that allowed a banjo player to play in a straight melodic style, without using rhythm notes that hindered the player's ability to reproduce complex melodies normally heard (in a bluegrass context) on the fiddle. A scale-based style in which every note is a melody note, the technique is now called "Keith-style" or "melodic-style," and it paved the way for the experimental banjo work of Fleck and Trischka.

"Bobby Thompson began doing that style in the mid-fifties, and Bill Keith didn't really start doing it until 1960," says Trischka. "He learned a lot from Carol Best, who was a farmer in Western North Carolina who was doing a melodic style in 1945. Carol showed Bobby how to play melodically in the key of 'D.'"

Born in 1937 and raised in the Converse mill community of Spartanburg County, Bobby Thompson left town in the late 1950s to work with bluegrass band Carl Story and the Mountaineers. With Story, Thompson recorded his first banjo tunes,

"Banjolina" and "Fire on the Banjo." He then joined classic bluegrass act Jim and Jesse and began incorporating the melodic style into his public performances and on two recorded songs, "Border Ride" and "Dixie Hoe-down." In Trischka's *Melodic Banjo*, Thompson reveals that bluegrass audiences of the day were not particularly accepting of his innovative new style: "When I'd play one of those tunes on stage, they'd just look at me like, 'What in the world are you doing?'. . . Everybody had just heard Scruggs and Reno in those days, and anything else just blew by them."

Discouraged by audience reaction, Thompson quit playing melodic-style on stage for a time. Bill Keith, a brilliant musician who had also been working to reproduce complex fiddle tunes by playing in a melodic style, then joined Bill Monroe's band and popularized the new form of banjo playing. Thompson grew tired of the grind of the bluegrass circuit and came home to Spartanburg County to work. During this time, Bill Keith came to visit Thompson in South Carolina.

"I'll tell you an interesting story," says Buddy Blackmon, a Nashville banjo player who worked with Thompson for years. "Bill Keith went down to Spartanburg with a friend named Steve Arkin and a guy named Fred Wise. Word had gotten back to Keith through Bill Monroe that there was a guy in South Carolina that could play 'Nola' on the banjo and do all this different stuff. Bill Keith drove down from Boston and played a jam session with Bobby. Keith had a briefcase with him, and there was a tape recorder in that briefcase. Bobby swears to this day that he had no idea that he was being taped. Since then, Keith has recorded every song that Bobby had on that tape: 'Nola,' 'Sugarfoot Rag' and so many others."

Trischka possesses a cassette copy of that jam session. "That tape is amazing," he says. "It's unfiltered Bobby Thompson. It's a slightly rough recording, and in the middle of some tunes they stop the tape machine, which is infuriating." Trischka's report that the machine stops and starts several times points to the possibility that Thompson may well have known that he was being recorded, but the fact that the tape is still being listened to today by some of the finest players in the world (Bela Fleck also has a copy) is indicative of Thompson's genius and of the importance of the recording as a historical document.

After his sabbatical from the road, Thompson rejoined Jim and Jesse for several years before moving to Nashville to find work as a studio musician. "The first time I ever heard Bobby Thompson play was with The Monkees," says Buddy Blackmon. "This was in about 1967, and Bobby played on a couple of Monkees songs that they recorded in Nashville, one of which was a single called 'Good, Clean Fun.'" The other players on that session included Wayne Moss, Charlie McCoy, and Elliot Mazer, musicians who would soon join Thompson (and a number of other studio pickers) in a group called Area Code 615. The group cut two records for Polygram around the turn of the decade. "The Area Code 615 records were cool because it was all the hot Nashville pickers really stretching out musically," says Tony Trischka. "They did a version of 'Lady Madonna' that still gives me goose-bumps when Bobby's banjo comes in. That banjo sounds so good, and he's throwing in some of those blues licks."

"Bobby was the first to really play the blues on the banjo," says Blackmon. "He and I had a long talk about this, and he said that it was due to his Southern heritage of growing up around blues musicians. Bobby grew up around the blues, and he applied that to banjo."

"The blues thing is probably his biggest contribution to the instrument," says Trischka. "Courtney Johnson of the New Grass Revival did a lot of that, but I think he got it from Bobby. He expanded the vocabulary of the banjo with his blues scales, and with a blues-oriented approach."

Thompson's blues approach was not the side of his playing known to most casual listeners: Thompson was a member of the "Hee-Haw" cast since the syndicated show's debut in the late 1960s, and his warp-speed banjo is heard on the "Hee-Haw" theme song. He was heard on the *Smokey and the Bandit* movie soundtrack, and his banjo also graced hit country songs such as Lynn Anderson's "Rocky Top" (released to great commercial success before the Osborne Brothers recorded the song), Dolly Parton's "Applejack," and Eddie Rabbit's "Smokey Mountain Memories." Realizing the dearth of session opportunities for banjo players, Thompson learned rhythm guitar and played that instrument on hundreds of songs, including "I'd Really Love To See You Tonight" by England Dan and John Ford Coley.

Thompson's successful career as a sideman found him recording with Danny Davis and the Nashville Brass, Chet Atkins, Hank Williams, Jr., and others, but the constant session work may have hindered his chances of recording his own music. "Bobby never did a solo album," says Blackmon, "although he did record one single for Capricorn Records in the 1970s. He was more concerned with making a living and keeping a family together. He didn't care about the ego part of the music business. I wish now that he'd had more of an ego, because then we'd have albums of material to listen to."

In the 1980s, multiple sclerosis slowly robbed Thompson of his playing ability and forced him into an early retirement. Buddy Blackmon took over the "Hee Haw" banjo duties, and Thompson slid quietly into the hills in Franklin, Tennessee, where he still lives today. "Bobby chose not to be in the forefront during his career," says Blackmon. "Here's one of the greatest banjo players of all time, but he never even did a solo album. I guarantee you that since Earl Scruggs there hasn't been another innovator like Bobby."

"The influence of the melodic style cannot be overstated," says Trischka. "It's so unfortunate that Bobby didn't get more credit for the development of that style. By all rights, he should have had the influence Bill Keith had, but Bobby was so far ahead of his time in the 1950s that people weren't ready for it. Also, Bobby's very shy and retiring, and maybe he didn't have the drive to get his name out there. What he was doing, though, was amazing. Bobby Thompson is the most underrated banjo player alive."

Born and raised in the Arcadia area of Spartanburg County, Buck Trent was a musical wild man, an instrumental innovator and a television star. As an eight-year-old, he took a number of lessons on Hawaiian guitar (dobro), then switched to five-string, Scruggs-style banjo. By his early teens, Buck was playing on WSPA with a bluegrass band, and as a seventeen-year-old he was a regular

on Cousin Wilbur's live television show in Asheville. From there, Trent traveled to California, Texas, Oklahoma, Georgia, and, in 1959, Nashville. After playing for singer Bill Carlisle for two years, Buck joined Porter Waggoner's Wagon Master Band, and thus became a regular on the *Porter Waggoner Show* in 1962.

It was with Waggoner that Trent broke out of the Scruggs-style banjo mode in a big way. In front of a national television audience, Buck Trent began using an instrument that he had asked Shot Jackson to build: the world's first electric banjo. The instrument sounded unlike any other, and guitarist Junior Brown, who years later became known for playing a unique instrument called the Guit-Steel (a combination Telecaster-steel guitar), remembers that "Buck did some of the wildest stuff this side of Jimi Hendrix, I guarantee you! That banjo was really closer to a steel guitar than

it was to a banjo."

RCA recording artist Jim Lauderdale, a South Carolina-raised, California-based singer/songwriter, was also watching those Porter Waggoner shows. "Buck Trent always stood out for me," he says. "He was a great player, and he had such a stage presence. I remember that when I heard 'I'll Go Down Swinging' on a Porter record I thought it was a steel guitar. Actually, it was Buck's electric banjo. It was a really new thing, and I loved that mix of pedal steel sounds, electric guitar sounds, and banjo sounds."

The specifics of the instrument are remembered in detail by Junior Brown. "It had a steel guitar pickup on it, and it had Scruggs banjo tuners that acted like steel guitar pedals. It also had palm pedals on it. Buck could raise and lower strings with these Scruggs tuners. He could change chords with those palm pedals. It's like no other instrument I ever saw in my life."

After eleven years of appearing and recording with Waggoner (and, of course, with Waggoner's "girl singer," Dolly Parton), Trent began a partnership with guitarist/banjo player Roy Clark. The two toured and recorded together for years, winning two Country Music Awards for "Best Instrumental Group." The association with Clark also led to a spot on "Hee-Haw," where Trent's South Carolina drawl and hillbilly persona were on

Buck Trent, Porter Waggoner, and Dolly Parton

Courtesy of Herald-Journal

display along with his musical talent. Those characteristics were never in short supply for Trent, who is as much of a cut-up in everyday life as he was on television ("The curtain's up a lot of the time with Buck," says Trent's friend and golfing partner Ollie O'Shea). Today, Buck Trent performs regularly in Branson, Missouri.

"The way Buck went about things really influenced me," says Brown. "He was doing wild things with timing, and always put little surprises in his playing. I've always been attracted to musicians who do the unexpected and make it work; Buck Trent is somebody who rides the edge."

"Sugarfoot"

Walter Louis "Hank" ("Sugarfoot") Garland is, without a doubt, the most important, innovative and accomplished of Spartanburg's guitarists. A major influence on jazz guitarist George Benson, and on practically every session guitar player in Nashville for over a quarter-century, Garland made his mark as a studio musician who played on hit records by Elvis Presley, Jim Reeves, Patsy Cline, and The Everly Brothers, as the writer of "Sugarfoot Rag," and as the author

(c) Fabry

of the brilliant instrumental album, *Jazz Winds From a New Direction*.

Born in Cowpens in 1930, Garland and his family moved to River Street in Clifton, just outside of Spartanburg, when he was a year old. Five years later, Garland's father drove into Spartanburg and bought a five-dollar

Encore guitar for the young boy who was already smitten with the rhythmic guitar of country great Mother Maybelle Carter's "Wildwood Flower."

When Garland was ten years old, he began listening to the Arthur Smith radio show on WSPA radio. Impressed by Smith's electric guitar sound, Hank tried to amplify his acoustic. Nashville producer and guitar great Chet Atkins, interviewed by music writer Rich Kienzle, spoke of Hank's recollection of this unfortunate brush with trial-and-error electronics: "He told me he hooked an electric cord to the strings and plugged it in the wall and almost burned the guitar up."

Garland began taking lessons from Jerome Fowler, who would later teach rockabilly artist Joe Bennett and country singer David Ball. By his early teen years, Garland was earning local exposure playing electric guitar on WSPA radio with Shorty Painter. With a reputation around town as a budding virtuoso, Hank dropped by Alexander's Music House on Main Street to buy a guitar string. There, he was introduced to Grand Ole Opry member Paul Howard, who was on his way through town with his Arkansas Cotton Pickers. Sales clerks at Alexander's told Howard about Garland's picking skills, then handed Hank a guitar. Paul Howard immediately offered Garland a job playing with the Cotton Pickers, and Hank and his family traveled to

Nashville a few weeks later to meet with Howard.

The night that he arrived in Music City, Garland was featured on the Grand Ole Opry. He played an instrumental boogie number that earned a standing ovation. After the show, Howard gave Hank his first professional nickname, "The Baby Cotton Picker," and reportedly said, "Kid, you have a job here as long as I got one." Two months later, though, the Nashville chapter of the American Federation of Musicians found out that Hank was one birthday short of legal working age. The round-faced teenager returned to South Carolina until his sixteenth birthday.

Sweet sixteen brought a call from Paul Howard, who asked Hank to come back to Nashville. Garland was happy to adapt, and he made his living from then on as a professional musician. If at first his playing was overly derivative of Western Swing guitar star Jimmy Wyble, he soon matured into a remarkable musician. He learned jazz licks from Harold Bradley and Billy Byrd and, as a seventeen-year-old, was recruited by steel guitarist Bob Foster (who today owns a gift shop next to Tootsie's Orchid Lounge in Nashville) to play country-style lead guitar in Cowboy Copas' band. Hank toured the country with Copas (and with Eddy Arnold), and played lead guitar on several Copas songs, including "Honky Tonkin'"

and "Don't Let Your Deal Go Down."

Hank Garland left Copas' band in 1949 and quickly emerged as a top session guitarist in Nashville. Working at Castle Studio in May 1949 with vocalist Eddie Crosby, Garland recorded a blistering instrumental number called "Sugarfoot Boogie." Impressed, producer Paul Cohen signed Hank to Decca Records that summer. In August, after some flawed attempts to record Hank as a singer, Garland recorded the instrumental that would bring him fame: "Sugarfoot Rag."

Written as a fingering exercise (and possibly based on an old fiddle tune), "Sugarfoot Rag" was blessed with a melody that stuck immediately in listeners' heads. Knowing a hit when he heard it, Paul Cohen commissioned Vaughn Horton to write lyrics for the song, then recorded a new version in November, utilizing the popular Red Foley on lead vocals. "Sugarfoot Rag," paired on record with "Chattanoogie Shoe Shine Boy," became a hit, reaching number five on the Cash Box country charts. Hank became known as "Sugarfoot," and from that point forward was, along with Chet Atkins, Grady Martin, and Harold Bradley, one of Nashville's finest and most sought-after session guitarists.

Garland was unable to parlay his hit single into a solo career, but the rent was more than paid by the constant demand for his guitar on records by other artists. His unique style of playing still owed something to the swing of Jimmy Wyble, but it was now shaded by other influences: Django Reinhardt, Charlie Christian, and Tal Farlow. The jazz stylings that emerged in Hank's playing would in a few years form the cultured basis of the much-heralded "Nashville Sound."

When Elvis Presley emerged in 1955 as a major force on the music scene, players like Garland were forced to acquiesce to the rhythmic sound of rock and roll or find themselves bereft of work opportunities. Sugarfoot had no problem with the transition: he listened to an R&B radio station to pick up the basics, internalized the style, and worked on classic rockabilly and rock and roll records such as Roy Hall's "Whole Lotta Shakin' Going On," which was recorded almost two years before Jerry Lee Lewis' version became a runaway hit.

Garland began working with Elvis Presley in 1958, and his distinctive guitar work is present on cuts including "It's Now Or Never," "Are You Lonesome Tonight?," and "I Got Stung." Hank's guitar also delivers the famous instrumental tag-line on Elvis' "Little Sister." Sugarfoot worked a number of concerts with Presley as well, most notably the famous 1961 benefit show in Honolulu that was Elvis' final show before an eight-year hiatus from live performance. On that night, Presley introduced Garland as "one of the finest guitar players anywhere in the country today."

In the late 1950s and early 1960s, Garland became the most recorded guitarist in America. He appeared on an astounding number of classic Nashville records, including Jim Reeves' "He'll Have To Go," "Mexican Joe," and "Billy Bayou," Brenda Lee's "I'm Sorry," Webb Pierce's "I Ain't Never," Don Gibson's "Sea Of Heartbreak," The Everly Brothers' "All I Have To Do Is Dream," "Cathy's Clown," "When Will I Be Loved" and "Stick With Me Baby," and Ferlin Husky's "Gone." Typically, when the material called for the fastest guitar in Nashville, Hank, not Chet Atkins or Grady Martin, would play the session.

Garland was known for his ability to adapt his style to fit the particular musical situation, and there may be no better example of this than in his work with Patsy Cline. "Hank played strange things," says 1990s guitar innovator Junior Brown. "I remember that echo with tremolo opening into 'I Fall To Pieces.'" Without upstaging Cline, Garland provided an eerie and intriguing addition to the song. His guitar is, save for Patsy's voice, the most memorable part of that song.

By 1960, Hank was often called on to play several sessions per day in a Nashville that was suddenly teeming with hit songs and hopeful singers. To break the monotony of session work, he and musicians such as Boots Randolph, pianist Floyd Cramer, bassist Bob Moore, drummer Buddy Harmon, and vibes player Gary Burton played often at Jimmy Hyde's Carousel club in Printer's Alley. Country music was a rarity at the Carousel, as Garland's guitar filled the smoky air with jazz, swing and be-bop. The Carousel sessions led to a gig in which the musicians, plus Chet Atkins and violinist Brenton Banks, were to perform at the Newport Jazz Festival. A riot canceled the festival, but Garland and his cohorts were nonetheless recorded by RCA Records for an album called *After the Riot at Newport* (lately reissued by Germany's Bear Family Record).

With the *After the Riot* sessions behind him, Hank entered a Nashville studio with Gary Burton, Joe Morello (Dave Brubeck's drummer), and bass player Joe Benjamin. The album that resulted, Garland's lovely, intricate *Jazz Winds From a Different Direction* (Columbia Records), became a defining influence in the guitar style of pop/jazz great George Benson and marked the full maturation of Garland as a jazz guitarist. His reputation was wide-

spread enough for the Gibson company to ask Hank to assist in the development of a new model of guitar. Named for Garland and Billy Byrd, the Gibson Byrdland is now a valued collectors' item.

1956 "Downbeat" advertisement

Less than a year after the recording of *Jazz Winds*, Garland was doing session work for a country record when he received a disturbing telephone call at the studio. Hank rushed out of the studio into his car and sped out of Nashville towards Springfield, Tennessee. He wrecked the car, sustaining severe brain damage in the accident. Unable to totally regain his coordination, Hank's career as a recording guitarist was ended. Had he escaped the accident unharmed, it is inevitable that Hank Garland would have continued to expand his already stunning talents in both the jazz and country fields. Many guitarists today consider Garland to be the greatest talent ever to emerge from Nashville's music scene. If he had continued to record through

Mark Olencki

Courtesy of Herald-Journal

the sixties and seventies, Garland might today be held in higher public esteem than the legendary Chet Atkins.

Garland's career ended in that automobile accident, but music was still very much a part of his life. In the 1970s, Hank's friend Colonel Gene Wyatt, a respected Spartanburg-area musician and teacher, began helping Garland to regain some of his lost skills. Garland was soon sitting in at Wyatt's Friday night Jamboree sessions and, by the latter part of the decade,

Hank was well enough to play at a ceremony held in his honor in Nashville. Wyatt played on stage with Garland that evening, and Hank cried as Chet Atkins and others spoke of Sugarfoot's undying influence in Music City. October 10, 1979, was designated as "Hank Garland Day" in Nashville.

Garland now lives quietly with his family, but his seclusion from the industry has done nothing to lessen his influence. "Hank Garland is one of the great players of all time," says Junior Brown, who has twice recorded versions of "Sugarfoot Rag." Garland's guitar style is studied, mimicked, and carried forward by a new generation of rock, country, and jazz musicians. When brilliant Dutch rockabilly guitarist Tjarko Jeen was asked recently about Garland, Jeen smiled and said, "You mean the great Hank Garland?" Yes, the great Hank Garland.

"Sparkle Boys"

Elvis' appearance at the Carolina Theater in downtown Spartanburg in 1956 changed forever the town's musical soundscape. The resultant rock and roll frenzy spawned a number of local Presley wannabes, but one group of young rockers stood out among the madding crowd: Joe Bennett and the Sparkletones. The Sparkletones became nationally known for their appearances on "The Ed Sullivan Show" and for their biggest hit, the rockabilly classic, "Black Slacks."

In 1963, the Sparkletones changed their name to The Clefs and took on a young drummer named David Haddox. Haddox's father was a jazz musician who played with Louis Armstrong before moving to Spartanburg, but David did not begin playing drums until the age of fifteen. He first played with a local band called The Originals, and then, after a year's stint with the Sparkletones, began teaching lessons at Alexander's Music House.

At least three of Haddox's students, Burt Hoffman, Mark Riggs and Paul T. Riddle, went on to great success. Hoffman drummed on the Grand Ole Opry for country legend Lefty Frizzell, Riggs played with Carole King and Rod Stewart, and Riddle went on to become the drummer for The Marshall Tucker Band and the manager of nineties rock band Albert Hill. "I worshipped David Haddox," says Riddle. "I used to buy jazz records because he loved jazz, and that's where I got my style."

Haddox also toured in the 1970s as the drummer for country

singer/songwriter Tom T. Hall and singer Jeannie C. Riley, and he worked in the studio with Dolly Parton and Billy "Crash" Craddock. He was attempting to forge a career as a drummer with his own band when the group's tour bus crashed, killing his bandmates and badly injuring Haddox. Told by doctors that he would never again play music, Haddox is today a fine drummer and a popular teacher in Spartanburg.

"From Spartanburg, South Carolina . . ."

Born of the post-Beatles rock and roll boom and nurtured by the open-minded audiences that came to drink and listen at The Sitar club, The Marshall Tucker Band released its first album in 1973 to a world that was well acquainted with the sounds, if not the names, of Spartanburg music. On the strength of songs like "Can't You See," "Heard It In A Love Song," and "Fire On the Mountain," the Tuckers sold more records than any group or solo act in Spartanburg history and helped to popularize a then-refreshing new genre called Southern Rock.

Southern Rock, a genre that encompassed bands such as The Allman Brothers, Wet Willie, Lynyrd Skynyrd, and Charlie Daniels, blended simple, country-influenced lyrics with long, blues-tinged instrumental jams and rock instrumentation. No one

Toy Caldwell with Hank Garland at Garland's Boiling Springs home (1977)

1993. "With Toy, it went way beyond 'chicken pickin'.' He was one of the greats," says Spartanburg musician David Ezell. "It was blues and country and rock all coming together, and those hands . . . that thumb was just phenomenal."

The success of The Marshall Tucker Band allowed Spartanburg to become a big part of the Southern Rock phenomenon, attracting musicians such as Thomas Delmar "Artimus" Pyle to the town. Pyle was born in Kentucky (though the *Rolling Stone Encyclopedia of Rock and Roll* lists his birthplace as

person better embodied Southern Rock's amalgam of rock and country than The Marshall Tucker Band's lead guitarist, Toy Caldwell. Caldwell, who claimed Hank Garland as his favorite guitar player, played in an unusual style, using his right thumb instead of a guitar pick. That style was eventually profiled in a cover story in a national guitar magazine, and it is imitated by lead guitarists in hundreds of bands across the country.

After leaving the Tuckers in 1984, Caldwell formed The Toy Caldwell band. His solo debut, *Toy Caldwell*, was released on Cabin Fever Music in 1992. That album featured contributions from Willie Nelson, Gregg Allman, and Charlie Daniels. The author of classic Marshall Tucker songs "Take The Highway," "Can't You See," "Searchin' For A Rainbow," and "Heard It In A Love Song," Caldwell died in his sleep in February of

Artimus Pyle

Spartanburg), but came to Spartanburg in the 1970s after a stint in the Marine Corps and made friends with Paul T. Riddle and George McCorkle of the Tuckers. In 1974, Riddle and McCorkle helped Pyle to meet and build a relationship with Ronnie Van Zant and Ed King of Lynyrd Skynyrd, a Florida band whose first two records had included FM radio hits "Free Bird" and "Sweet Home Alabama."

Pyle lent his double bass drum to Skynyrd's next four albums (1975-1979), before a plane carrying the band from Greenville, South Carolina, to Baton Rouge, Louisiana, crashed in Mississippi, killing Ronnie Van Zant and Steve Gaines and injuring Pyle and the others. Pyle returned to Spartanburg and played locally in a group called Studebaker Hawk. When Skynyrd's remaining members decided to regroup in 1979 as The Rossington-Collins Band, Pyle was involved in a motorcycle crash that precluded his involvement with the new group. Upon his recovery, Pyle formed The Artimus Pyle Band and recorded two albums that were produced by McCorkle, Jerry Eubanks, and Doug Gray of the Tuckers. In 1987, Lynyrd Skynyrd reformed and Pyle rejoined the band for several years, leaving after recording and touring behind an album called *Lynyrd Skynyrd 1991.*

Fiddler Charlie Daniels, who toured often with The Marshall Tucker Band, played on several of the Tuck-

Charlie Daniels

ers' records and forged his own career as a country artist, was not a Spartanburg native, but he did attend the city's Jenkins Junior High School. The lyrics to Daniels' "The South's Gonna Do It Again" referenced the Tuckers. Daniels is best known for his epic, "The Devil Went Down to Georgia."

A Spartanburg native who went away to find her small portion of fame was Fayssoux Dunbar. Dunbar took classical piano lessons as a child, but it was her exposure as a teenager to banjos and acoustic guitars that helped enable her to participate in the recording of some of Emmylou Harris' classic records of the 1970s. After learning about bluegrass music through high school beau Julian Josey (now Marshall Chapman's brother-in-law), Dunbar left Spartanburg in the late 1960s for the University of South Carolina, where she met future bluegrass star John Starling. "When I met John, he couldn't believe that this young girl knew anything about Don Reno or The Stanley Brothers," she says. "He couldn't believe that I could sing harmony in the same style that Ralph Stanley used."

After Starling and Dunbar were married, the couple moved to the Washington, D.C., area, where John helped form the groundbreaking contemporary bluegrass band The Seldom Scene. It was while in Washington that the Starlings met a young Emmylou Harris. "John went down to Clyde's (a popular bar) in the Georgetown section of D.C., and he saw Emmy singing solo," Fayssoux says. "He brought her home that night, and we sat up until 4:30 or 5:00 in the morning, singing and having a wonderful time. She called me a 'harmony genius,' and we sang together a lot after that."

Later, when Emmylou was offered a solo recording contract with

Warner Brothers Records, Fayssoux Starling was called in to harmonize on Harris' first album, *Pieces of the Sky*. That record, along with Harris' subsequent four albums, are regarded as classics, and the mass-market popularity of Emmylou's early recordings helped country music to obtain new credibility and influence with pop audiences. Fayssoux was in on each of those recordings, singing on number one hits "Together Again" and "Beneath Still Waters." The Spartanburg native was also given an arrangement credit on "Satan's Jewel Crown" (from *Elite Hotel*), and she sang a duet vocal with Harris on "Green Rolling Hills" (from *Quarter Moon in a Ten Cent Town*).

"When I hear those songs today, I get so nervous," says the woman now remarried and known to her Spartanburg neighbors as Fayssoux McLean. "It's a wonderful feeling to hear them, but it's an emotional experience." Removed from the music business for many years, McLean is now a teacher at Cannons Elementary School. Most of her students don't realize that their teacher's voice has been heard by millions of radio listeners and record buyers across the world.

Another contributor to the Southern Rock scene was Flournoy Holmes, son of jazz musician Ross Holmes. Flournoy painted album covers for Capricorn Records acts The Marshall Tucker Band and The Allman

Courtesy of Fayssoux McLean

Fayssoux performing with Emmylou Harris at a Washington, D.C., nightclub following the release of "Luxury Liner" (January 1977).

Brothers, among others. His most famous cover graces the Allmans' *Eat a Peach* album, which received a plaque in the Rock and Roll Hall of Fame as one of the one hundred greatest album cover designs of all time.

The Tuckers came out of a Spartanburg music scene that was heavy on country, psychedelic rock, and 1960s soul, emerging from a pack of groups that included The Rants, The Kaks, The New Generation, The Toy Factory, and Pax Parachute. Franklin Wilkie, whose father's Spartanburg store was frequented by blues legend Pink Anderson during Franklin's childhood, played bass in two of Toy Caldwell's pre-Tucker bands, The Rants and The Toy Factory. Known as one of the town's premiere musicians since he was in high school, Wilkie became more widely known in the late 1970s while playing in Garfeel Ruff, a group which also features Greer, South Carolina's Alan Pearson and Greenvillians Buddy Strong and Ronnie and Rick Godfrey. Loosely categorized as Southern Rock, Garfeel Ruff favored rhythm and blues and Southern boogie. They played regularly in the late 1970s at Spartanburg clubs including Arthur's, Hooley's, and The Andiron Club. The band secured a contract with Capitol Records, released an album in 1979, recorded the soundtrack to a movie called *The Hitter*, and opened shows for The Marshall Tucker Band and The

Charlie Daniels Band.

When Marshall Tucker bassist Tommy Caldwell was killed in a 1980 automobile accident, Wilkie was asked to join the Tuckers, playing bass on the *Dedicated*, *Tuckerized*, and *Just Us* albums. He went on to play in The Throbbers, a locally popular instrumental group that featured Tucker drummer Paul Riddle. Today, Wilkie remains in demand as a studio musician and live performer. "Frank Wilkie is a unique and versatile player," says George McCorkle. "He can adapt to any style, and he's got a lot of soul."

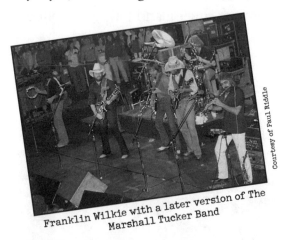

Courtesy of Paul Riddle

Franklin Wilkie with a later version of The Marshall Tucker Band

Two other major acts, Marshall Chapman and Uncle Walt's Band, left the east side of Spartanburg and arrived on the national scene in the 1970s. Chapman, born into one of the town's most prominent families, went to Nashville to attend Vanderbilt and stayed there to hang out with the Music City outlaw crowd that included Cowboy Jack Clement, Waylon Jennings, and Billy Joe Shaver. Twenty years in the music business have found Chapman recording for

Marshall Chapman

Uncle Walt's Band

Columbia, Rounder, and Island/Margaritaville Records and writing songs for Emmylou Harris, Jimmy Buffett, John Hiatt, Sawyer Brown, Crystal Gayle and others.

The formation of Uncle Walt's Band owed something to the rise in popularity of a new acoustic music venue in Spartanburg: The Wofford College Coffeehouse. The Coffeehouse staged early performances by young acoustic acts including David Ezell, Collins McDowell, and The Hyatt Consort. "It was a pretty big thing for a high school kid to be able to go somewhere and see live music," says Spartanburg music promoter Chip Smith. "See, they didn't serve alcohol there, so all ages were allowed in. It was dark in there, and they had black light posters and a little stage. I went in there one night and listened to Walter Hyatt play with Champ Hood, and David Ball was there watching them. Just after that, David started playing bass with Walter and Champ."

The group Smith speaks of became Uncle Walt's Band. Comprised of David Ball, Champ Hood, and Walter Hyatt, Uncle Walt's took their acoustic-swing sound from the Wofford College Coffeehouse to Austin, Texas, and became a favorite of such musicians as Lyle Lovett, Shawn Colvin, Guy Clark, Junior Brown, and Jimmie Dale Gilmore. A short breakup of the trio in 1975 begot The Contenders, a Nashville-based folk-rock band that included Hood and Hyatt. Uncle Walt's regrouped several years later in Austin, packing Texas clubs and appearing on PBS's "Austin City Limits," but the band was unable to secure a major-label recording contract.

Hood, Ball, and Hyatt dissolved the

David Ezell (1970s)

David Ball

AmVets club located in the bottom of the Franklin Hotel, Hooley's was a local center for acoustic and electric music.

"David used to play down there during the time that Uncle Walt's was broken up in the seventies," says Chip Smith. "He was in a combo with Johnny Morgan and David Haddox. It was a neat little scene." Smith remembers Texas folksinger Townes Van Zandt, bluesman Panama Red, Hood and Hyatt's Contenders, rock and roll singer/songwriter David

group again in the early 1980s, with Champ finding work as a fiddle and guitar-playing sideman to Guy Clark, Jimmie Dale Gilmore, Lyle Lovett and others. Ball and Hyatt each pursued solo careers, and Ball scored a number one country music hit in the mid-1990s with "Thinkin' Problem." Hyatt recorded a lovely solo debut, *King Tears*, for MCA Records in 1990, and followed with the country/swing-flavored *Music Town* in 1993. Three years later, while flying from a Florida performance to his eldest daughter's college graduation in Virginia, Hyatt was killed in a commercial airline crash.

"In the wake of the Tuckers— Local Heroes"

Uncle Walt's string bass player David Ball also contributed heavily to the Spartanburg music scene in the seventies in his position of part owner (with current Nashville booking agent Bobby Cudd) of a club called Hooley's. A former

HOTEL FRANKLIN

Hooley's

Olney, and Garfeel Ruff performing at the Spartanburg club.

In addition to drawing national talent to Spartanburg, Hooley's was a venue of choice for local rock acts, though business was also strong at east-side clubs Arthur's and El Cid. "At the time that David and Bobby Cudd had Hooley's, I was working at the El Cid, which was a bar below the New China restaurant," says Chip Smith. "We just threw some gravel on a parking lot, put up a fence, put out some tiki torches and built a stage. The first act I had down there was a band called Lightwood, with John Cobb and Kym Shurburtt."

"When I was a teenager, I'd go to Charlotte or Columbia to see a big concert at an arena," says Spartanburg musician and photographer Steve Stinson. "Then I'd come back to Spartanburg and see a band like Garfeel Ruff or Lightwood in a small club and think, 'These guys blow that band in Charlotte out of the water.' Kym Shurburtt with Lightwood was a great frontman; a good-looking guy who had the crowd where he wanted them." Shurburtt now performs year-round at a music theater in Myrtle Beach, South Carolina.

Steve Stinson's teenage years were not limited to watching other people's bands. The bass player for a successful club act called Jericho when he was in high school, Steve is one of four brothers in what must be one of Spartanburg's most musical families. Scott Stinson, now a drummer in Nashville, played throughout his teen years

with Shatter Act, a group for which mother Kay Stinson served as manager. A student of The Marshall Tucker Band's Paul Riddle, Scott eventually became known as one of the town's best drummers. Greg Stinson has played guitar in a number of local bands, including Ten Grand (with singer/songwriter Paul Finger), and Little Harbor. In the early 1990s, Steve, Scott, and Greg played together in The Stinson Brothers. Younger brother Vic is a bass player and vocalist who led 1990s quartet Somebody's Cousin.

"There was so much going on in Spartanburg in the 1970s," says Steve. "Jericho would play at Hooley's when I was sixteen. We'd all turn our heads when the cops walked in the door. We were just glad to be there, because all of our favorite bands played there: Lightwood and Garfeel Ruff and The Contenders."

Most of the local musicians who played in the wake of Marshall Tucker

The Stinson Brothers Band: Steve, Scott, Rick Willis, Dinah Cauldwell, and Greg (1992)

would not sustain careers in music, but the explosion of interest in rock and roll and the resulting abundance of talent was a shot in the arm that helped carry the tradition of Spartanburg music through the 1980s. Bands such as Shatter Act, Jericho, The Daily News (led by Mark and Chip Cromer), The Big Horn Saddle Distillery Band (which featured Barry Smith and Freddy Brown), and Lightwood ensured that Spartanburg retained a music scene even while Marshall Tucker, Marshall Chapman, and Uncle Walt's Band were off making a name for themselves in distant cities. The musicians who stayed in town also did double time as mentors for the younger crowd.

"I used to go to Frank Wilkie's house and just hang out with him," says Steve Stinson. "He'd teach me things on the bass. One time, we were riding around outside of town and I asked him, 'Why is it that there are so many great musicians in Spartanburg?' He said, 'I don't know why that is, but I know what you mean. It's just kind of special around here.'"

"The 1980s"

The 1980s were dominated in Spartanburg by two rock and roll clubs: Clancy's and Dawg Gone. Clancy's, a rock pub on Union Street, played host to bands including Rob and the Mob and The Killer Whales in addition to providing

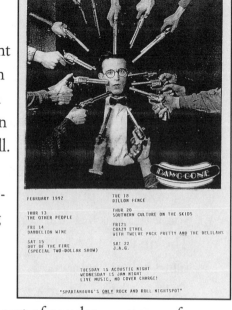

a stage for less frequent out-of-town guests such as bluesman Drink Small. Owned by Jesse Cleveland, Dawg Gone was operated and populated by its cast of regulars: a group of musicians who worked behind the bar or in front of the grill during the day and graced the stage at night. The most notable of that regular crew was Matthew Knights, a gifted rock and roller who spent much of the decade seemingly on the cusp of a career breakthrough that never came.

Called "The Dawg" by most of its patrons, Dawg Gone was the venue for concerts by performers such as Doc Watson, Taj Mahal, Jimmie Dale Gilmore, and The Shades, and it was the home club of perennially steady Homeboy Madhouse (later called Pop Gun), a group that included Jim Denton, Sander Morrison, and the Volianitis brothers, Tommy

Mark Olencki

and Johnny. The Dawg was also known for its "Jam Night," a weekly rock and roll open stage. Jam Night was hosted by Sander Morrison and was the occasion for initial or early public appearances of Spartanburg bands Crazy Ethel, Fluffy, 12-Pack Pretty, Out of the Fire, and The Cunninghams. Among the best of the musicians to play regularly at Dawg Gone were ex-Accelerators members Doug Welchel and Mike Johns, blues guitarist Allen Heavrin, father and son team Gene and Wes Wyatt, and bandleader/keyboardist Bruce Joyner.

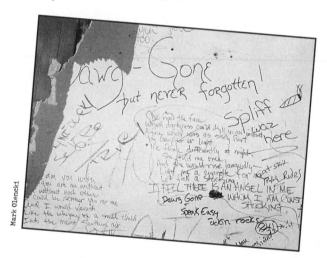

Mark Olencki

A brother duo that was not associated with either club was called The Taylor Twins. The Taylors, Todd and Allen, released a 1987 album that included appearances by Marshall Tucker lead guitarist Toy Caldwell and drummer Alan Pearson. Todd ("Banjo Man") Taylor went on to gain national exposure, appearing on ABC's "Live With Regis and Kathie Lee" and also on The Nashville Network.

Another native Spartan who

recorded a nationally-distributed album in the eighties was Daryle Ryce. Ryce's *Carolina Blue* was a collection of music that accented her folk and jazz leanings and served as a showcase for her rich vocals. She went on to release several albums both in the United States and in Europe. Ryce got her professional start playing bluegrass music, a genre that was in no short supply at one of Spartanburg's 1980s musical celebrations: Barney Barnwell's Moonshiners' Reunion and Mountain Music Festival. Barnwell and his band, Woodstick, hosted the yearly festival at the Woodstick Farm in New Prospect. The Moonshiners' Reunion was a celebration of the nearly lost art of moonshine production and 'shine runnin',' and it featured groups such as the Radiation Blues Banned, Broken Home, and The Prograsstinators.

Singer Aaron Tippin, a hard country singer from Greer, just west of Spartanburg, left South Carolina in the 1980s and hit the national charts in the early nineties with hit songs "Blue Angel," "Working Man's P.H.D.," and

Courtesy of Daryle Ryce

Daryle Ryce

"There Ain't Nothin' Wrong With the Radio." A muscle-bound performer with a South Carolina crescent moon and palmetto tree tattooed on his right arm, Tippin rocketed to stardom when his "You've Got To Stand For Something" became identified with the military's Operation Desert Storm effort in the Persian Gulf.

One of Tippin's competitors on the country charts is North Carolinian Randy Travis, a "new traditionalist" singer whose late 1980s road band was bolstered by a Spartanburg County guitarist named Ronald Radford. "Ronnie is an incredible guitar player who can play just about anything," says Joe Bennett. Radford presently teaches aspiring guitarists at Spartanburg's Smith Music.

Wofford College was the scene of a dubious admissions situation that helped to spark one of the top-selling rock bands of the *next* decade. In the late 1980s, a prospective English student from Georgia named Chris Robinson was given conditional entry into Wofford. Robinson was told that he would have to pass summer school classes at the Spartanburg campus in order to be admitted. He was unable to fulfill his end of the bargain, falling victim to Dr. Tommy Thoroughman's research methods class. Forced out of

Wofford because of his academic ineptitude, Robinson moved back to Georgia and went on to write hit songs "Twice As Hard" and "Jealous Again" for his multi-million selling band, The Black Crowes. Possibly as a tribute to the town Robinson hardly knew but surely grew to love, The Black Crowes called their second album *"Southern Harmony and Musical Companion,"* after "Singin' Billy" Walker's shaped note hymnal of the same name.

A friend, contemporary, and musical compadre of the musicians in The Marshall Tucker Band and Uncle Walt's Band, David Ezell provides a bridge of experience that connects twenty-five years of Spartanburg music. Ezell, a singer, bandleader, and songwriter, has been a force on the South Carolina rock and roll scene from the 1970s to the present day.

Inspired by the seemingly disparate sounds of soul, folk, rock, country, and punk music, Ezell fronted the group in the late 1970s called The Driveways, which became the 1980s band The Rage of Europe. Since the breakup of that group, the Spartanburg native has played as a solo act and as part of a Charles

Mark Olencki

David Ezell (1996)

Mark Olencki

Ezell relaxing during a sound check (1996)

ton, South Carolina duo with bass player Jim Orr. Ezell also spent time in Nashville as a songwriter, and his "When Will I Ever Learn," written with ex-Foster and Lloyd member Bill Lloyd, appeared on Lloyds' 1995 *Confidence Is High + 4* CD.

"...The Here and Now"

Seven hours to the west, in Nashville, Marshall Chapman continues to make fine rock and roll records on the Island label, and David Ball records country albums for Warner Brothers. In Austin, Champ Hood continues to tour with various roots

Spartanburg-bred Debbie Pilley's 1996 CD release

musicians and to release albums with his Threadgill's Troubadours on Watermelon Records. In Charlotte, Daryle Ryce is an acoustic favorite, and David Ezell plays his consistently excellent original songs in Charleston. Debbie Pilley, a conservatory-trained pianist and native of Spartanburg, released an independent CD with her band, Ila's Dress, in 1996. The band is a regular on the Manhattan club scene. In town, the emergence of John Dannert's Magnolia's Pub has been a factor in the popularization of pop/punk band Albert Hill.

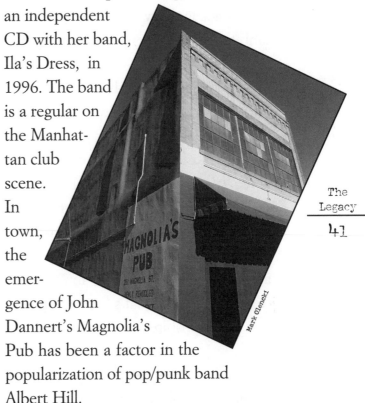

Mark Olencki

For now, Spartanburg's straight rock and roll scene is practically vacant (save for Matthew Knights), there are few acoustic musicians of consequence (though solo guitarist Brian Keenan has recently made a local stir), there is no venue for

Brian Keenan
Performing Live at
Gallery 522

original soul music, and the country/ blues styles played by Pink Anderson and Baby Tate are unheard in the county limits. The one thriving scene is alternative and punk rock. The Jitters and Jokestick have played original music to enthusiastic young audiences, and Jeremy Shlemenda's Utah Package may be the next Spartanburg band to merit attention from major record labels.

The mid-1990s have been a kind of purgatory for a town whose influence on the twentieth century popular music landscape is undeniable. "It's a shame for Spartanburg, because there are almost no venues for local musicians," says David Ezell. "You need a place for people to be able to go and hear things. You need to be able to see what's happening, so you can be inspired and influenced."

"Postscript"

This book cannot show what is happening, as a musical existence is by nature one of instability. Musicians change record labels and stylistic direction; bands develop, destruct, rebuild, and dissolve while the printed page remains static. There is, however, something to be gained in understanding what *has* happened to some of the people who have attempted to make their lives in music. The profiles that follow are as much cautionary tales as they are celebrations, detailing the dangers inherent in any attempt to live the artist's life and, hopefully, the brief moments of triumph that give reason to the struggle. It is that struggle, along with a pervading sense of place, that binds the Hub City music makers.

"Different wines come from different regions, and I think the place where you come from is completely influential," said Walter Hyatt. "The dust of this place is in me; there's no doubt about it. Spartanburg is a mix of real strong blue-collar culture and people who are into the old-time religion of Bach, Brahms, and Beethoven. There are places that have a certain energy, and this may be one of them. I think Spartanburg is a lively sort of place. It's got a lot of soul."

Mark Olencki

3 PINK, LITTLE PINK, SIMMIE, PEG, AND BABY

Alvin "Little Pink" Anderson, son of the most important blues musician in Spartanburg history, meets me on a Sunday afternoon in the parking lot of The Beacon drive-in restaurant on Reidville Road in Spartanburg. Two weeks after his release from a Greenville prison, Anderson is glad to be a free man and pleased to answer questions about his life as the son and sidekick of Pink Anderson. We drive to Alvin's girlfriend's apartment for the interview, and I present Anderson with a compact disc called *The Blues of Pink Anderson: Ballad and Folksinger, Volume 3.*

The disc, recorded in Spartanburg in 1961, thirteen years before Pink's death, contains liner notes in which Pink is called "one of the greatest of the Piedmont-style guitar-picking songsters, an inspiration to the British art-rock band Pink Floyd and to such folk-blues troubadours as Roy Book Binder and Paul Geremia." The photo-

graph on the cover depicts Pink, then sixty years of age, sitting on the steps of his Forest Street home with his smiling, suspender-clad, six-year-old son, Alvin. Alvin has never seen the photograph before, though he remembers precisely the situation and time of day that it was taken. We put the disc on the stereo, and the memories return in a flood.

"As we're listening to this, I can see that little boy that's in that photograph," he says. "Samuel Charters came to our house to record those songs. I can see that little boy sitting on the floor in front of the coal heater, listening to my father in complete awe. I was sitting there, trying to be as quiet as I could. Hey, they were making a *record*, like you bought in stores."

Pink was not the only Spartanburg bluesman to make a record—the others were Simmie Dooley, Baby Tate, and Peg Leg Pete—but Anderson was a sort of common denominator for a century of musical activity. A protégé

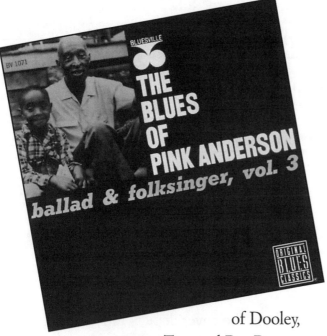

of Dooley, a mentor to Tate and Peg Pete, and a performing partner of each of the three men, Pink favored a musical approach that was highly informed by his forty years of traveling with medicine shows and playing Spartanburg street corners. Mississippi bluesmen such as Robert Johnson and Skip James knew how to draw a tear from a listener, but Anderson and his kind knew how to draw a chuckle. A tear was good for nothing in Pink's world; a laugh was often good for a thrown quarter.

A month after my conversation with Alvin Anderson, Roy Book Binder and I are sitting in Roy's R.V. after his concert at The Handlebar in Greenville, South Carolina. The vehicle is truly a home on wheels, with photographs of some of Book Binder's musical heroes prominently displayed. Pink's photo is in the kitchen area, while a picture of the Rev. Gary Davis,

a bluesman who hailed from Greenville and who learned to read at Spartanburg's School for the Deaf and Blind, is located just behind the front passenger seat. Book Binder first traveled with a friend from New York to Spartanburg in order to meet the man who had made those living room records, and he recalls his surprise at some of the other activities that took place in Pink's small home:

"Pink was selling whiskey at the time. You could always wake up Mr. Pink if you needed a drink. He'd sell it to anybody. I remember one time I was there and Pink had one of his albums on the mantelpiece. I said, 'You only have one album?' He said, 'I only made one album for Mr. Charters.' I said, 'They put *three* out.' The next time we came down, I brought him the other albums. I brought the records in, and there was this drunk lady in the living room. She was a mess: sprawled out on the couch, trying to get a drink from Pink, but she didn't have any money.

"Me and my buddy were sitting there talking to Pink, and this lady woke up from a stupor and said, 'You boys want to get straight for a quarter?' I said, 'Do *what*?' Then she looked down from the couch, and I had two Pink Anderson albums. She picked one up and looked at it, looked at me, looked at Pink, and said, 'Pink Anderson done made records!' She went up and down the street yelling, 'Pink

Anderson done made records!' I guess she had no idea."

Such was the life for Pink Anderson and for his young son. "Yeah, he was a hustler," says Alvin. "I grew up around all this. As a matter of fact, I grew up a part of all this, because he didn't hide anything from me. He used his music to hustle, he played cards, and he sold liquor. In the art of surviving, he was a genius."

"When I asked Rev. Gary Davis whether he knew of Pink, he said, 'Oh yeah, Simmie's Boy,'" says Book Binder.

"Simmie" is Blind Simmie Dooley, the first mentor to a young Pink Anderson. Neither musician was born in Spartanburg—Dooley was born in 1881 in Hartwell, Georgia; Anderson in 1900 in Laurens, South Carolina—but the two met in Spartanburg in 1916. Dooley and Anderson were playing as a duo at local parties, dances and picnics, and on city streets by 1918. By this time, Pink was already a part of W.R. Kerr's Indian Remedy Company Medicine Show, and Simmie eventually began playing with Pink on some medicine show tours. Anderson also performed during this period with the Spartanburg String Band, which often traveled to play Greenville's Textile Hall. In 1928, Simmie and Pink traveled together to Atlanta to record four songs for Columbia Records.

Those four tunes, originally issued on two 78 RPM records, are now available on a CD compilation called *Georgia String Bands (1928-1930)*. The musicians alternated lead and harmony vocals, with both performers playing guitar and Dooley chiming in on kazoo. The first song issued was "Every Day In The Week Blues," which would be a part of Anderson's repertoire for the remainder of his career. The other songs were "Gonna Tip Out Tonight," Dooley's own "C.C. and O. Blues," and the witty "Papa's 'Bout To Get Mad," in which Pink threatens, "You been flirting with the butcher/ Flirting with the baker/ Now, Mama, you're flirting with the undertaker."

Unimpressed with Dooley's high-pitched voice, Columbia was interested in Pink recording more sessions as a solo act. Anderson decided not to take the solo offer as a show of loyalty to Simmie. Though Pink had been taught to play guitar in an open tuning by a Laurens man named Joe Wick, he considered Dooley to be his true teacher. "Simmie was the one that molded him," says Alvin Anderson. "My daddy was dedicated to Simmie. I remember three or four people asking about the times on Columbia, but he never would discuss it. He'd say point-blank, 'This is none of your business.' The only thing I remember him saying about it was that Simmie *made* him. Simmie was like a second father to him, and his dedication to Simmie was

Mark Olencki

Alvin "Little Pink" Anderson on the porch of his father's house (1996)

out Dooley's life, and Alvin remembers that "when Simmie died (in 1961), my daddy helped pay for the funeral. Really, when Simmie died, a part of him died, too."

The 1930s and 1940s found Pink traveling extensively with W.R. Kerr's show, where he danced, sang, and performed comedy routines. He was not interested in non-musical work. "He told me that he worked one job in his life, and it was for a feed company," says Alvin. "He worked fifteen minutes, and they told him that he had to push a wheelbarrow maybe two hundred feet. He told them to give him his money—it was something like a quarter a day—and he left them. He said he'd been playing ever since."

While certainly more appealing than hard labor, the medicine shows were not always a great money-maker for Pink. "He'd tell me stories about the Hoover days," says Alvin. "The medicine shows wasn't doing no good, 'cause nobody had any money. He said he was so hungry he seen roast turkeys flying through the air!"

Anderson's work with Kerr's medicine show had a palpable effect on his music and performing style. He learned that, in Alvin's words, "In order to entertain, sometimes it's not

only surpassed, I would say, by his dedication to me."

Alvin remembers Dooley as "a real small fellow who wore suspenders," though Simmie must have been somewhat of an intimidating presence when the six-year-old Alvin was first learning to play. It seems that Dooley's preferred teaching method, and the one by which Pink was "molded," involved a stick. Pink later lamented to Samuel Charters that Simmie "gave me the devil when I missed one," and Simmie attempted to use the same methods on young Alvin before Pink put a stop to that. Regardless, Pink and Simmie remained friends through-good enough just to be a musician." Comedy became a large factor in Pink's act, and his songs were, unlike traditional Mississippi-style blues, more likely to provoke a grin than a tear. "Pink was doing *schtik*, as they say," says Book Binder. "He exaggerated his accent, and he rolled his eyes. In a lot of ways, he was doing a parody of a black singer. You couldn't call it blackface, but in a lot of ways that's what he was doing."

It was 1950 before Anderson would record again. Playing at the Virginia State Fair in Charlottesville, he was recorded by Paul Clayton in May of that year. Those seven performances, compiled along with eight songs by the Rev. Gary Davis on a CD called *Gospel, Blues and Street Songs*, are often considered the finest of Pink's sporadic recording career. "He was at the top of his form on that record," says Book Binder. The song selections were typical of Anderson's medicine show and street singing sets, mixing traditional folk songs "John Henry" and "Wreck of the Old '97" with humorous minstrel tunes such as "Greasy Greens" and "I've Got Mine." Pink's playing was vibrant, and his

vocal delivery was impeccable as he boasted in song that "Ever since that big crap game/ I've been living on chicken and wine" and hypothesized about proper collard preparation: "That meat you use must be fat/ To keep them greens greasy like that/ If you don't use nothin' but natural lean/ You can't cook no good greasy greens."

It was the Charlottesville recordings that, unknown to Pink, became influential to country music's Johnny Cash. The connection is documented in at least two places. In the liner notes to his *American Recordings* album, Cash writes, "When I heard a Carolina street singer named Pink Anderson and a gospel singer named Sister Rosetta Thorpe, it was confirmed in my mind that I didn't have to learn to play like Chet Atkins. As a matter of fact, I didn't even have to use a pick." Freed from concerns about technical prowess, Cash went on to record sparse, musically rudimentary hits like "I Walk the Line" and "Folsom Prison Blues."

One Cash hit from the 1950s, "Big River," may have been inspired directly by Anderson's music. In his 1996 autobiography, Waylon Jennings writes that Cash wrote that particular song "after listening to Delta-influenced blues singers like Robert Johnson and Pink Anderson." While Anderson was not in any way Delta-influenced, it appears that Cash was smitten with his conversational singing and spare folk ballads.

By now, Pink was working with Chief Thundercloud's medicine show, often playing with harmonica player and fledgling comedian Arthur Jackson, who was known as "Peg Leg Sam" or "Peg Leg Pete" (so-called ever since an unfortunate situation involving Jackson's right leg and a train). Anderson and Peg Leg had begun working together in the late 1930s, with Peg acting as the straight man in their routines. "They got 'Peg Leg Sam' on the album cover, but nobody ever called him Sam," says Alvin. "His name was Pete. Peg Pete was the first one to ever take me fishing. He lived in Jonesville, but he hung out in Spartanburg a lot."

In his 1971 book, *Crying For the Carolinas*, folklorist Bruce Bastin reported that Peg referred to himself as "'the ugliest damn Negro in the world,' a statement which has some claim to accuracy." Bastin went on to describe Peg's appearance in the following manner:

> *He has a severe cut across the right side of his face which was incorrectly treated and left a bad scar on his cheek, disfigured one of his ears, and appears to have affected his vision, pulling down the*

corner of his eyes. Another, rather less damaging scar adorns the other cheek, and a further cut is on his left breast. He has lost his right leg above the knee in an accident in Raleigh and has a Sonny Boy Williamson goatee . . . an altogether remarkable sight.

BORN: DECEMBER 18, 1908 OR 1911
PLACE: SPARTENBURG, S.C.
DIED: NOVEMBER 1978
NAME AT BIRTH: ARTHUR JACKSON
NAME AT DEATH: PEG LEG SAM.

"Pete was the only man I'd ever seen play harmonica with his nose, and that's the God's Heaven truth," says Alvin. "I even seen him take it around to his ear and get a note out of it. This man blew the harmonica with his ear! How he did it I will never know, but I saw this and heard this. Peg was one of the biggest clowns I ever saw in my life, and he could tap dance his butt off with that peg leg."

The mid-1950s found Pink spending much more time at home in Spartanburg. The medicine show seasons were shorter now that W.R. Kerr's show was no longer in existence, and heart troubles caused Pink to cut back on traveling. He played many days for thrown quarters, dimes, and nickels on the streets of Spartanburg, and he also profited from selling bootleg whiskey. It was during this time period that Alvin was born. By the time the son was five, tensions began to develop between Pink and Alvin's mother, who were not married, over the young boy's inclination towards following in his father's footsteps.

"I remember him and my mother falling out once. They had a fight about a possum. See, my daddy ate possum, but my mama was scared of a possum. Daddy had this lady staying up on Highland Avenue, behind Franklin Wilkie's grocery (Wilkie's son, Franklin Jr., would later become a member of The Marshall Tucker Band and of Garfeel Ruff). That lady would cook possum for him. This is before I was even old enough to be in school. I was with him, and we went up to the house and ate possum, 'cause whatever he did, I wanted to do. We come out the door, and there stood my mother. My mother asked me what I'd been doing, and I told her I'd been eating, and Jee-sus Christ did all Hell break loose! I remember her swinging at my daddy and saying, 'You got that boy eating that ol' nasty stuff!' See, I just wanted to follow him and do what he was doing."

In 1961, when Alvin was six years old, his mother died. "When my mama died, I was crying. He said, 'I can't stop you from crying, and I know you're gonna miss your mama, but you still got me.' When he said that, he proved it. He was mother and father to me from 1961 to 1974. He was everything to me. I can remember hearing him praying: he would ask to be able to take care of me, and to live long enough to see me get grown."

Samuel Charters came to Spartanburg to record Pink Anderson later in 1961, and Alvin was there for those sessions. The boy also tagged along with Pink on gigs in and out of Spartanburg. "He'd play up at Franklin Wilkie's store. He used to set up in front of the store with his guitar and his records. I'd get my little guitar and my little hat, and I'd try to play. Mostly,

I'd collect money. Even today, a lot of older people from that time remember my face. My name has never been Alvin in Spartanburg: it's always been Little Pink.

"When I'd play with my old man on the street, the people would give me quarters and dimes and nickels. So my pockets were fatter than any kid's in this town. He made me accustomed to guns and money. Both of them will get you into trouble, and he thought if you were used to them as a child that you'd know how to handle them when you got older. I'd walk around the house with real pistols strapped on my side, or play 'Cowboys and Indians' with real guns."

Alvin also became well-acquainted with the non-musical addendums to Pink's income. "He sold white lightning, and for every quarter shot of liquor I sold, I kept the quarter. Fifty-cent shots and up, he'd keep. He kept the liquor buried beneath the ground, and he had a dog named Dad that would lay on top of the ground where that liquor was. Back then, the young boys would come along and steal the bootleggers' liquor. They came up on that dog one night, pushed the dog off the stash, dug it up, covered the hole back up, and put the dog back over the hole! That sorry dog never even barked: he wouldn't do nothing but eat, but my daddy was crazy about that dog. He used to tell me, 'That's all you do, too,

and I'm crazy about you.'

"He also had a pen by the side of the house where he kept his turkey. He had a turkey named Henry, and that turkey was just like a dog. That turkey would run me to school in the morning. My old man would say, 'Henry, take him to school,' and I had to go. I would run all the way to school, and that turkey would follow me there and then go back home. One time, a policeman named Wyatt came over to search the house for white lightning. That policeman went in the turkey pen and bends over, and the turkey took his beak and stuck it in the policeman's leg! The policeman was getting ready to shoot the turkey, and my daddy was looking out the window, saying, 'You shoot that turkey, I'm gonna kill you.' The man left."

Pink's Forest Street home was the center of all sorts of activity, legal and otherwise, and it was a gathering place for musicians. Pink's friend (and another of his medicine show side-kicks) Baby Tate, with whom he began playing in 1954, was often around, as was Peg Leg Pete. "You'd be surprised at what you would see on any given day at my house," says Alvin. "At any time, Daddy, Peg, Baby Tate, another guy called Pete Taylor . . . they would all sit around. If it's

summertime and you catch 'em sitting outdoors, they got a jug full of ice water and a jar of white lightning, and there would be a crowd out there! The whole neighborhood would be there, with kids out dancing. Those men ain't tryin' to sell no snake oil, but they're putting on a show. It would last three or four hours sometimes. I think it was a better show than any concert I've been to in my life. When I sit back and look at it, I see the history that was there. Not just the history of black people, but the history of music."

Those front yard concerts featured three musicians whose recordings would eventually be released on compact disc. When Sam Charters came in 1961 to record Anderson, he also recorded Baby Tate. A Spartanburg bricklayer when he wasn't traveling the medicine shows, Tate's blues guitar playing was closer to Piedmont bluesmen like Blind Boy Fuller than to Anderson's vaudeville-styled work. His *See What You Done Done* featured an impressive version of "Dupree Blues," and the album, while not as original or inspired as the best work of Pink Anderson, is a credible example of traditional Carolina blues.

Peg Leg Pete's harmonica style, while it was based on the traditional, was often quite inventive. He was prone to lightning quick bursts of musical emotion, and his medicine show upbringing had taught him how to gain and hold the listener's atten-

tion. Playing two harps at once, one through his mouth and one through his nose, was a good start towards that end. In his exceptional book, *Red River Blues*, Bruce Bastin writes "there cannot have been too many performers of the equal of Peg Leg Sam." Several albums' worth of material were released under the name "Peg Leg Sam," including Trix Records' *Peg Leg Sam: Medicine Show Man* (which boasts backing guitar by Baby Tate, who often served as Peg's medicine show partner), Tomato Records' *Joshua*, featuring Louisiana Red, and Flyright's *Carolina Country Blues and The Last Medicine Show*. Peg also appeared in Tom Davenport's film, *Born In Hard Luck*.

As for Pink's three albums that were recorded in 1961, they are excellent summations of the breadth of his artistry. The first volume, called *Carolina Blues Man*, includes a number of traditional Piedmont blues tunes (many of which were learned from Baby Tate), and adds the vaudeville numbers "Every Day in the Week" and "Try Some of That." Volume three, *Ballad and Folksinger*, features folk songs such as "The Titanic," "Wreck of the Old '97," and "Boweevil." The second volume, currently out of print, is by far the most interesting. Titled *Pink Anderson: Medicine Show Man*, it contains his best-known original song, "Travelin' Man," as well as a new version of "Greasy Greens." Six-year-old Alvin Anderson makes his debut on the album, singing with Pink on "Old Cotton Fields Back Home."

None of the three albums were big sellers, even for blues standards, but they were fairly influential. British art student Syd Barrett heard the material and became a fan. Barrett went on to include Anderson's first name in the name of his enormously successful rock band, Pink Floyd. Fledgling bluesmen Roy Book Binder and Paul Geremia bought copies in the late 1960s, and they both became interested enough in Anderson's vaudeville-styled blues to seek Pink out in Spartanburg. "Charters recorded thousands of people," says Book Binder. "Out of the 300 albums he put out, there were maybe twenty important records. Volume II of Pink's (*Medicine Show Man*) was *very* important. Pink's style of playing had been all the rage in the black community from about 1927 to 1937, but Pink didn't realize until Charters came down that there was an interest in this archaic art form."

Pink was paid $300 for his efforts on the records. Unaware until years later that Prestige Records had issued more than one album's worth of material from those living room sessions, Pink, normally the hustler, was being hustled. It is difficult to blame Samuel Charters, who was simply on a quest to record as many blues performers as he could as

quickly as possible. Prestige Records, however, could certainly have done a better job keeping Pink apprised of the efforts being made to market his music. At the least, the record company should have been sending statements to Pink concerning albums sold and money made, and those statements should have been accompanied by royalty checks.

Sam Charters came back to Spartanburg in 1962, working with his wife on a documentary film called *The Blues*. Charters shot some footage of Baby Tate and also filmed Pink in his back yard giving Alvin a music lesson. Finally, Charters and Anderson recorded some final sides of material that later ended up on a Folkways Records album called *Pink Anderson: Carolina Medicine Show Hokum and Blues*. This record was not released until after Pink's death. Charters' liner notes for the Folkways album concluded by saying, "Pink's music died with him, and though what he sang was part of a small, out-of-date, half-forgotten song tradition, our own musical experience is poorer without him."

For a total of one film appearance and six records that influenced Johnny Cash, Pink Floyd, Roy Book Binder, Paul Geremia, and perhaps many others, Anderson's career recording earnings amounted to less than $1,000. It's a good thing the man knew how to peddle whiskey, for otherwise he might have starved to death.

Having concluded his career on record and in movies by autumn of 1962, Pink went back to playing the streets of Spartanburg, often setting up at Franklin Wilkie's grocery, and back to traveling with Chief Thundercloud's medicine show. Pink's son, now seven, had begun traveling sporadically with his father on the medicine show trips when the boy was five years old. He was now a Chief Thundercloud regular, playing pint-sized side man to his father's practiced "draw" man (meaning Pink's performance was "the main draw"). "I got paid about five dollars per show, which was a lot of money for a little kid," says Alvin. "I would come out on stage after his first song, and by my being so young it was a gimmick. I'd go up there with my little black Stella guitar. By the age of six, I could read a crowd easy. They even taught me how to do my own makeup. I could paint his face and mine at that early age without messing up.

"One time, he said he was too sick to go on. To this day, I don't believe he was sick: I believe he faked it as a confidence builder to me. There wasn't but one person there to take his place, and that was me. I was six years old, and I'm just dying to do this! I'm dying to do this because I'm getting to do what he did, and I'm getting

to do it by myself. That made me feel as tall as he was."

The dynamics of the relationship between Pink and Alvin are difficult to grasp for people separated by years and social station from the carnival life. No parenting guides would condone allowing a six-year-old to walk the neighborhood with real pistols strapped to his waist, using a small child to sell bootleg liquor, or even taking a kid of Alvin's age on the road with the medicine show. Alvin's later problems with the law might seem traceable to those formative years, though he protests that "he didn't raise me to do those crazy things that I did. I wasn't raised to want to go out and fight and do all this other crazy stuff: I was raised to play music. I was raised walking the streets with a black Stella guitar in my hand."

In fact, most of Alvin's troubles seemed to occur when he was not around Pink. The father and son lived in a dilapidated neighborhood where trouble was easily found. "I hurt him," says Alvin. "I hurt him because I got

Pink Anderson's sidewalk at 383 Carpenter Street (1996)

Mark Olencki

wild. But it was partly survival. He provided everything I needed, but I couldn't stay in the house all the time.

I had to fight. If you didn't fight the big boys back then, they would jump on you and take everything you got."

There were advantages to being Pink Anderson's son that extended beyond the easy acquisition of quarters and dimes. Unlike most of Spartanburg's black citizens, Pink's reputation as a musician allowed him access to all parts of town and discouraged overt (read: violent) racism towards Alvin. "When people started talking about segregation and racism, I was lost," says Alvin. "I couldn't associate segregation because I never had to deal with it because I was Pink's son. He could pick up his guitar and walk anywhere, and nobody ever bothered him. He was a man who tended to break the barriers.

"There was a hot dog stand here called Pearson's, and he used to go in there and play. There was a black side and a white side to that restaurant, but there were no boundaries as to which side we had to be on. I had a free hand in Spartanburg because of him. I could go up to Montgomery Ward and get a bicycle. He didn't even have to be there. They knew to give it to me and put it on his bill. I could go anywhere, and I was always recognized as Pink Anderson's son."

Alvin was almost ten years old when his father suffered a stroke that severely hampered his ability to play music. The stroke, which hit Anderson some months after playing a "legiti-

mate" gig at Clemson University with Baby Tate, was extremely serious. "The doctors said he would never play again," says Alvin, yet Pink eventually regained about ninety percent of his skill. "After the stroke, he stopped trying to play much in front of crowds, but he still played at home."

For years after the stroke, Pink was basically confined to his home, where he still sold liquor by the drink, gambled, and rented his back room by the hour to amorous neighbors. Alvin learned to play electric, Albert King-style blues guitar and spent more and more time out of the house. By the late 1960s, the name of Pink Anderson was known to acoustic blues enthusiasts around the United States and Europe, the Pink Floyd rock band had been formed in England, and Johnny Cash's "Big River" had long since become a part of the rockabilly and country music canons. Still, few people in Spartanburg realized the legendary status of the old man who used to play street corners but who now stayed in his home. Alvin estimates that less than ten people came by the house in those years who were interested in meeting Anderson the musician as opposed to Anderson the illicit entrepreneur. "The one person that came by that impressed him was Roy Book Binder," says Alvin. "I think he loved Roy 'bout as much as he loved me. Those two were special to each other."

"I was on a mission to find Pink Anderson," says Book Binder. "I had bought the three Prestige records in New York for five dollars, and I had the other records, too. This was in 1970 or so, and I was living in the South Bronx. I can't remember whether or not I'd made my first record yet. Me and this friend of mine decided we were going to find Pink. I had two weeks' vacation, and that's how I used it. We had beards and long hair at the time, and we got to Spartanburg and tried to stay at the big hotel downtown on the square. The one that's now been knocked down, over by Smith's Pawn Shop (he is almost certainly referring to the Cleveland Hotel).

"We checked in and went up to the fifth floor and there was only one bed. We came back down and they gave us another room. We went up to the tenth floor and it was the same thing. Took us three rooms before we realized they didn't want us in the hotel. We asked around to see if anybody knew Pink, then somebody suggested we look him up in the phone book. That's exactly where he was. We went over there and he was playing Georgia Skin. Pink was a gambling man. There was a lot of money on the table, too."

Thus began a friendship that on the surface seemed improbable, yet was, in retrospect, almost certainly inevitable. Roy Book Binder was a white Yankee bluesman who had been performing in Rhode Island and New York since he got out of the Navy in the mid-sixties. Roy was in his late twenties when he traveled to Spartanburg to meet Pink, and he had toured for the past three or four years as a companion to the Laurens-born, Greenville-raised Rev. Blind Gary Davis. In Pink Anderson, Book Binder saw a musician of vastly different abilities than Davis. "Gary Davis was a genius of a guitar player, and Pink was not," he says. "Pink was all right, but guitar wasn't exactly his thing. He was an entertainer first. He was a comedian, really: the last minstrel man. He tickled us. That's what my whole life is today: making people laugh and forget their problems. Pink was great at that."

Today, much of Book Binder's act revolves around stories of his times with Pink Anderson. "Not a night goes by on stage that I haven't said the name 'Pink Anderson' and related an anecdote or experience," he says. Book Binder also plays some of Pink's songs in concert, and Anderson's "Travelin' Man" has become Roy's signature tune. Roy has also recorded a number of the songs that Pink used to play, including "Travelin' Man" and "Every Day In the Week."

"In the stories that I tell on stage, I always look at the brighter side of Pink's life. When we first met him, though, I think he was really malnourished, not in great shape. We bought him some groceries and stuff. Alvin was there the first time we went down to Spartanburg. He couldn't have been more than fourteen then. He was playing guitar, but he was more into being a Jimmy Reed or B.B. King-type player, because that was hip then. His father was not very hip; his father was old-fashioned."

"When I first started to play on my own," says Alvin, "I was uncomfortable playing his style of music. I've always loved it, but I wasn't comfortable playing it. I played electric blues, and I used to think that the guitar was just good to get a few extra dollars and a woman. He told me, 'One day, you gonna pick up that guitar and you gonna take it serious. That guitar will feed you when nothing else will.' You know, if I had it to do over again there's a lot of things I would do different."

With Pink still primarily bound to his house because of health problems, Alvin got, as he puts it, "wilder and wilder." Alvin's musical stature around town was growing, but so was his penchant for trouble. In the early 1970s, Alvin was sentenced to a fifteen-year jail term at the same time that his father was reclaiming the guitar skills that had been depleted by the stroke.

Every spring, Roy Book Binder would drive to Spartanburg to visit Pink. On one of those trips, he brought along Fats Kaplin, a teenage fiddler who would later become one of Nashville's most respected multi-instrumentalists. Kaplin was a white Northerner who had not spent much time in the South. "It was culture shock," he says. "We drove down a dirt road and pulled up outside Pink's house. There were chickens running around on the road, and the houses were dilapidated. It was a Sunday when we got there, so Pink was selling little half-pints that he would buy during the week. He'd sell them on Sundays to people who really needed them.

"After that, we went over to see Peg Leg Pete in Jonesville. He lived in a total shack. I was seventeen years old at this point, and I was pretty amazed."

Book Binder remembers that trip to Peg's house. "Peg was laid up in his bed because he had gotten shot," he says. "He didn't seem too upset about it. He put his leg on and got out of bed. I was playing guitar—Pink didn't play much at that point, but he started playing more by the next time we came down to Spartanburg—and Peg was playing harmonica. Pink was looking at Peg's set-up. Peg had three shacks on his property out there in Jonesville. Pink said, 'We could have gambling in that first one, women in this one, and we could be brewing whiskey over in that other one.' He thought Peg was wasting what could

be a great situation. Pink was an entrepreneur."

The idea to take Pink Anderson on a Northern tour began with a phone call from Book Binder to his friend and fellow bluesman Paul Geremia. "Paul Geremia is the greatest country-blues guitar player alive today, and he's one of my oldest friends," says Book Binder. "I called him up from Pink's house. I said, 'Guess where I am.' He said, 'Oh God, you're not back with *her* are you?' I said, 'No, I'm in Pink Anderson's living room! Here, talk to him.' Paul got real excited about it. He was living in Newport, Rhode Island, and he had a lawyer friend who owned a place called Salt Coffeehouse. That

summer, the summer of '73, Paul and his lawyer friend drove to Spartanburg, picked Pink up, and drove him to Newport for a gig with Paul, myself, and Fats Kaplin. They got some good press up there, and the place was packed. It was a magical night."

"When we played Salt, Pink hadn't played on stage in years," says Kaplin. "We were all sweating it, because we didn't know how he would do. He walked on, swung his guitar behind his back, tilted his hat back, and just started going into his medicine show rap. He told jokes and did his whole routine, just like he'd never stopped playing. There were other shows he did up North where he didn't feel so well and was not as *on*, but that gig was really amazing."

The show at Salt Coffeehouse went so well that more Northern performances were arranged for Pink. "We started to piece it together, but I was worried about Pink's health," says Book Binder. "I told Pink, 'I gotta have a note from your doctor that says you're not gonna die on me.' He sent me this great letter—all his letters read like telegrams—that I still have. It said,

> *Spartanburg, July 23. 7:00.*
> *This is Pink Anderson. I got your letter.*
> *How are you? The doctor says I am fine.*
> *If there's any work, he said I can go.*
> *P.S. I hope you get this letter.*
> *Bye now.*
> *Pink Anderson.*

I sign all my letters 'Bye now' at the end, 'cause Pink used to do that."

He played shows at the Folklore Center in New York City, Harper College in Binghamton, Kirkland College in Clinton, New York, and even Yale University in New Haven, Connecticut. "After the gig at the Folklore Center in Greenwich Village, we went to this bar and Dave Van Ronk was playing," says Book Binder. "Pink and I sat in a booth, and all the other celebrities came over to our table. Danny Kalb from The Blues Project (a band that helped start the blues revival of the late 1960s) was there. Danny said, 'Oh, Pink, I've got all your records!' Pink couldn't believe it. He didn't know who The Blues Project was, he didn't know who Dave Van Ronk was, he didn't have a clue about any of these people."

Alvin Anderson remembers that Pink made $2,300 on the Northern tour, and Book Binder confirms that figure. "We were pretty tickled when we sent him home with that pile," Book Binder says. "The next time I came down, he had two refrigerators, a new gun, a guitar, and beer and wine in the refrigerators."

"He sent $1,500 of that to me," says Alvin. "I sent it back to him, because with the skill he taught me with a deck of cards I was doing real well. He came to visit me when I was doing a fifteen-year bid in the worst penitentiary in the state of South Carolina, and I gave him something like $6,000.

He used to say, 'Boy, you need to slow down. Somebody is gonna kill you.' I used to say the same thing he'd say: 'I ain't going nowhere 'til it's my time.'"

Pink's time came on October 12, 1974. "The day before he died, I called home," says Alvin. "He said, 'Boy, I ain't gonna be with you much longer. I'm dying.' I tried to tell him that he wasn't dying, and he said, 'All I ever wanted out of life was to see you be grown. I don't like where you are, but you're a man. I know you can take care of yourself now, so if I die tonight I'll die happy.' The next day, he died."

"When he first died, (bluesman) Brownie McGhee told me that Pink was dead, and I couldn't believe it," says Book Binder. "I called up the welfare department and checked it out, and they told me he was dead. When my (ex) wife and I came down, I wanted to go to the cemetery. We called up someone and they told us where it was. It was an unmarked grave. They said, 'Take twenty paces south from the Smith grave, then go east, then go west, then whatever else. I was walking around the graveyard, saying, 'Pink, this will never do.'"

Disheartened by the lack of a marker, Roy arranged for a stone to be placed on Pink's grave at Spartanburg's Lincoln Memorial Cemetery. "Paul Geremia was all for it, and he chipped in, too. It was a cheap thing to do: I don't think it even cost us sixty dollars. We wanted to put up a monu-

Mark Olencki

ment, but they said we could only put up this flat stone. I said, 'Okay, I'll take it.' We didn't have any money at the time, anyway.

"The stone says, 'Pink Anderson,' and has the date of birth and the date of his death. Then it says, 'Recording Artist.' I really should have said, 'Medicine show man,' but at the time I figured so few people knew he made records that I'd just put that down. I figured maybe one day one of his relatives or friends would walk by and say, 'Wow, Pink Anderson got a stone!' Kind of like that lady that said, 'Pink Anderson done made records!'"

Baby Tate was already dead and gone by the time Pink passed away, although Peg Leg Pete lasted until October 1977. "The last time I saw Peg was at the Mariposa Folk Festival in Toronto," Book Binder says. "I wasn't scheduled to be on the bill. Peg remembered me after I rein-troduced myself. He said, 'Maybe you'll come up and play with me.' We were backstage rehearsing and I said, 'We ought to do one of those routines that you and Pink used to do.' We went on stage together, and it was great: we did the whole routine. It was really hot up there, though, and he went back to his room after the show and didn't even come out the next day. Then he went home and died."

Few wept when Peg died, and few mourned the culture that ended with his passing. As Alvin Anderson put it, "The lifestyle of a medicine show musician was just as different as day is to night from the life of any other musician." That lifestyle was neither well-known nor well-documented, but it was a vital, inventive, and entertaining strain of American musical history that can never be recaptured. "Chief Thundercloud was possibly the last medicine show of them all," says Book Binder. "They were talking about having me go out with the Chief. He was moving up to a tent show—that was going to be the Chief's big move—but the tent broke down. I might have had a story to tell if that had worked, but I never got to do a real medicine show.

"Pink and Peg were great guys, and the sad thing is that they're gone. There's nobody like them left: there *can't* be. It's a piece of Americana that's long gone."

Alvin Anderson continued to play music even while in prison, though it was not the country-blues of his father. As the lead guitar for the traveling penitentiary band, The New Coronets, he began to garner a good bit of attention. He played an electric guitar that Pink had bought for him. "I was doing fifteen years, but we went to the streets four nights a week to play," says Alvin. "On my guitar case, I had 'Pinkie' written on it, and the state ordered this light especially for me: they would turn a pink light on me when I would play a solo."

Released from prison in the 1980s, Alvin began the process of trying to put his life back together but relapsed after his baby son went into a coma and died. Soon after his son's death, Alvin was sent back to the penitentiary. The year 1996 found "Little Pink" back out of prison and determined to make a better life for himself. "I'm finally screwing my head back on straight, and I know life has to go on," he says.

Alvin is also beginning the process of rediscovering and relearning his father's style of music, and he speaks of carrying on the legend of Pink Anderson. "I'm at peace with myself now, and his style of music is now my style of music. See, that's my roots. I'm not going to try to walk in his footsteps, because I need to make my own tracks. I can still walk in his shadow, though. I've always been there, and that's where I'll stay.

"He's influenced a lot of people, and he never even knew it. He didn't know about Pink Floyd, or about Johnny Cash. I just want people, especially in his home, in Spartanburg, to know who he was and what his name really meant. It wasn't that he was the world's greatest singer—to me, he was—but he has passed on

"Little Pink" performs at a blues jam session in The Handlebar, Greenville, S.C. (1997)

Roy Book Binder,
Pink Anderson,
unidentified fan,
and Fats Kaplin
(c) David Gahr

something that needs to be kept alive. I think the racial situation from the 1920s to the 1970s caused a lot of the world to miss something that he shared with me, and that he would have shared with anybody. I won't be satisfied until I'm standing in front of audiences again, telling the story of growing up with that ol' fool, as I used to call him sometimes when he'd get crazy."

Until Alvin is able to realize his intentions of performing his father's medicine show blues, Paul Geremia and Roy Book Binder will continue as the sole purveyors of the Pink Anderson legacy. "I guess we've done more to keep his name alive than anybody, because we talk about him all the time," says Book Binder. "He was a part of our lives. Really, our position in show business today is not that far from Pink's medicine show days, except we've got fancier cars.

"The music game is a tough game. I've thrashed on for thirty years, and I have a decent career. But sometimes I'm driving down the highways pondering it all and thinking, 'If I got murdered tonight, would it make the *Rolling Stone*?' Probably not. We're on a small-time circuit. At this level, the whole thing is a carnival: a hustle. You play shell games with promoters and record companies and club owners. You have to wonder what success is. It would be cool to make $100,000 a year, but it would change things. I don't know if I want to change things. I do a hundred dates a year and travel around in my own house on wheels with a picture of Pink Anderson in my kitchen."

Whatever success Book Binder has achieved, it has allowed the name of Pink Anderson to spread. Audiences still laugh at the old routines and smile at the old songs as they take in lyrical advice such as "If you got one woman/ You sure better get you five/ 'Cause the two might quit you/ And the other three might die." Roy returns to Lincoln Cemetery a couple of times a year to see his old friend:

"I stop by and grab the biggest bouquet of flowers off somebody else's grave. I bring it over and put it on Pink's. I know he'd like that."

ACE RICKENBACKER

"Hi again, Gates. Let's spin 'em at a 78.
This is your old platterboy . . ."

With a show called "Ace's Wax-works" as his bully pulpit and *Cab Calloway's Book of Jive* as his hep-talk Bible, Herbert Lee "Ace" Rickenbacker, Jr. was the Right Reverend of big-band jazz in World War II-era Spartanburg. Ace was not a musician, though his contribution to the town's musical heritage would not be any greater had he been skilled at an instrument. Rather, Ace's place was as a quick-witted, zoot-suited propo-nent and educator of a music that would heavily influence the Spartan-burg-bred sounds of Hank Garland, The Marshall Tucker Band, Daryle Ryce, and Uncle Walt's Band.

Now almost eighty years old, Rickenbacker resides in the sleepy mountain town of Tryon, North Caro-lina, where he lives with his wife of many years. It is in his Tryon home, in an upstairs room filled with pictures of fighter pilots and airplanes, that he sits for an interview. Ace sees himself as a relic of a music that is now practi-cally forgotten by a country that once screamed for the likes of Benny Good-man and Duke Ellington; a music that he feels was taken away from the peo-ple who loved it. "Radio today . . . I don't dig it," he says. "I think it stinks. They want to tell you what to play and when to play it, and I can't work that way. Back then, radio was just a way I had of expressing my love for music, and I think it showed."

Before he was a disc jockey, Ace was a fan. As a student at Mount Airy High School in North Carolina, he collected records by the performers of the day, and he sought out those performers when they would appear in nearby towns. "That was the start of the big band era," he says. "Back in those days, you had names like Benny Goodman and Duke Ellington. Those guys were starting playing jazz back in those days, and I was learning about them even at the time. I didn't think about being involved with music as a career back then, though, because my forte back then was flying. I started flying when I was twelve."

Rickenbacker held to a dream of becoming a fighter pilot, though that dream was made considerably more far-fetched because of an eye injury (as a twelve-year-old he was shot in the eye with a BB gun). Nonetheless, he attempted to scheme his way into the Air Force after high school graduation.

"The draft board sent me to Camp Croft," he says, "and I flunked the eye test because I couldn't see out of my left eye. While I was there, I got a copy of the eye chart and wrote it all down. Then I had them send for me to take the test a second time. Well, I knew that when they closed my right eye, they'd want the third line. I had memorized the third line, so I passed with flying colors. After the IQ test, they asked me if I wanted to go into the Air Force, so I said, 'Sure.'"

The ruse only worked for a short time. Rickenbacker learned that the flight school eye exam was more intense, so he requested a placement at the aircraft and engine school in Amarillo, Texas, where he learned

about engines. "Later, when I was stationed in Maine, I hurt my eye again, and they sent me to a doctor," he says. "He saw that my eye was in bad shape and gave me a discharge, and I came back home."

Rickenbacker's father was with Duke Power, and Ace was sent by his dad to work in the meter department in Spartanburg. In 1942, while living at the YMCA across the street from the studios that then held WSPA and WORD radio, Ace was asked to audition for a job as a broadcaster. "A guy was going into the Navy," Rickenbacker says, "and they gave me his slot from six to twelve at night on WORD. I wound up making $35 a week, which wasn't bad in that era. I had a car, had clothes, and I could buy records once in a while. After a while, I quit Duke Power, because I was doing so well in radio."

Back then, WSPA was a powerful station, and "Ace's Waxworks" could be heard as far off as Florida, Alabama, Virginia, and Ohio. The show became known not only for its music, but also for Ace's insistence on giving out information about the artists behind the songs. Rickenbacker became more than a platter spinner: he was a teacher and a taste-maker. "Even before I was on the radio, I knew about the music," he says. "The records that I played when I started my show were the records I'd been listening to since high school: Tommy Dorsey, Cab Calloway, people like that. Many of the listeners didn't know much about those guys until I started talking about them.

"I was really a workaholic. I made myself learn the musicians, who they were, where they came from, what their style was, and what records they'd made before. Eventually, some of these things would just come to me naturally. You could mention Duke Ellington, and I'd say, 'Washington, D.C. His artists were Lawrence Brown . . .' and so on. I made sure to give out that information on the air, and maybe that enlarged the listeners' scope a little. They seemed to appreciate the fact that they could listen and learn."

Had Rickenbacker commandeered Spartanburg airwaves a decade earlier, he might have found his radio audience considerably more educated. The 1930s were a time of immense activity for jazz musicians in town, though the scene gradually receded as the players left one by one for out-of-town opportunities. The center of the scene was the downtown Sanitary Cafe, a haven for musicians and listeners, and Spartanburg's sole purveyor of 3.2 beer during prohibition time. A number of excellent jazzmen passed through during the thirties, playing lucrative gigs at The Cleveland Hotel or The Strand Theater and then retiring to the Sanitary Cafe for beer and more music.

WORD'S ROCKIN' PAPA 1400
ON YOUR DIAL

SOLIDLY YOURS Ace Rickenbacker

One player who used Spartanburg as a stepping stone to bigger and better things was jazz drummer Johnny Blowers, who went on to play with Frank Sinatra, Louis Armstrong, Billie Holiday, and scores of others. Blowers' father, John Sr., was a professional drummer who played at The Strand, The Rialto, and other vaudeville theaters in downtown Spartanburg, and John Jr.'s mother, Adabelle, played piano in silent movie theaters.

"The population of Spartanburg back then was about 9,000 people," Blowers says. "Strangely, being such a small town, Spartanburg was highly recognized in music. You had all kinds of theater and all kinds of music going on." The music going on in the Blowers house was primarily jazz, and Johnny remembers listening at a young age to his father's Paul Whiteman records. "I would practice by those

records," he says. "Playing music was always what I wanted to do."

It was the end of silent movie pictures that began Blowers' push towards playing professionally. "When Al Jolson made the first talkie, my dad said, 'This is the end of vaudeville and the end of the silent movie.' He and my mom organized a dance band, and when I was sixteen (1927), I started substituting for Dad at little dances at hotels from Greenville to Spartanburg. There were dances at these places on the outskirts of Spartanburg, places like Glenn Springs. I'd never seen anything like it. People just mobbed the place."

Blowers attended Spartanburg High School, where he says he was kicked out of class many times "for playing drums on the desk with two pencils." He also held a brief summer job at the already vibrant Alexander's

Music House. "I didn't last too long at the store," he says. "Mr. Alexander was getting these jazz records in from people like Tommy Dorsey, Duke Ellington, and Red Nichols. When the new records came, you could go back to a cubicle in the back of the store and listen to them. Mr. Alexander would be looking for me to wait on customers, and I was always in the back listening to records. That happened three times, and then he fired me!"

At age seventeen, Blowers left Spartanburg to finish high school and learn music in Ft. Myers, Florida. After that, he toured with a big band out of Hendersonville, North Carolina, and spent time at Oglethorpe University in Atlanta. He came back to Spartanburg briefly in the 1930s but left soon thereafter. "I knew I had to go one of three places: New York, Chicago, or California," he says. "I needed exposure, and I knew nobody was going to find me down South."

His analysis was correct—no one would have found him in Spartanburg—and within a few years of his move to New York in 1937, he was playing with Sinatra. Spartanburg couldn't hold Johnny Blowers, any more than it could hold any of the scores of other excellent players who passed through town. By the time Ace Rickenbacker took over a microphone at WSPA, the town's days as a Southern jazz hotbed were decidedly over,

although some players remained and worked whatever gigs were still available at hotels and lounges. By the end of World War II, though, it was obvious that if big-band jazz was going to remain a part of the listening lives of Spartanburg's populace, it would be the airwaves, not the live music scene, that would be responsible for keeping the genre alive.

"Hi again, fellows and gals. Is everything mellow with you'se? Do you feel groovy, hepped up, and comin' on? I'm here to put down a dash of salt on the latest in wax, and I want you to be diggin' in for a few ticks and pick up on it."

As Ace Rickenbacker's popularity rose, WSPA allowed him to develop several shows and segments, including "Waxworks," "Ace's Platter Chatter," and a segment he invented called "Fresh Air Time." "'Fresh Air Time' was a street broadcast," he says. "One day, I got a long microphone cord and just walked out onto Main Street. Cars started honking, and people started coming by to see what was going on. It got to where I knew everybody who would drive by there, and I'd mention their names on the air.

"I'd squeal on people, too. I'd say, 'Who's that girl with Jim Rose this morning? I don't think that's his wife!' Boy, a lot of people would avoid driving by there just so I wouldn't see them."

An important element in Ace's popularity was gimmickry, a quality found in spades on the 1990s radio dial but not so common in Rickenbacker's day. Put simply, he was willing to try anything to amuse an audience. He would climb radio towers, hold contests in which listeners were to guess how long it would take a block of ice to melt on Main Street, and even broadcast while flying an airplane. "I did that on the 50th anniversary of the Wright Brothers' flight," he says. "I got to about 1,500 feet and said, 'Now, when the Wright Brothers started, they had no engine in their aircraft, so I'm going to cut this engine off and fly into the airport without any power.' I was never afraid of flying. I

would fly in one seat, climb outside the airplane, and climb in another seat. It sounds crazy, but it's been a darn good life for me."

The plane-flying and ice block-melting seemed to have nothing to do with music, but they helped to increase Ace's visibility and celebrity quotient enough for ratings of his music shows to rise. Rickenbacker became a recognizable figure in the community, and that figure was made more recognizable by the fact that it was often clad in a zoot suit and saddle shoes. He

dressed similarly to the top big-band performers, a habit that made him appear to be "one of them" when he would do live interviews with musicians who were appearing at Spartanburg venues such as Memorial Auditorium, the armory on St. John Street, or Wofford College.

"Anita O'Day, Mildred Bailey, Chick Webb, Ella Fitzgerald, Harry James, Dizzy Gillespie, Duke Ellington: these were people who I met and enjoyed talking to," says Ace. "I could talk hep talk to them—like today we're using 'cool' and 'gross' and so on—and in conversation they would swing right along with it, because they were digging me and I was digging them. Duke Ellington was very nice; he was a real cultured guy. Louis Armstrong was another musician that I particularly enjoyed meeting. It was always a thrill to talk to these people."

Rickenbacker would routinely step outside the jazz world for interviews and in-studio guests, and two musical legends from the Spartanburg area played his Saturday morning show as teenagers. "Don Reno and Hank Garland would both play live in the studio on my show," says Ace. "Reno was in his late teens at the time, and he was real good. My show was the first show that Garland ever played: he was just a kid." Reno remained a bluegrass man all his life, while Garland went on to play country music in Nashville studios and jazz music on

Ace interviewing Elliot Lawrence and vocalist Roz Patton

his own records.

"I've often wondered how Garland got influenced by jazz and big band when all he played in the studio was country music," says Rickenbacker. "I lost contact with Hank after he went to Nashville, but a friend of his from Converse used to call me at the station and give me updates on how Hank was doing. He said Hank always remembered the name 'Ace Rickenbacker.'"

Ace continued to broadcast big-band sounds on WSPA through the mid-1950s, bringing the sounds of Ellington, Calloway, and Dorsey to older listeners who loved the music, and to younger listeners who didn't know any better but to listen and learn. Spartanburg-born songwriter

Walter Hyatt said in 1996 that he and fellow Uncle Walt's Band member Champ Hood had the sounds of big-band music in their ears "since baby-hood," and the disc jockey that spun those records during Hyatt and Hood's baby-hood—the man who put those songs on the airwaves—was Ace.

By 1956, though, a new form of music had begun to turn the ears of Spartanburg's young people away from big-band jazz and towards performers like Elvis Presley. Partly due to the popularity of Rickenbacker's show in the 1940s and 1950s, big-band would remain an influence on a number of Spartanburg musicians who grew up during that time, including Hyatt, Hood and Toy Caldwell of The Marshall Tucker Band. Those influences would usually appear as subtle musical references within a rock and roll context, though, and Elvis's 1956 appearance at the Carolina Theater in Spartanburg was a decisive blow in the fight for the heart of the city's

Ace interviewing wherever the story happens to be

youth. When Presley came to town, it was none other than Rickenbacker who conducted a WSPA interview with the King of Rock and Roll.

"Yeah, my program director told me to go down to the Carolina Theater and talk with Elvis Presley," says Ace. "I wasn't real excited about it—I didn't really go for Elvis Presley—because his music had no relation to the kind of music that I liked. I remember that Elvis had two shirts: one was soaking wet after the first show, and he threw that one aside and put on the dry one for the next show. I went down and recorded the interview, and the station played it on the air. After that, I guess somebody put the tape back in the rack at WSPA and it was recorded over for something else. Think what that tape would be worth to me now, but it's long gone."

After Presley's Spartanburg appearance, it became obvious to WSPA that the big-band music that Rickenbacker worked so hard to keep alive would not withstand the onslaught of drums and guitars that had begun to scream from AM radio stations across the nation. As the musical times changed, Ace attempted to change with them. "I played country music, rock music, Elvis, you name 'em," he says. Though he gave the new sounds a try, Ace was attracted to radio because it gave him a chance to play the music he loved, not attracted to music because it gave him a chance to

be on the radio. In 1958, after sixteen years in Spartanburg, Rickenbacker left town to become program director at WTYN in Tryon, North Carolina, where he could program the music that he wanted to hear. "I had the opportunity to run a radio station in my own way," he says. "I took that opportunity, and I'm glad I did. I spent the rest of my career doing my thing, and I was accepted for it."

In Tryon, Rickenbacker found an older audience that was pleased to have radio access to songs and performers who couldn't be heard on other stations. He spent thirty-seven years broadcasting in the Tryon area, bringing "Ace's Waxworks" and "Fresh Air Time" with him to WTYN. All in all, Ace spent over fifty years in radio, but it was his time in Spartanburg that he claims as the highlight of his career. "For the kids of that era, I was the guy they listened to," he says. "Those people remember me after all those years, and that fact means I must have done something to impress them. From the people I saw on the street during 'Fresh Air Time' to the Converse College girls that would call me all night to request songs and talk about music, this was a part of their life."

"That's the session, guys and gals, so I'm gonna cut out and widen the gap. I'll be diggin' you later. I'm Ace Rickenbacker, your old platterboy. Good-bye."

Mark Olencki

5 FREDDIE "CARELESS" LOVE

red "Careless" Love is the only Tucapau Mill kid ever to grow up and become a Hollywood television star. No question about it. Between 1950 and 1955, "Careless" was an international recording artist for Decca Records, a *TV Guide* cover boy, and the singing star of an Emmy-winning show. Love can give first-hand accounts of stories involving Frank Sinatra, Fred MacMurry, Bob Hope, Betty White, Roy Rogers, and countless others.

When Fred was growing up in the thirties, it was considered a long way from Tucapau to Spartanburg, much less to California. Only twelve miles separate the two Spartanburg County towns, but without easy access to transportation, most residents took advantage of the mill-owned stores and housing. Except for the radio, the mill town was nearly as isolated as it had been at its founding in 1898.

Tucapau (the name means "strong cloth" in an Indian tongue) was a company town where workers lived in the mill village and walked to work. Now known as Startex, only a small percentage of the town's current mill-workers actually live in the village: most employees drive in to work their shift and drive out at closing time. Sixty years ago, to be a mill kid was to see your present and future spread before you in the form of a big building where cloth was produced. Escaping the shadow of that building for a life somewhere else was no easy feat. Emerging as a star of stage and screen was nothing short of amazing.

Perhaps the most amazing thing about Fred Love is that few people in Spartanburg have ever heard of him. The reasons for this are inexplicable, but they have something to do with the lack of respect the Piedmont city has shown for its popular musical history, the rise of rock and roll, and a brutal murder that took place in the

Freddie
"Careless"
Love

75

foothills above the Mojave Desert.

Fred's nephew, Larry Turner, has sought for years to tell people in Spartanburg about Careless Love. "They just don't understand the importance of what he did," he says. In addition to playing guitar and bass, Turner is a walking encyclopedia of the names, dates, songs, and records of twentieth century American popular music. Larry, better than anyone else, fully understands Fred's accomplishments in the context of modern country and Western Swing music, and he peppers Love with questions about the old days at every available opportunity. Today, Fred resides in an Anderson, South Carolina, veterans' home, and, though health problems have stolen his singing voice and his ability to play guitar, he is able to remember (with some prodding from Larry) the specifics of a remarkable career. First, some background.

To understand Fred Love's career, you must know about a musician named Donnell Clyde ("Spade") Cooley. A quarter-Cherokee born on an Oklahoma ranch in 1910, Cooley studied classical cello and violin in what was then known as "Indian School." By the mid-1920s, he began working hillbilly dances and hoe-downs in an attempt to turn a Depression-era buck. After a particularly successful card game, he took the nickname by

Courtesy of Larry Turner

which he would be known throughout his life. The late thirties found Spade in Hollywood, playing music and assisting Roy Rogers as an arranger/stand-in/manager. By 1944, Cooley was under contract with Columbia Records as leader of his own band (in which he played fiddle) and proponent of a new sound called Western Swing.

Bob Wills had been recording for years with his Texas Playboys, but he hadn't yet come up with a fitting name for the Playboys' sound. Spade's band was slicker and more classically influenced than Wills', but twin (and sometimes triple) fiddles and wry lyrics placed the two groups into one camp. Spade called the music "Western Swing," an almost perfect description of the amalgam of big-band, country and western, and boogie music. A battle-of-the-bands between Bob Wills' Texas Playboys and The Spade Cooley

Orchestra ended with the assembled audience choosing Spade's group as the winner. From then on, Spade Cooley called himself "The King of Western Swing."

Cooley's orchestras of the mid-1940s included vocalist Tex Williams (whose "Smoke, Smoke, Smoke That Cigarette" would later become a smash hit), guitarist Smokey Rogers, and two of the most influential steel guitar players in the history of country music, Joaquin Murphey and Noel Boggs. That group chalked up the number 1 country record of 1945, "Shame On You," and another number 1 in 1946, "Detour." The latter part of the decade brought the departures of Williams and Murphey, a shift from Columbia to RCA Victor Records, and a damaging ban on recordings (due to war-time shellac rationing) that lasted from 1947 to 1949. With his career as a recording artist stopped in its tracks, Cooley found a new angle: he would perform via a new medium called television.

KTLA in Los Angeles gave The Spade Cooley Orchestra its own television show as the forties came to a close. With this arrangement came several changes. First, Cooley wrapped his Western Swing in a setting that was more pop than country. Next, he left RCA for Decca Records. Finally, Spade realized that to be popular on television, he needed a lead vocalist who could impress an audience both vocally and visually, someone who sounded

good on records and looked good on camera. A singer named Les Anderson won the gig for a time, but that didn't work out so well. Spade's search would end when he discovered a young Naval officer named Freddie Love.

"It all started as a way to get out of classwork in grammar school," explains Fred Love. "The teacher would say, 'We're not gonna have class today. We're gonna let Fred sing instead.' I'd get up and sing for the kids, and I've been doing it ever since."

Larry interjects. "Tell him about the ice man, Freddie."

"Oh, yeah. Back in Tucapau, the ice man would come around. This was before people had freezers, and the kids would try to get some free ice to eat as a treat. It was like ice cream to us. The other kids would go out there and try to get ice and they couldn't get any. The ice man would say, 'Go get Fred and his ukulele.' I'd go out there and sing, 'How'm I doin', hey, hey' and I'd get me a piece of ice big enough to share. We'd all sit out there and eat it."

Several of the eight Love kids were known around Tucapau for their musical skills. Fred's brother Lindy is a jazz guitarist who worked professionally for years. Brother Joe also played guitar and sang. Fred, the third oldest, remembers a childhood filled with music. "Daddy would buy guitars and fiddles and clarinets and everything else. He'd get 'em at the jockey lot. We picked 'em up and started playing because there was really nothing else to do. You could play baseball or play music. Later, I started practicing music so hard because I wanted to get out of Tucapau, and music was a way to make it out of there."

Surprisingly, *country* music was not particularly favored in the Love household. "None of us ever did sing hillbilly music. Lindy played country for awhile, until he learned to play the guitar good. He elevated himself. Anybody could play country, but there weren't many that could play jazz. He liked a challenge." Fred learned many songs from sheet music bought by his brother Joe, and he learned some from a medicine show man named Jay White. "That's where I learned a talking blues about 'Barefoot Boy With Shoes On,'" Love says. Asked to recall the lyrics, he does so without hesitation:

> The night was dark and stormy
> The moon was shining bright
> Stars were casting burning rays
> On a storm that raced the night
> The lightning struck the cow sheds
> The cows all chewed their cudds
> Moonlight set the prairie on fire
> In the middle of the woods

"That one won me a lot of prizes," he says. "I knew songs like that, and I knew songs like 'Cross-eyed Nancy Jane' off records. I could listen to records and learn the chords

on guitar."

When Fred and Joe started their own band as teenagers in the 1940s, they called their group "The Hawaiian Beachcombers." Fred played ukulele while Joe played guitar, and the brothers made appearances at local functions and, sporadically, on WSPA radio until Fred entered the Navy.

Fred was well-liked in the Navy for the same reasons that he was popular in Tucapau. The only difference was that the part of the ice man was played by a bartender. "The men would fight to go to shore with me," Love remembers. "They knew if they went with me they could get drunk for

Freddie Love

The SAILOR COWBOY SINGER *and his Guitar*

Courtesy of Larry Turner

free! I'd go in them bars, get up with a guitar, and start singing. I'd do stuff like 'Hong Kong Blues' (a Hoagie Carmichael number) and the drinks would start coming!"

One of the artists that Fred

Love liked to hear during his Navy days was a man known as "The King of Western Swing," Spade Cooley. Cooley's Armed Forces Transcriptions were favored by many servicemen, and Love was no exception. Before too long, the two men would cross paths at a sailor bar in California and Spade would ask Fred Love to appear on "The Spade Cooley Show." Later, Spade would actually hear Fred sing.

Larry Turner begins the story: "Freddie told me about how he and Spade hooked up. When he was in the Navy, Fred would go in and sing sometimes at a place called Hollywood on the Pike. It was a tough place to work, the crowd could get pretty rough. Fred would sing there when he was on leave, and he got to where he was pretty popular there. Spade was a guest at that club one night, he just came to watch, but they asked him to get up and play something. He said he'd play fiddle if somebody would get up there and sing."

"Yeah, they were yelling for Spade to play 'Texarkana Baby,'" Fred Love recalls. "Everybody started hollering, 'Let the sailor sing it!' They kept up with that. Well, I didn't get to sing it! There was an old boy that had a little trio and he got up and sang while Spade played: that old boy wouldn't let me up there. When Spade got through, he went back to the club office, talked to the owner, and said, 'Call that sailor back here. I want to meet him.'

"I went back there and he said, 'Come up Saturday night and be on my television show.' I said, 'You ain't even heard me sing yet!' He said, 'I heard them people hollerin' for you, and that's good enough.'"

Fred appeared on Spade's show wearing his Navy uniform. The appearance was a success, and the sailor was asked back for return visits. Spade gave him the nickname "Careless" after the classic song, "Careless Love" ("Love, oh love, oh careless love"). Upon his discharge from the military, Fred signed on officially as a lead vocalist for The Spade Cooley Orchestra.

"I don't think it was my voice," says Love. "I think it was my smile. Back then, I had some perfect teeth. I showed 'em, too. I told Spade, 'There's lots better singers than me. What do you want me for?' He said, 'I want a new face, for TV.' That's why he got me.

"There wasn't even no TV back in Tucapau then. People back home didn't have any idea about what I was doing, but we were on top back then, buddy. It was like being a movie star."

By now, Spade Cooley was not only "The King of Western Swing," he was king of West Coast television, the Ed Sullivan of the West Coast, pulling down an over fifty percent share of the

8746 SUNSET BOULEVARD
HOLLYWOOD 46, CALIFORNIA
BRADSHAW 2-4493

June 3, 1955

TO WHOM IT MAY CONCERN:

Freddy "Careless" Love has had an exceptional background in so far as the entertainment field is concerned; especially in television, since he was with me for several years here in Los Angeles.

I think "Careless" would be a natural for a kiddy show of some sort because he has a huge fan club out here on the West Coast and most of the fan club members are youngsters.

Sincerely hoping you can spot him with his own show, I remain

Sincerely your friend,

Spade Cooley
SPADE COOLEY

SC:mf

market. Cliffie Stone's "Hometown Jamboree" show, which aired in the same time slot, was the direct competition, but even at KTLA there were a number of challengers to the throne. "Lawrence Welk was on the same channel we were on," says Love. "He was just getting started. Liberace was on the same channel: he was sponsored by the bank. Johnny Carson had a fifteen-minute show called 'Carson's Corner.'"

Before long, Cooley had a nationally broadcast radio show to go along with his TV gig. Both shows were recorded on Saturdays, and they were followed by a midnight dance at the Santa Monica Ballroom. The orchestra would start rehearsing at noon, then record the radio show, then record the television show, then play at the dance until two in the morning.

The dance was wildly popular, drawing more than eight thousand people for seventy-four straight weeks, and there were usually some young wannabes in the crowd trying to hustle some stage time:

"Ferlin Husky, his real name is Terry Preston. I'd call him up on stage and let him sing when he was first starting out. Then he went to Louisiana and recorded 'Dear John' and changed his name to Ferlin. Later on, he had a hit on 'Wings of a Dove.' I remember his eyebrow would go up and down when he'd sing. Johnny Horton used to come out there, too. He had an old overcoat that he wore all the time. I guess that was all he had. I'd call him up on stage sometimes. He went on and recorded 'Battle of New Orleans.'"

The biggest stars appeared on Spade's television show, which won local Emmy awards in 1952 and 1953, and Fred has stories to tell about many of them. "Pee Wee King, Dean Martin, you name 'em. If they could make Spade money, he'd bring 'em on. Spade hated Roy Rogers, but he'd bring him on the show, 'cause he'd draw people. Roy was a nice guy, but I didn't care too much for that wife of his.

"Count Basie was on there. Lionel Hampton, too. Maynard Ferguson played in Spade's band for a while. We had Harry James on the show. We had to set up a separate bar for Harry. Frank Sinatra was on there, too. Sinatra was real good. We got him for $1,500. He came up to Dee, my wife, and said, 'How 'bout painting in my bald spot, doll?' She painted that little ol' bald spot with an eyebrow pencil. Dee never did forget that."

For all of the star power on the show, Love says the best act he ever saw on Spade's program was Peg Leg Bates. "He was from South Carolina. He was a one-legged black guy that would tap dance with that wooden leg. He had pegs that would match every one of his suits, and he'd get up and dance all the way across the stage on that peg leg. I said, 'I ain't followin' you!' Peg used my dressing room. He called me 'The Home Town Boy' because we were both from South Carolina."

At the height of his success, Fred was making over $10,000 a year from Spade. In addition, he put his own bands together and worked during the week playing gigs all over California. "I'd play all over. Before Spade's show, I'd say, 'Spade, when you introduce me tonight, ask me where I'm going to be appearing this week.' See, I had already worked something out with the club owner. I'd say, 'You give me this amount of money and I'll give you a free plug on Spade's TV show.' I played places like the Palomino Club, George's Round-

Up, Irish World . . . places all around the area."

Love also played shopping center openings up and down the West Coast. For those gigs, he would often use Jimmy Bryant and Speedy West as a backing band. Bryant and West also played as a duo, producing some of the most influential guitar and steel work in country music history.

The Cooley Orchestra traveled at times to play venues such as The Apple Valley Inn. Fred's brother, Norman, remembers going along on one such road trip: "I was kind of green," he says, "just out of high school. Ginny Jackson, one of Spade's girl singers, said, 'Let's dance.' I said, 'I don't know how to dance.' She said, 'That's all right, we'll do the "Why" dance.' I said, 'What's that?' She said, 'We'll just stand here and rub. Why dance?' Well, I could do that! I tell you, those people were characters."

Fred's visibility as a TV and radio performer and touring musician led to "star" status around Hollywood. "Fred had his own fan club and everything," says Norman. "When I'd visit, we'd be walking up the street and the girls would ask for his autograph." Fred appeared on a number of talk shows, including one hosted by the future star of "The Mary Tyler Moore Show" and "Golden Girls," Betty White. ("She gave me fifty dollars' worth of after-shave for being on there.") He also made the cover of

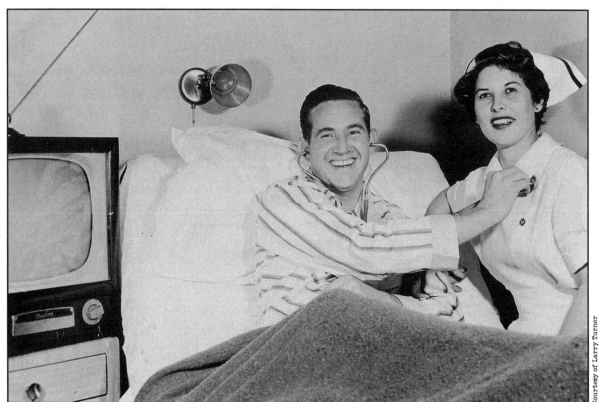

This <u>Los Angeles Times</u> publicity photo was taken when Careless was in the hospital for stomach ulcers.

TV Guide and performed on "The Bob Hope Show."

"Martin, Lewis, and I were on the Hope show with Spade," he says. "Some old woman called in a thousand dollars if I'd sing, 'Whoa, Sailor.' Spade said into the microphone that he'd loan me to her for the *weekend* for a thousand dollars. Fred MacMurry was on that 'Bob Hope Show,' too. After the show, he said, 'Come on, Careless, let's go get a beer.' I didn't even know he knew who I was. He was one of the nicest guys I met. Old Hoot Gibson was at the bar. He was so old he couldn't hardly stand."

Love also saw his private life affected in some strange ways by his celebrity. "I remember that I was in a grocery store one time and this little boy said, 'Look up, Mama. There's Careless Love!' She said, 'Careless Love wouldn't be in here!' and she slapped him. I wonder what that woman thought I ate."

"The Spade Cooley Show" was a runaway success in Hollywood, but the show was never syndicated nationally. Fred's friends and family in Tucapau were, however, sometimes able to pick up the Spade Cooley radio show. On one occasion, Fred dedicated a song to his father via the radio waves. Larry Turner has copies of some of these shows, and a listen to the first national broadcast in 1951 reveals this exchange:

Bob LeMond: *Say, Spade, don't you have a male vocalist? One that I haven't met?*

Cooley: *We sure do, Bob, and that's the boy that does the rhythm songs: Freddie Love.*

LeMond: *Oh, you mean the one you call Careless Love?*

Cooley: *That's right, but there's not a thing careless about the way he sings the tunes. Careless, meet Bob LeMond.*

Love: *Hi, Bob.*

LeMond: *Hello, Careless! (applause) Say Careless, what part of the West are you from?*

Love: *I'm from Spartanburg, South Carolina.*

LeMond: *Mighty fine country out there. What was your first musical job?*

Love: *Playing ukulele with The Hawaiian Beachcombers. (audience laughs)*

LeMond: *With that history, how did you ever get with a Western band?*

Love: *Just lucky, I guess.*

The radio show was broadcast from CBS studios in Hollywood. "They had a pretty big live audience there," says Fred. "A Mexican woman came in to watch one time. She said, 'I want to hear Carlos Love sing one.' I thought I'd die laughing."

The Cooley band also taped transcriptions for Armed Service Radio to be used overseas. Larry Turner re-

members that Fred's brother, Lindy, was in the service at the time. "Lindy was over in the Pacific and the guys would say, 'Hey Love, your brother's on the radio!'"

Though his voice could sometimes be heard through the radio static, people in Spartanburg had little idea of Fred's celebrity. He was, however, not above trying to have a little fun on trips back home by playing the big shot. "One time I drove up to The Beacon wearing a cowboy suit and driving a Cadillac," he says. "I let Norman borrow that car to date in on a Saturday night. He come back and had it full of girls!"

At the height of his popularity, Spade Cooley auditioned his band at Paramount Studio for what would have been a coast-to-coast television show. About this, Fred says, simply, "They didn't pick us up." If the show had been bought by Paramount, it would have greatly expanded the popularity of Western Swing, and it would almost surely have enabled Careless Love to lengthen his singing career. The failure at Paramount, however, was soon followed by a drop in advertising revenues for the show. Before long, the gig at the pier was gone, and the popularity of a new kind of music called rock and roll sealed the fate of "The Spade Cooley Show."

"You don't last forever on TV," says Fred. "I guess the ratings started falling off. That's why we got canceled.

The band broke up, and Spade just went crazy after that."

Fred's analysis of Spade Cooley's mental state is no exaggeration. Cooley did, in fact, "go crazy." He tried in vain to revive his sagging career (even hiring an all-girl band to perform as his orchestra), then retreated in 1960 to a plot of land on which he envisioned building Spade Cooley's Water Wonderland, a vacation resort consisting of artificial lakes.

It was on this land, just above the Mojave Desert, that Cooley beat and strangled his wife to death in front of his fourteen-year-old daughter. He was found guilty of this crime, jailed, and granted parole in 1969. In November of that year, he performed at a benefit concert for the Alameda (California) Country Sheriff's Associa-

tion. He was given a standing ovation and died immediately afterwards of a backstage heart attack.

Perhaps because of his brutal act, Spade's past achievements fell out of the public consciousness. He was never inducted into the Country Music Hall of Fame, his recorded output was not kept in circulation, and the contributions of his bandmates, such as Careless Love, were never properly honored.

Love gigged around California for a while after the Cooley band broke up, painted houses for a time, then returned to the East Coast. "When I quit was when rock 'n' roll came out," he says. "I didn't like that, and I still don't." He operated TV cameras for WSPA, played music at supper clubs in Georgia, and per-

Careless on stage in Apple Valley, California (1952)

formed on the occasional radio show. Ferlin Huskey offered to knock down some Nashville doors for Fred, but Love found it hard to give up something for what might turn out to be nothing.

I ask Fred Love if he wants people to remember that he was once a singer. "It doesn't matter to me," he says. "I'm done over the hill and down the valley." Fred's family members, however, are eager for the story of Careless Love to be told. Larry recalls a conversation with steel guitar virtuoso Noel Boggs, just before Boggs passed away. "Noel said, 'Larry, I've worked with Bob Wills, Spade, Roy Rogers, and Jimmy Wakely. Freddie was a good singer, but what put him over was his personality. He had better stage presence than all of them.' Now that's saying a lot."

Larry continues, "I read where at one point Spade was getting seventy-five percent of all the television ratings in Hollywood, so a lot of those actors and actresses and musicians had to be familiar with that. They *must* have known Careless Love. I read where one of the Beach Boys, when he was learning music, would jump around the room and act like he was playing fiddle like Spade Cooley."

Today, multiple strokes have taken Careless Love's singing voice, and most of the residents at the veterans' home where he resides have no idea of his musical past. "I don't talk about it much," Fred says. "They'd never believe it if I told it to 'em."

Still, Fred Love is proud of his music career, and satisfied with his place in history. "I'd rather be a has-been," he says, "than a never-was." With that humble assessment, Careless Love flashes the *TV Guide* smile that must have inspired many a "Why" dance. ᛗᛗ

Mark Olencki

6

JOE BENNETT
AND THE SPARKLETONES

Somebody made a funny noise, and it worked out real well. It was the kind of noise made by small, bored children or by frustrated adults; a rapidly repeated "b" sound: *"Bbbbbbb."* A sound unlikely in normal circumstances to do much good or much damage.

"Yeah, but it was in harmony," says Joe Bennett.

It was, in fact, in harmony, and it was followed by enough catchy lyrics and hot guitar picking to propel it into the national consciousness in 1957. The song with the funny noise, "Black Slacks," was the vehicle that took four Spartanburg kids, who carried the name "Joe Bennett and the Sparkletones," from their homes to the Ed Sullivan Show in New York City, beamed their teenage faces across the nation, and gave them a tantalizing, temporary view of the big time.

Nowadays, Joe Bennett is a guitar teacher—the only teacher in town who receives regular royalty checks from the Walt Disney Company ("Black Slacks" was a featured song in a Disney movie called *Rescuers Down Under*)—and it is in his Smith Music office that he greets a visitor and speaks with affection towards both his teenage glory days and his quieter life of late. Bennett is in a fairly unique position among musicians, in that he had a year's worth of head-spinning success and forty years to think about it. Having lived a fairy tale and watched it unravel, Joe talks about his life in music with hard-won knowledge that shows no trace of the bitterness that might be expected.

"The music business looks like a fair in the daytime to me, like Las Vegas at high noon," he says. "I can see the facades, and it's just phony. But the music part of that . . . you take the 'business' away from the music and you get the genuine article. That's the core right there, and it's real. It's real, and it's a part of all our lives. It's been a part of me since I was a kid, and I've never been able to get away from it."

"My mama was a piano teacher," says Bennett, who grew up in Cannon's Campground, a mill area just outside of Spartanburg proper. "When I was six, which was about 1947, she'd play piano at the elementary school, and I'd put Coca-Cola bottle stoppers on the bottom of my shoes and tap dance. I'd never had a dancing lesson in my life, but I could make those clipping sounds in rhythm with the piano. I always liked putting on a show."

Bennett's proclivity towards show business resulted in a series of back yard "concerts" in his neighborhood beginning when Joe was thirteen years old. "My mother got an old Gibson guitar from my Aunt Lottie in Glendale," he says. "Mama showed me the three or four chords that she knew, and that did it. It hurt my fingers like the dickens, but I learned to play those chords. Ronnie and Jerry Cooksey lived across the street from me, and they had a mandolin and a banjo that they wanted to learn to play. We learned to tune our instruments from this little book and we started a little group called The Jamborettes."

Ronnie and Jerry's father, Doc Cooksey, a carpenter, built the boys a stage in his back yard. The Jamborettes would borrow a P.A. system from Cannon's Campground Elementary School, hook up the system on their homemade stage, and put on concerts that included country music standards such as Hank Williams' "Your Cheatin' Heart." The kids called the show The Saturday Night Jamboree, and it wasn't long before the Jamboree was drawing crowds.

"People started pulling in the driveway," says Bennett. "They'd sit in their cars and listen. After a song, they'd honk their horns. Eventually, this thing got so big that the highway patrol was out there on Saturday nights directing traffic. People were lined up on both sides of the road going up to Cannon's Elementary. It was madness! We were just these little kids."

Among the "little kids" playing in the Jamborettes were Ronnie and Jerry Cooksey, a Cannon's Campground singer two years Bennett's junior named Wayne Arthur, and Cowpens drummer Jimmy Denton, who was a year younger than Bennett. Joe's rapid improvement on guitar was aided by the private lessons he was taking from Jerome Fowler, a Clifton, South Carolina, mandolin player and guitar teacher who had taught guitar legend Hank Garland and who later tutored both banjo virtuoso Bobby Thompson and country musician David Ball. Almost certainly, there is not another small town instructor in America to have taught such an impressive array of talent at such early

Joe Bennett (top), Jimmy Denton (left), Howard "Sparky" Childress and Wayne Arthur

ages. A count of records sold that feature Garland, Thompson, Ball, or Bennett totals over five million.

"Fowler had been a vaudeville performer and had been a drummer on Broadway," says Bennett. "He had a wreck and his shoulder never hinged properly after that, so he couldn't throw his left arm far enough out from his belt to play guitar. He ended up having to play mandolin, because he couldn't reach the end of a guitar. Even though he never played guitar, he could teach it, and he could teach other instruments. When you studied with Mr. Fowler you had to study note reading, and he was a real old-pro musician. I don't know his whole story, but I know he helped a bunch of musicians.

"Mr. Fowler was one of the only instructors in town, and he was located in Clifton, which was close to the mill areas of Glendale, Converse, Cowpens, Cannon's Campground, and Chesnee. There were a lot of young players in those areas, and Mr. Fowler taught a lot of them. Even if he didn't play their instrument, he could always teach them something. He knew theory backwards and forwards, and timing was his specialty. He was a great teacher of syncopation and timing, and that really shows up in the music of Bobby Thompson and Hank Garland."

Under Fowler's tutelage, Bennett blossomed into an excellent young lead player, and he and the Jamborettes used their back-yard stage experience to full advantage in local talent shows. "In those days, they'd have a talent show at Roebuck Elementary and Cowpens Elementary and Boiling Springs and so on," he says. "Every weekend there was a talent show somewhere. You could win fifteen bucks, so we'd make the circuit.

"During one of those shows, we saw a little kid from Clifton with a guitar that was bigger than he was! He came out there and sang 'Davy Crockett,' and he never missed a lick on the chords. He must have been ten or eleven years old, with great big ol' blue eyes and great big ears. We beat

him in that show, but he placed second. We had to split the first place money among the band, so he actually made more than we did. We got fifteen for first and he got ten for second." That kid, Howard Childress, who was also a student of Jerome Fowler, would soon figure prominently in the life and career of Joe Bennett.

Asked about his early guitar influences, Joe recalls several key figures. One of them, Lindy Love, is the brother of Fred "Careless" Love, a Western Swing singer who performed with Spade Cooley's orchestra in Los Angeles in the early fifties. "Lindy Love was my hero," says Bennett. "Lindy had a green guitar, as I remember it, and, gosh, he played just like Les Paul. I said, 'Oh man, I want to be like that.' I guess Lindy was only about twenty years old then, but he could really play. I always wanted to go up and talk to him, but I was afraid because he was bigger than I was and played better than I did.

"Then I saw Arthur Smith in the mid-1950s. He was a fantastic guitar player, and he played stuff that I'd never seen anybody play before. He had a TV show every afternoon, and I'd come home from school and watch it. When I was taking lessons from Jerome Fowler, my dad told me if I finished the course, which was three years long, that he'd buy me any guitar I wanted. What I wanted was a Fender Stratocaster just like

Arthur Smith, and that's what Dad bought me.

"The last thing that really inspired me as a player was a show I saw at The State Theater in Spartanburg. Little Jimmy Dickens came there when I was fourteen. We went in and sat down and Jimmy Dickens' band came out first. That was the part of the show that really moved me. Buddy Emmons was on steel guitar, and he was awesome. There was a guitar guy named Spider, and another guitarist named Jimmy Wilson. Both of the guitars played lead, and they would do runs with Emmons in three-part harmony.

I just could not believe it. That show made chills go up my backbone. I decided then to get serious about music."

As Bennett entered Cowpens High School, he found that his female classmates were more smitten by the sounds of rock and roll and doo-wop than by country music. "Here we were playing country, and they said they didn't really like that country stuff," he says. "I guess I probably got influenced by that." The country stylings of The Jamborettes were soon put to rest in favor of a rock sound, with Jimmy Denton and Wayne Arthur making the transition with Bennett from hillbillies to rockers.

"I went to Wayne's mom and I said, 'Buy Wayne a bass,'" says Bennett. "She swallowed her bubble gum! She wouldn't do it, but Wayne and I kept working on her 'til she finally bought him one. We didn't know a thing about the bass, though. I said, 'Wayne, we're just gonna tune it like a guitar,' which turns out to be how you tune a bass. I didn't know that at the time, but it worked real well. We'd put pieces of tape on the fretboard to show Wayne where to put his fingers. Well, Wayne got to really *playing* that bass! He was slapping the thing, and he put on a ring to try and make it click like Elvis's bass player."

Deciding that the newly-formed trio needed a lead singer to free Joe up to concentrate on guitar, Denton,

Arthur and Bennett turned to the little kid who had placed second to The Jamborettes in that elementary school talent contest. "We wanted that kid with the big ears," Bennett says. "His name was Howard Childress, and later on we started calling him 'Sparky.' The four of us would practice in my house, right in the middle of Cannon's Campground."

The group needed a name that they could use in the local talent competitions, but the boys were unable to think of a fitting moniker. "My mom finally thought of the name," Bennett says. "She said, 'Why don't we make you guys some little vests? I'll put a musical note on there with sequins on it, and you can call yourselves "The Sparkletones." We said, 'Not bad!' See, in those days 'Sparkletones' wasn't rinky-dink. You'd never name a group that now, but back then they had the Twin-Tones and the Mono-tones and all other kinds of tones. So the parents made us costumes, and we got together and painted Jimmy Denton a bass drum head that said, 'The Sparkletones' and had 'J.D.' in the middle of it."

The origins of the group's name is one of the more misunderstood parts of the quartet's story. Most of the Upstate town's citizens now assume that The Sparkletones were named after Spartanburg, a town that is today often referred to, albeit at times with sarcasm, as "Sparkle City" or "Sparkleberry."

"No, the band's name was not taken from Spartanburg," says Bennett. "Later on, we were on the Ed Sullivan Show and people began to know that The Sparkletones were from Spartanburg. So people started calling Spartanburg 'Sparkle City.' That was where that nickname for the town came from: the whole thing was based on that little sequin on the vests. My mom wanted the clothes to match the name."

Rock and roll was a new thing in 1956, and many in the community felt it to be something of a threat. The locals were supportive of The Jamborettes singing Hank Williams songs, but the heavy beat of rock and roll seemed something entirely different and much more dangerous. "Some of the churches around back then frowned on dancing, and dancing went along with the whole rock and roll scene," Joe says. "I guess because of that, I had some reservations about it myself. Then somebody said, 'Well, it's in the Bible where they danced,' and I figured it must be okay after that."

The Sparkletones continued to play at talent shows around Spartanburg County, until the band's big opportunity came in the form of a major show at Spartanburg's Memorial Auditorium in January of 1957. First prize was a television appearance on

the "Ted Mack Original Amateur Hour." A Northern talent scout named Bob Cox, who later earned limited fame under the name Guitar Muvva Hubbard, came to Spartanburg for the event in order to ferret out any local boys who might be capable of entertaining a national audience.

Over the years, members of several other bands that played at the Memorial Auditorium show have claimed that The Sparkletones should not have won first prize that evening and, therefore, that the group's later achievements are tainted. Bennett defends his band's performance in the show, but allows that it is difficult to judge music as good, better, and best. "I don't doubt that there was a certain amount of luck in our winning," he says, "and all the groups that played that night were good."

One group in particular stands out in Joe's memory. "I'll tell you who was a heavyweight: Joe Dean Haywood. He was a black kid from Spartanburg, and they called him 'Joey.' I mean, that guy sang like Sam Cooke, only better. He and his band got up there and did about three or four songs. They had old, beat-up drums, and an old, beat-up saxophone, but they played in tune, and those guys could wail! Man, they were good. I heard them and said, 'Oh, forget this. We're out of here.'"

No audio or videotape exists of that show, but Bennett says it was

Howard "Sparky" Childress that put the band over the top. "Yeah, you should have seen that little kid. He was just a live wire. The boy was all over the stage, and it was natural. Nobody choreographed this stuff, it was just his internal enthusiasm. I think Sparky, combined with the fact that we had three-part harmony, really helped us out." At the time of that performance, Childress was not yet a teenager, and Bennett, the band's elder statesman, was only sixteen.

The Sparkletones were declared the winner of the show, and were, as promised, awarded a spot on the Ted Mack show. An off-shoot of the victory was the interest shown by talent scout Cox, who soon quit his job to become the band's full-time manager. "Bob Cox is the guy who is really responsible for The Sparkletones' success," says Bennett. "There were a lot of groups around who were better than us, but we had one heck of a manager. He's the guy who ram-rodded us all the way through to 'The Ed Sullivan Show.'"

Before they could play for Ed Sullivan, though, the band had to do well for "The Ted Mack Amateur Hour." By all accounts, they did just that. For that appearance, the band's rockabilly sound was bolstered by a female singer. "Yeah, we had a beautiful girl named Sandra Vest. She was real good, but in those days a girl just couldn't go on the road without a

chaperone. When we went to New York to try for a contract, we couldn't afford to carry an extra member of the band, plus another adult. Our manager told us that there was just no way."

It was around this time that the band began, at the urging of Bob Cox, to write their own material. One of the first—and it could have *been* the first, Joe isn't sure—songs that they put together was called "Black Slacks."

"We didn't like to write, because it was boring," he says. "Bob Cox kept telling us to write songs, though. So one day, me and Jimmy Denton were on my porch in Cannon's Campground, trying to write a song. Jimmy's mama called over, and he told her, 'Bring my

The Sparkletones made the cover of Rock and Roll Songs (1957).

black slacks by.' Then Jimmy and I looked at each other and said, 'Let's write a song about black slacks.' That's the way it happened. We sat there on the porch and made it up.

"We were really just writing gibberish. You know, making words rhyme and trying to be bad boys. The song said, 'When I go places, I just don't care/ You'll know why if you see what I wear/ Black slacks/ Peg fourteen/ And the parents don't like.' You know what 'peg fourteen' means? That's where you take a pair of slacks for alteration and they cut the seams out so you end up with the pants real tight: fourteen inches around. The pants had a cuff on them, but they were pegged. You had to be careful just to get your foot through there."

Denton and Bennett finished the song that day, but they were not terribly impressed by their new creation: "We went on and wrote other stuff that we thought was a lot better than that," says Joe. With several new compositions in tow, "Joe Bennett and the Sparkletones" (manager Bob Cox decided that the group needed a name out front, and Bennett was the oldest) accompanied manager Cox to New York City, where they would audition live for ABC Paramount Records. The audition was a success, and the record executives were impressed by the band's vocal harmonies and instrumental prowess. The boys immediately signed on ABC Paramount's dotted line, and they were quickly trotted into Bell Sound recording studio to cut their first single.

When they arrived at the studio, the 'Tones did not rush to play Denton and Bennett's front porch song about the pegged pants. "It was down towards the end of the session, and the producer was asking us if we had anything else for them to hear," Joe says. "We said, 'Well, we got one called 'Black Slacks.' Don Costa, the producer, said, 'Black Slacks? What does that sound like?' So we did it for him, but it didn't sound right yet.

"Costa heard the song and said, 'Well, that's got possibilities, and it's got a good beat to it. Can you slow that down a little?' See, we played everything like it was a hoe-down." Even the slowed-down version of the song was found lacking by band and producer, and the group struggled to find a combination of musicality and gimmickry that would allow the tune to find favor with its intended audience of dance-happy teenagers.

"We couldn't think of anything good to try," says Bennett. "Then somebody, I don't know who it was, made that noise: 'Bbbbbbb.' He went, 'Bbbbbbb, black slacks.' Right then, Don Costa said, 'That's neat! Let's try that. Can you do that in harmony?' So me and Sparky worked it out—'Bbbbbbb'—in harmony, and that was it! We laid it down: did it in maybe four or five takes."

Joe credits producer Costa with shaping the song into a national hit. "Don Costa made that song. He knew all of the right pieces of the puzzle, and he knew how to put them together. He kept telling us, 'Slow it down, now. You've got to be able to dance to this thing, boys.' He also told us how to pronounce the words. I remember distinctly him telling us, 'Don't say *black*,' say *buhlack*.' *'Buhlack slacks.'*"

Another artist making his ABC Records recording debut that day in 1957 was sixteen-year-old Paul Anka, who recorded "Diana," a song that would become a number 1 hit, just before Joe Bennett and the Sparkletones began their session. After he finished the vocals on "Diana," Anka stayed in the studio to watch The Sparkletones. He even joined in the recording of "Black Slacks," adding his voice to the chorus of the song.

"Black Slacks" was quickly pressed as a single, and the song was debuted on Cliff "Farmer" Gray's morning radio show on Spartanburg's WSPA radio. Another Spartanburg station, WTHE, was also supportive of "Black Slacks," with morning disc jockey Rick Rogers interviewing the band on several occasions and spinning the record until the grooves wore down. When the song began climbing the charts, the Upstate quartet, who had been playing a series of one-nighters with a theater chain, signed

on as a part of Art Mooney's Las Vegas show. It was while working in Las Vegas that the most popular rock and roll artist of them all, Elvis Presley, paid a visit to the 'Tones dressing room, posing for a picture with the band and commenting on the boys' unique, sparkly stage attire.

Manager Bob Cox had taken over as legal guardian for The Sparkletones, who by now ranged in age from fourteen to seventeen, and the growing success of "Black Slacks" helped Cox to land the band a slot on "The Ed Sullivan Show," one of the most popular television programs in America. A large proportion of TV-viewing Spartanburg tuned into Ed Sullivan every week, but The Sparkletones' first appearance on the program was viewed by a number of people who didn't normally watch television on Sunday nights: church-goers. "This is gross to say, but the Sunday night that we did that show a lot of the churches shut down," says Bennett. "We were all church-going boys, and we felt a little weird about that. I guess that shows you about how the town was watching what was going on with us, though."

The appearance on Sullivan's variety show pushed Joe Bennett and the Sparkletones into the rock and roll forefront and boosted "Black Slacks" into the top 20 of the Billboard pop chart (by the end of its run, in 1958, the record had sold over a million

Courtesy of Joe Bennett

The group toned down the sparkle by wearing black jackets during their first "Ed Sullivan Show" appearance.

copies). Another television performance, this one on Nat King Cole's show, also helped the song's popular cause. The Sparkletones embarked on a national tour, visiting AM radio stations and performing with big-name stars in theaters and dance-halls before crowds of screaming teenagers. The hit record became an exciting and at-times frightening ticket into the crazed world of early rock and roll.

"If we got out of there with our clothes on, we were lucky in a lot of those places," says Bennett. "We played at a record hop with Fabian one night, and it was madness. We came out there and the crowd just went wild. We had those shiny suits on, and those kids would just yell and scream. It was deafening. You felt like your head was going to cave in. We couldn't hear ourselves play, but we got up there and played anyway.

"The only place where the crowds were pretty reserved was Spartanburg. They'd go nuts for us in Pennsylvania or New York, but Spartanburg was quiet. We had a lot of friends in town, but a lot of the young guys were kind of jealous, and they'd make wise remarks. So many people here play music, and a lot of them don't care if you've been on 'The Ed Sullivan Show.' They think, 'I could have played those licks as good as he did,' or 'I could have sung as well as that guy.' A lot of times they're probably right. When you're young and pretty innocent, you don't think about stuff like that: we were just happy to be home. I think the older we got, the more hang-ups we got. We'd think, 'Hey, they ought to respect us more for the things we've done.'"

As quickly as The Sparkletones were thrust into the spotlight, they were pulled back into the shadows. Though it hadn't reached number one, "Black Slacks" was the most played and requested song in certain areas of the country (rock and roll record distribution was quite spotty in the 1950s, and even hit songs tended to find popular favor one region at a time). Even today, hundreds of thousands of people remember the tune and lyrics that Bennett and Denton strung together on Joe's Cannon's Campground porch. The problem was in achieving a second such success, and The Sparkletones were unable to do that.

"We were hot for a year," Bennett says. "See, the second hit is what you need to make a career. The first one gets your name out, but the second one gives you a toe-hold. Then it's easier to get the third one, and then you stick around. We couldn't get that second hit."

The band's lack of a second hit was due as much to unfortunate misunderstanding as to any musical reasons. The Sparkletones were offered a chance to play "The Ed Sullivan Show" for a second time, just after the release of their second single,

"Penny Loafers and Bobby Socks." Says Bennett, "That record had already hit the charts at number forty, but we didn't know that. We ended up doing a song on the Sullivan show called 'Cotton Pickin' Rocker.' Our manager said that we should do a new song, because he didn't think 'Penny Loafers' was going anywhere. Now, this was just ridiculous: you've got a song that just hit the Top 40 and you don't do it on Ed Sullivan?!! We should have done that song, and then we would have had the second hit and been established and had a chance of lasting longer than we did."

Bennett claims that manager Bob Cox knew of the chart position of "Penny Loafers and Bobby Socks," but that Cox withheld the information for some reason. "I've been told that ABC Paramount threatened Cox that if we didn't do 'Penny Loafers' on the show, they were not going to renew our contract. I don't know exactly what the problem was, but something strange was going on there. Cox knew what the situation was."

Whatever the reason, Joe Bennett and the Sparkletones were dropped from ABC Paramount's roster, but subsequently picked up by the ABC branch of the company. ABC released four singles of the band, then decided that the 'Tones would not record again for the label. "They kept Lloyd Price, Paul Anka, and Johnny Nash, and we went the way of the world," Bennett says.

Bob Cox was by this time taking on other acts, including Spartanburg's Tony McCorkle, whose brother, George, would later play rhythm guitar for The Marshall Tucker Band. Most of The Sparkletones' members decided that a change in managers might help the band revitalize its career, but Sparky Childress remained loyal to Cox. "We dropped Cox, and Sparky dropped out of the band," says Bennett. Childress stayed with Cox and took part in at least one musical tour of Korea in support of American military troops. The remaining Sparkletones took on local boy Gene Brown as a replacement for Sparky. Then, when Denton left to finish high school, Brown moved to the drums and Donnie Seay joined the band as rhythm guitarist. Rick Dunn also played in one of the group's final incarnations.

The last hurrah was a song called "Boys Don't Cry" that Bennett and Wayne Arthur recorded for Paris Records, a company best known for releasing a song called "See You In September." "Boys Don't Cry" made the top 50 of the Billboard charts, but Bennett and Arthur soon decided to

Courtesy of Joe Bennett

Elvis Presley visited their dressing room in Las Vegas (1957).

call it quits. Feeling washed up at nineteen, an age where most musicians are just starting out, Joe Bennett left Spartanburg and entered the Air Force.

"I tried to get away from playing music, but I couldn't. The pull was too strong," says Bennett. "I had been in the service about a year when I called Daddy and asked him to send me my Stratocaster guitar. We had a little group over in Europe called 'Joe and the Jaguars.' We were pretty good, especially the drummer."

Turns out that the drummer for Joe and the Jaguars was none other than Mickey Hart, who later catapulted to fame and fortune as the drummer for a band that was among the top-grossing tour attractions in all of rock and roll: The Grateful Dead, whose pro-LSD stance in the 1960s and 1970s became as well-known as any of their songs. Upon his release from the Air Force, Hart went to New York and then to California, while Bennett returned South.

"Mickey called me from California one day and said, 'My dad's got a music store out here. Come on out and I'll give you a job.' He said he'd give me $350 a week, plus whatever I could make from teaching. He and I had a little group together around San Francisco in the mid-1960s, up in San Carlos. We were playing Sonny and Cher stuff, and songs by The Animals.

We were just a cover band, but Mickey was like a young Buddy Rich. He was a tremendous drummer. I worked out there for about a year with him, and then I went back in the Air Force."

It was not until the 1990s that Bennett knew about his former drummer's fame as a member of The Grateful Dead. "I never knew anything about that band," Joe says. "I thought by their name that they were headbangers, you know, hard rock. Later, I heard some of their stuff, and it turns out they're real mellow. Well, I'd heard of the band, but I'd never seen them. One day, about three or four years ago, I picked up a *Rolling Stone* magazine, and there was a giant, blown-up picture of The Grateful Dead on there. Right in the middle of that picture was Mickey Hart!

"A guitar student of mine was a big Grateful Dead fan, and he got in touch with Mickey in 1995 through the Internet and told him where I was. One day, I got a phone call and it was Mickey. We got together in Charlotte the last time that his band came through, right before Jerry Garcia died. Mickey was such a clean-cut kid when I knew him. I never figured out why he did all that drug garbage. I said, 'Mickey, what did you do that for?' He said, 'I wanted to see what was on the other side.' I said, 'Well?' He said, 'Nothing, man. There was nothing there. I don't do none of that stuff now: I'm clean. I got my own yoga man that travels with me now.' I'm glad that he came out of that period, and I'm a Mickey Hart fan today."

Joe Bennett is nearing sixty years of age, but he still makes music. Around his Smith Music office are cassette tapes of recent recording projects, and those tapes attest to Joe's skill, speed, and inventiveness as a guitarist. Forty years removed from fame, his playing is sharper and cleaner than it was on songs such as "Black Slacks" and "Penny Loafers and Bobby Socks." Other musicians in Spartanburg are inclined to view Bennett as a gifted and knowledgeable player: any notion of Joe as a lucky participant in a fun but musically vapid fifties musical scene has long since vanished.

Bennett has also solidified a reputation as a teacher. In the 1970s, he helped two Spartanburg teenage bands, Shatter Act and Jericho, to develop musically and to learn about stage presence and repertoire. "Joe had something to do with Shatter Act and Jericho," says Steve Stinson, former bass player for Jericho. "He'd help both of those bands to figure out songs that were on the radio. One time, Jericho had a gig at some apartment complex for probably $100. Our guitar player had his appendix out, and Joe said he'd sit in with us. We were playing on a flatbed truck, and we

were all longhairs with our jeans and boots and cowboy hats, and there's Joe playing killer guitar with a bunch of kids. We were pretty good to be so young, and I think maybe Joe saw a little bit of his old band in us."

As Bennett's teaching and playing reputation has prospered, so has his bank account. "Black Slacks" sold well in the 1950s, but the royalty money that songwriters Bennett and Denton received was not exactly mind-boggling. Recently, though, the Walt Disney Company decided to use "Black Slacks" in its *Rescuers Down Under* movie. Thus, every time a video store in Missouri or New Mexico decides to carry a couple of copies of that film, Bennett and Denton get a proportionally small but surprisingly lucrative piece of the pie.

"They used the original Sparkle-tones recording of that song," Bennett

Mark Olencki

says. "John Candy was the voice of the Albatross, who is the bird that these little mice fly on to rescue these people down in Australia. The Albatross is up there dancing and singing along to 'Black Slacks!' That was a neat deal, right there."

Joe Bennett's recordings are still treasured by rockabilly fans in America and in Europe. Dutch rockabilly guitar virtuoso Tjarko Jeen claims Bennett as a major influence, as does California hillbilly rock quartet The Dave and Deke Combo, and Joe is periodically approached about regrouping the band for domestic or foreign reunion tours. While he doesn't discount the possibility of getting together with Denton, Arthur, and Childress for one last run, Bennett is pleased with his current position as a player and teacher. Of all the Hub City music makers, Joe seems the most outwardly content.

"I've tried to do lots of other things to run away from music," he says. "I joined the Air Force twice, got other jobs, worked as a salesman . . . I used to think, 'Ah, forget this music stuff. I'm going to get a real job.' But I'm so blessed to be able to make a living at what I'm doing now. I get to play music and teach people about the guitar. I'm still writing and I'm still teaching, so I'm a happy dude."

Joe Bennett at Smith Music, Spartanburg, S.C. (1997)

Mark Olencki

7 THE MARSHALL TUCKER BAND

No musical act has been more closely associated with Spartanburg, South Carolina, than The Marshall Tucker Band. The Tuckers' six original members—Toy and Tommy Caldwell, Paul Riddle, George McCorkle, Jerry Eubanks and Doug Gray—all called Spartanburg home, and during the band's 1970s heyday, the city was mentioned in *Rolling Stone*, *Circus*, *Creem*, *The New York Times*, and the hundreds of other local and national newspapers and magazines that ran articles and reviews of Marshall Tucker. Spartanburg was not only homebase for the group and its road crew and entourage, it was a marketing tool for the Capricorn Records promotion department. "They're just a bunch of talented, good ol' country boys," the press kits implied. "Just look at where they're from."

In the Tuckers' hands, Spartanburg became linked to Southern Rock in the same way that Luchenback,

Texas, was connected to Waylon Jennings' and Willie Nelson's Outlaw Country movement. "I'd love to haul 'em all down around Spartanburg/ And show 'em how to raise Hell in Caroline," sang Hank Williams, Jr., who for a time seemed more influenced by Marshall Tucker's sound than by his own legendary father's honky-tonk legacy. The result of all the hoopla was a simplified canonization of a town that was more complex than Southern Rock fans or Northern liberal presses realized. There was undeniable power and giddy fun, though, in witnessing the roar of a sold-out Madison Square Garden crowd as a New York City master-of-ceremonies announced, "From Spartanburg, South Carolina, The Marshall Tucker Band!"

Today, Toy and Tommy Caldwell are gone, victims of a heart attack and an automobile accident, and vocalist Doug Gray is the only one of the original six band members still performing with the current version of the Tuckers. Flute and saxophone player Jerry Eubanks has recently sold his share of interest in the group, drummer Paul Riddle teaches drum lessons and manages Spartanburg's Albert Hill band, and rhythm guitarist George McCorkle, who penned "Fire on the Mountain," one of the Tuckers' most enduring hits, is a professional songwriter in Nashville.

More than a decade has passed since McCorkle left the band along with Toy Caldwell and Paul Riddle, and he is now able to look back on his career in rock and roll with the detachment of time if not of feeling. It is in McCorkle's drawling voice that much of this, a story of The Marshall Tucker Band, is told. The look on George's face when the talk turns serious suggests his belief that neither he nor his former band is to be taken lightly, while the laughter that frequently punctuates the conversation implies that the trappings that came with the Tuckers' success are far less sacred to him than the music they made. The music room in the Peagram, Tennessee, home that George shares with his wife Mary is free of Marshall Tucker paraphernalia, save for the collection of 1970s Tucker CDs that takes up a healthy portion of space in his CD rack. When a visitor requests a look at a few of his framed gold and platinum records, McCorkle pulls them out of a closet and sets them on the music

room floor, eyeing them once in a while in a manner both proud and suspicious. The shiny records are tokens of the Tuckers' enormous popularity and of the heavy cost that came with the money and attention. That cost was paid in a number of ways

The McCorkles' music room (1996)   Mark Olencki

by each member of the band. For McCorkle, the problems surfaced not in the group's rocket launch to stardom or the freefall from grace: the trouble was in the landing. When Toy, Paul and George gave up the Tuckers' ghost in 1984, McCorkle found himself back in Spartanburg with no cheering fans, no charting records, too much empty time and too many empty bottles. There was a time in the late 1980s when George appeared to be, in the words of his most famous song, "Shot down in cold blood/ By a gun that carried fame." Turns out it was only a flesh wound.

None of the six could be considered children of privilege, most having grown up in Spartanburg's rougher sections: the south or west sides, or the mill villages that surround Spartanburg proper. When McCorkle says, "Marshall Chapman's daddy owned the mill where my mama worked," it is not without pride in his mother or in his background, or in himself for having risen to such heights from meager beginnings.

"My mother and father divorced when I was real young, and my mother raised me and my brothers," he explains. "It was kind of a rough neighborhood, and I had to learn to fight early on. My mama worked at the cotton mill and I knew I didn't want to do that, but I didn't have the funds to get a college education."

If hard-scrabble upbringings had something to do with the band's ability to work up to ninety days at a time in later years, then so be it. In the fifties and early sixties, none of the six were thankful for lessons learned or karma points; they were simply struggling to keep a few dreams alive before the impending reality of work-a-day life set in. For McCorkle, music was both a means of escape and an end in itself. "All I cared about was that guitar," he says. "With that, you could take a black world and turn it into white; a red world and turn it green. You could shape it anyway you wanted to."

At first, McCorkle and his friend Toy Caldwell chose to shape their musical world into something vaguely reminiscent of the music that was associated with the British Inva-

The Marshall Tucker Band at The Ruins, Spartanburg (1970)

Les Duggins

sion bands, groups like The Beatles or The Rolling Stones. The two high-schoolers (Caldwell was at Dorman; McCorkle at Spartanburg High) played in The Rants, a band that also included future Marshall Tucker member Franklin Wilkie. Publicity photos of The Rants depict Toy in a mop-top wig, with the rest of the band checking in with more pedestrian haircuts. The

Courtesy of the estate of George McCorkle

The Rants (1964)

group played a number of gigs in and around town, and was even brought to Nashville in 1964 for a recording session that resulted in no real break-through.

The New Generation, which favored a soulful, rhythm and blues sound, was led by singer Doug Gray and solidified by drummer Ross Hannah and Toy's little brother, bassist Tommy Caldwell. "I'll never forget

The New Generation," says Spartan-burg-bred musician David Ezell. "I was in a soul band with (future Marshall Tucker manager) Joe McConnell called The Kaks. There was a real competition between The Kaks and The New Generation back then, and right after I was asked to join The Kaks, there was a March of Dimes talent show in Spartanburg. The New Generation came out for that talent show and they did 'When A Man Loves A Woman.' It was a band of white kids doing a black soul song, and Spartanburg had only recently been integrated. Doug Gray sang the hell out of that song, and the white and black kids in the audience just went crazy. That put any competition between the two bands to rest: The New Generation was on top after that."

The New Generation cut one record, a 45 called "Because of Love, It's All Over" that was recorded at Reflections Studio in Charlotte. In 1966, the two Caldwells, Gray, and McCorkle joined together in the first edition of The Toy Factory, but that line-up was soon altered by the Vietnam War. Upon finishing high school, The Toy Factory's oldest member, George McCorkle, went into the Navy, and Doug Gray joined the Army. The Caldwells, first Toy and then Tommy, followed in their father's footsteps and became members of the United States Marines, though Tommy's stay in the service was brief.

In the late 1960s, there were several versions of The Toy Factory, most of which included Tommy Caldwell on rhythm guitar and Franklin Wilkie on bass. When McCorkle returned from his Navy stint, he did not rejoin the Factory, instead joining up with junior high school drumming whiz Paul Riddle in a band called Pax Parachute. That band was playing Spartanburg's Sitar club one night in 1970, soon after Tommy had returned from the Marines. Singer/songwriter David Ezell was at the club with Tommy that night. "Tommy had on this long olive-drab trenchcoat," Ezell says. "He had just come back from the Marines, and he still had real short

hair. I think he had a hat on that night. I remember Tommy and I were standing off to the side of the stage at one point, and Tommy looked up at Paul playing drums and said, 'That's my drummer right there.'"

"I don't remember much about that night," says McCorkle, "but I remember that after Pax Parachute played, Paul and I started talking with Tommy. We finally said, 'Hell, why don't we get up there and play one.' We did, and that was the start of it all."

By this time, Toy Caldwell had returned from Vietnam, and he worked for a short while to lead a new version of The Toy Factory. Soon, however, he decided to quit music altogether and concentrate on his job at the Spartanburg Waterworks. "At first, the band was just Paul on drums, Tommy on bass, and me on guitar," says McCorkle. "Actually, Toy was the one that suggested to me that me and Tommy should put something together. He told me, 'I'm tired of this music stuff. I don't want any more of it, and I'm not playing anymore.' I said, 'Hey, that's cool.'

"Well, we were at our practice place out on Spring Street one night and we heard someone banging on the door. We looked out and it was Toy. He was going, 'Let me in! Let me in!' He had his guitar and his amp with

Pax Parachute (1970)

him. It was just like that: he couldn't stand it. We knew that night when we all started playing that we had something really good."

Toy may actually have been attempting to get back into music *before* interrupting that Spring Street rehearsal. "At the time, we were attempting to develop a group with myself and Toy on guitar, Frank Wilkie on bass, Ross Hannah on drums, Carol Cox on keyboard, Jerry Eubanks on sax and Doug Gray singing," says David Ezell. "We had two or three rehearsals together. One Saturday, we were supposed to rehearse and Doug and Jerry decided that they were going to go to the beach. That pissed everybody off. All it took was one missed rehearsal. One week after that, Toy said, 'Forget this, I want to play with my brother.' He didn't say, 'I want to play with Pax Parachute,' he said, 'I want to play with my brother.'

"They did that four-piece thing with Tommy doing lead vocals for a while and they realized they needed another singer, so they brought Doug on. Then Doug brought Jerry in and that was the band. That is the group that became Marshall Tucker."

Though not a virtuoso player like Toy Caldwell or Paul Riddle, Jerry Eubanks was an important addition to the group. His instantly identifiable woodwind sound would help to separate the Tuckers from other acts that emerged from the South in the 1970s,

and he is today one of only two memorable flautists in rock and roll history (the other is Ian Anderson of English progressive rock band Jethro Tull).

The sound that resulted from the combination of the group's six members embraced various elements of Spartanburg culture and music: jazz, country, loud rock and roll, soul, gospel, bluegrass, blues, and swing. That mix was later labeled by record companies and music writers as "Southern Rock," but, in many ways, the Tucker band was a culmination of Spartanburg's twentieth-century musical history. Lead guitarist Toy Caldwell was a country and jazz fan who would later name Hank Garland as his favorite player. Rhythm guitarist McCorkle was a rock and roll fan whose oldest brother, Tony, was a contemporary, friend, and musical competitor of The Sparkletones' Joe Bennett, and whose older brother Chuck also played guitar in rock and roll bands. Drummer Paul

Jerry Eubanks (1977)

Riddle is a direct product of the city's jazz scene, having played his first paying gigs with local favorites Stanley and the Stardusters.

"They each brought their own thing to the table," says David Ezell. "It was a combination of styles that had not been tried before. Paul was a jazz drummer, Tommy was a funky, back-beat, straight R&B bass player, Doug was kind of a soul singer, and then you had Jerry on flute and sax. The only reason they did country/rock was because that's what Toy was writing. Toy's father played guitar, and played a lot of country music, so that was always a big part of Toy. The sound wasn't predicated on any movement, it was just pure Spartanburg. It was the result of high school buddies growing up and growing out and growing back together through a common bond, which was Toy's songwriting."

Just before Woodstock in 1970, the new band had scheduled a gig at a drive-in theater on Asheville Highway in Spartanburg. "We played that gig on a flatbed truck," recalls McCorkle. The group was in their practice room on Spring Street, preparing for the gig, when they decided they needed a name. Toy Caldwell preferred that they not be known as The Toy Factory, because he wanted to emphasize the band's newness (versions of The Toy Factory had been playing in town for years) and de-

emphasize his role as group leader.

In an occurrence that pushes the limits of believable symbolism, Tommy Caldwell found a key on the floor. Attached to the key was a tag on which the name "Marshall Tucker" was written. Supposing that to be an adequate moniker, The Marshall Tucker Band went to supper and came back to rehearse for their flat-bed truck concert.

As word got out around town about The Marshall Tucker Band, a number of curious locals began to sit, watch, and listen while the band practiced. "The people who would come to hear us were mostly a bunch of hippies back in those days," remem-

Courtesy of Don Bramblett

One version of The Toy Factory

bers McCorkle. "We weren't your typical hippies, but they liked us anyway. We had long hair, but we'd whip your ass. They smoked dope and everything was cool; we drank liquor and fought."

After recording some demo tapes, one in Muscle Shoals and one at Mark V Studio in Greenville, the band found themselves in a position to win a record deal. An opening gig for Capricorn Records act Wet Willie led to members of that group going back to Macon, Georgia, and talking the Tuckers up to Capricorn President Phil Walden. Toy and Tommy soon made a visit to Capricorn and, after some wrangling, managed a personal audience with Walden. The label boss then booked the band into Grant's Lounge, a tiny Macon bar where The Allman Brothers often held court.

"That was the opportunity," says McCorkle. "We set the whole band up on that little stage and blew that place in half." Phil Walden and the Capricorn staff were at the gig, as were the Allman Brothers. "They were all in there, staring at us, thinking, 'All right, boys, what can you do?' We went in there and blew their asses away. If it was

ever left up to our band to prove something, it wasn't a problem. Bring 'em on."

Following the Grant's Lounge gig, The Marshall Tucker Band was offered a record deal with Capricorn. The contract stipulated that Phil Walden would be the band's manager and publisher. Walden also received royalties as record company owner and collected thousands of dollars more as owner of the Macon studio where the band

Toy and Tommy at San Francisco's Winterland (1974)

recorded. "He couldn't do that today," says McCorkle, "because it's a conflict of interests. We signed everything we had to him, but that's okay. Ol' Phil was a slick man. He knew how to do it, and, you know, that's great. So we gave him every-thing. Who cares? A couple of guys in the band bucked that pretty hard. They were like, 'We're gonna give him everything?' Well, sure we are! We're gonna have a record deal! How many other bands can say they've got record deals?"

Several years after signing the deal with Capricorn, the Tuckers were able to right some of the contractual wrongs by pressuring Walden to step down as manager. After more haggling, Joe McConnell took over as manager and restructured the contract so that the band members received a fair share of the money collected from album sales and live appearances. All this was in the future, though, as The Marshall Tucker Band began playing club dates throughout the Southeast in preparation for its first album.

"Once we got that record deal, work became the window to success," says McCorkle. "We said to ourselves, 'If you want this, you will go out and work hard,' and we did. I think that has a lot to do with that true South Carolina upbringing. Nobody in that band was afraid of work; it didn't scare

us. A lot of guys in the music business would say, 'Work twenty days in a row? You must be crazy.' Hell, we worked ninety. Didn't bother us. It beat the cotton mill."

On stage, George McCorkle was the smiling Tucker, usually standing near the drum set with a grin on his face, playing in, out, and around any number of rhythm patterns on acoustic and electric guitar, and freeing Toy to play most anything without worrying about the band losing any momentum from a sound that George describes as being "like a freight train unleashed all of a sudden." It was with the intention of capturing that sound on tape that the six young men from Spartanburg entered Capricorn Sound Studios in Macon in the summer of 1972.

The first album, called *The Marshall Tucker Band*, was recorded by a fledgling producer named Paul Hornsby. That album, written entirely by Toy, contained some of Tucker's best songs, including "Can't You See" and "See You Later, I'm Gone," but it also betrays Hornsby's studio inexperience. The recording of "Take the Highway," a strong showcase for the band in concert, was marred by Hornsby's intrusive synthesizer. Nonetheless, it became immediately apparent to all who heard the album that Marshall Tucker was both very different and very good. The Capricorn Records hierarchy was first apprehensive about the pervasive nature of the former: in an interview with Rick Clark for the liner notes of *The Best of The Marshall Tucker Band: The Capricorn Years*, Hornsby said that the label first attempted to shop the album to other record companies because "it didn't sound like anything they were used to and they couldn't put a

Mark Olencki

Doug Gray (1977)

Paul T. Riddle (1977)

us, The Allman Brothers included. We knew what we had to do: we went for the throat."

As their professional lives were on the upswing, band members saw relations with friends and family altered by the intrusions of fame. "One of the last really personal conversations I had with Tommy Caldwell was when their success was beginning to happen," says David Ezell. "Tommy lived in a concrete block house on the west side of town, and I went over to see him one day. We were standing out in the yard, and he said, 'I went to this party the other night and there were all these old friends there, and they

name on it."

On April 1, 1973, Capricorn released the record to critical success. The record company press kit described the band's sound as "a blissful package of easygoing country, full soaring rock, and a melange in between of gospel, blues, and Carolinas funk." Not an immediate hit, the album began picking up commercial speed after the group hit the road for an unending stream of live dates. Well after its original release, *The Marshall Tucker Band* reached number 29 on the Billboard Album chart and became the first of the group's gold records. The Tuckers toured all over the country, playing with complementary acts like The Allman Brothers and less-than-compatible bands like Bachman Turner Overdrive. Says McCorkle of those opening gigs, "We could blow anybody's ass away that was in the arena, and we'd do it ninety percent of the time. We took no prisoners. We'd kick anybody's ass who got near

Toy Caldwell (1977)

Tommy Caldwell (1978)

money in the world that can buy that: everybody that tries to buy it loses."

In today's pop music world, record sales fuel concert sales. In the Tuckers' case, the opposite was true. Each of their early albums, *The Marshall Tucker Band, A New Life, Where We All Belong*, and *Searchin' For A Rainbow*, sold slowly at first and gradually moved towards gold or platinum status (a gold record is one that sells at least 50,000 units, while a platinum record sells at least 100,000). There were no successful singles until 1975, when the McCorkle-penned "Fire on

were all acting weird and treating me different.' He was really disturbed about this. He said, 'What do people expect? I'm just me.' I said, 'Tommy, these people will always be your friends, but they're as proud of you and wrapped up in the thing and awestruck by this as anyone.' I think he was worried that people would think he'd changed. Well, of *course* you change. Success changes your perspective on things. Maybe that's just growing up, but it changes you."

The years 1974 through 1977 were spent almost entirely on the road or in the studio. In those years, the band played about three hundred shows per annum, and found time to record six albums. "We did three hundred dates a year for four straight years," says McCorkle. "We starved out there for a long time, buddy, but we weren't in it for the money. That world up there on stage is something that nobody can touch. There ain't no

George McCorkle (1980)

the Mountain" hit number 38. The albums sold not because of the record company's publicity efforts, which were modestly budgeted, but because people who went out to hear the band opening for big-name acts or headlining at smaller venues went home impressed enough to purchase the records.

A tape recorded straight off the club's mixing board from a concert that Marshall Tucker played at Austin's World Armadillo Headquarters on November 2, 1975, provides a sense of the energy and musicality of the group's live shows. On that night, songs like "24 Hours At A Time" and "Can't You See" were athletic in their intensity. Toy's guitar solos spiral over the gritty soundscape like passes thrown from a strong-armed quarterback, and the rhythm section sounds like the runaway train that McCorkle remembers. "24 Hours" builds to a fury, breaks down to near-silence, held together only by Riddle's cymbal and Tommy's bass, then explodes once again until notes and voices and chords and beats are flying everywhere. Never released to the public, the tape is both a lasting proof of the band's dominance and a forgotten relic of a time over twenty years past. "That tape moves me when I hear it," says Riddle. "I can remember that show: the music stirs my soul so much that it makes me remember."

As the band played on that

Greg Savalin

Toy, Paul, Tommy, and 50,000 fans in Callaverous County, California (1979)

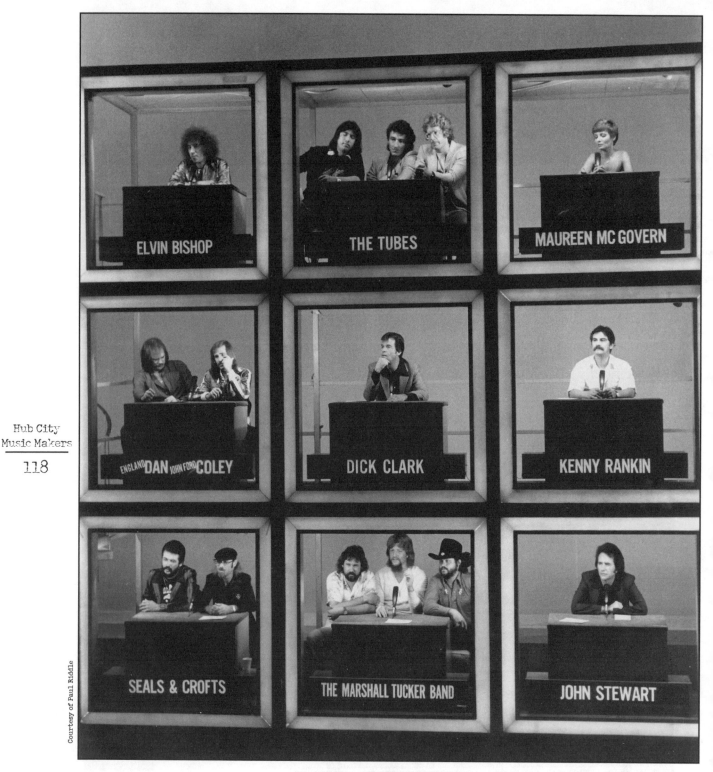

ELVIN BISHOP

THE TUBES

MAUREEN MC GOVERN

ENGLAND DAN JOHN FORD COLEY

DICK CLARK

KENNY RANKIN

SEALS & CROFTS

THE MARSHALL TUCKER BAND

JOHN STEWART

Courtesy of Paul Riddle

"The Hollywood Squares" TV program

November evening in 1975, their just-released *Searchin' For A Rainbow* album, produced (as were each of their first six records) by Hornsby, was on its way to becoming the Tuckers' best-selling record. The album eventually hit number 15 on the Billboard album chart and earned platinum status. The title song found Dickey Betts of The Allman Brothers soloing on guitar while Toy played steel, an instrument that he dearly loved. Riddle says that Caldwell enjoyed playing steel because, unlike electric guitar, it *didn't* come easy.

The next album, 1976's *Long Hard Ride*, included the Grammy-nominated instrumental title song, as well as three songs not written by Toy. "That was a conscious effort," says McCorkle. "Toy was getting a little burnt. Writing four records is a lot of work, a lot of pressure." Spurred on by McCorkle's success on the previous album with "Fire On the Mountain," all of the band members except Riddle had songwriting credits on *Long Hard Ride*. Tommy wrote what some consider the record's best song, the raw, bluesy "You Don't Live Forever."

That year also saw the group's first extended European tour, as they played cities like London, Hamburg, Frankfurt, Brussels, Paris, and Amsterdam. Spartanburg musician Marshall Chapman, by then signed to Epic/Columbia Records, asked Toy in early 1977 about the places he'd been on that tour. "I asked him, 'Where'd you play?' He just said, 'Theeyaiters mostly.'" To Caldwell that must have been how it seemed on the road: The Tuckers had been playing almost constantly since the release of their first album in 1973, and the stage of an arena or theater in Des Moines looks a lot like an arena or theater in Paris. Of course, there were days off—two of them between November 9 and December 2.

It was a Toy Caldwell composition, "Heard It In A Love Song," that

helped the band's next record, *Carolina Dreams*, to become their second platinum album. In 1977, that tune climbed to number 14 on the singles chart, while the album hit number 23. The band started off the year by playing Jimmy Carter's inauguration, but ended it richer and less happy than ever. The late 1970s were the group's wildest years, and drug and alcohol abuse had begun to exact a toll on both internal and external relations. There were problems between the Tuckers and Capricorn and problems between the Tuckers and producer Paul Hornsby.

For 1978's *Together Forever*, Hornsby was dropped in favor of Stewart Levine, to this day a professional role model for Paul Riddle. That album was recorded in Miami and sounded considerably more "uptown" (Riddle's word), and it reached as high as number 22 on the charts and was certified gold.

Wanting a change, and feeling that Phil Walden was not proceeding with the band's best interests at heart, the band made a switch to Warner Brothers Records and, in 1979, released *Running Like The Wind*, another Stewart Levine production that embraced some of the slicker arrangements of the day. *Running* included McCorkle's "Last of the Singing Cowboys," a song that Riddle considers among the best songs in the MTB catalogue.

Throughout the lifetime of The Marshall Tucker Band, the group succeeded in making their affiliation with Spartanburg a marketing advantage. The band's members and crew all resided in Spartanburg County, and most articles written about the band dwelled at length on Spartanburg. An article in *Circus* magazine written by Kurt Loder, perhaps the best-known rock journalist of the past twenty years, begins, "The town of Spartanburg, South Carolina, isn't much impressed with gold records."

Most of the write-ups used Spartanburg as a kind of Southern everyplace: a naive, backwoods town that wouldn't allow a few hundred thousand record sales to go to the heads of its rock and roll boys. The hometown provided newspaper and magazine writers with a foil for the Tuckers, and the scribes would frequently contrast a quiet, reverent town with a sextet of loud, long-haired musicians. Both sides of that equation are, of course, caricatures of the city and its sons, yet neither is particularly damaging or patently untrue and the publicity helped both parties substantially. Wofford College spent a football halftime honoring the Tuckers with a community service award (to which

McCorkle replied in his acceptance speech, "Not bad for a kid who used to have to climb the fence just to watch these games"), and the band members spent many interviews playing up the hometown angle.

In 1980, the band released *10th* (the band had by then recorded eight studio albums, and Capricorn had released a *Greatest Hits* album that eventually went gold). *10th*, like *Running Like the Wind*, contained some good songs but no hits. The Marshall Tucker Band was by now struggling: substance abuse remained a divisive factor, and, although the group was still able to sell out concert venues across the country, record sales had dried up considerably. Troubles were mounting, but the perspective brought about through the tragic events of the spring of 1980 would reveal the group's professional difficulties to be insignificant in the face of greater tragedy.

In March of 1980, a wreck on a rural Spartanburg County highway claimed the life of Toy and Tommy's younger brother, Tim Caldwell. A lover of horses, Tim was in charge of the daily operations at Toy's Southern Music Farms. "Tommy and Toy were two Marines, but Tim was a real gentle soul," says David Ezell. "He was an excellent horseman and a really nice young kid." It was a hard time for the Caldwell family, and for The Marshall Tucker Band, and it was about to get much harder.

The band attempted to play through the pain through mid-April, performing a memorable show to a sold-out Nassau Coliseum crowd in Long Island, New York. Then another car accident, this one taking place in Spartanburg less than a month after Tim's wreck, claimed the life of Toy's last remaining brother, Tommy. His death stunned his hometown, saddened fans across the country, and devastated his bandmates. "I didn't even have a suit of clothes to my name until 1980," says George McCorkle. "The only reason I bought one then was 'cause Tommy died. That probably tells you a good bit about it. Tommy's

death always bothered me, probably more than anything I've ever been through in my life."

According to McCorkle, Riddle, and Joe McConnell, Tommy Caldwell was the heart of The Marshall Tucker Band. "He was the wheel around which everything turned," says McConnell. Riddle says, "Tommy and I were inseparable. If you look around my studio, you'll see Tommy's pictures more than anyone. I miss him every day, and it's been sixteen years since he died."

Musically, Tommy anchored the rhythm section, playing a prominent bass guitar and at times taking bass solos. He also played guitar on some studio tracks, sang backing vocals, and

Les Duggins

The Marshall Tucker Band with friend/guest musician Charlie Daniels (June 1977)

played *drums* on the album version of "See You Later, I'm Gone." As important to the band as his musical contributions were, his backstage leadership was perhaps his most valued attribute. "Tommy Caldwell had the biggest heart of anybody in the world," says McCorkle. "He'd give you the shirt off his back anytime you asked for it."

The "shirt off his back" expression is often used and seldom literally intended, but in Tommy's case it holds true. Joe McConnell offers an example: "When we first took Charlie Daniels on the road to open for us, we were out for a forty-five-day tour. After the first week, Tommy was talking to one of the guys in Charlie's band, and that fellow was saying, 'I need to send my wife some money, and we're just not getting paid any money for being out here with Charlie.' Within the hour, we were having a band meeting and Tommy was saying, 'My suggestion is, we pick up the payroll for Charlie Daniels and his band and crew for the rest of this tour. They'll pay us back one day, and if they don't then we're doing the right thing anyway.' Who the hell else would say that? Who'd even think that, much less take it to the point of writing checks? Tommy was very special like that. It's such a great quality, and I wish I had more of it. Tommy was real caring; absolutely a man of compas-

Franklin Wilkie with The Marshall Tucker Band

sion. I'd love to see him again."

Badly shaken, the Tuckers regrouped, drafting former Toy Factory guitarist Franklin Wilkie into the group to play bass. Wilkie had been playing in Garfeel Ruff, a Greenville-based band that released one major-label album on Capitol Records and scored a movie soundtrack as well. "I love Frank to death," says McCorkle, "and Frank Wilkie is a great musician, but it just wasn't the same. We played some wonderful shows after Tommy died, but Tommy was just that . . . I don't know, man. He was a wonderful human being who lived and breathed music, and when you took that part of the unit away, it just wasn't ever the same again. At that point, the band got way too heavy into drugs and alcohol."

The Tuckers recorded three albums after Tommy's death, released a few videos, and played to sell-out crowds, but they were never to match the creativity or the record sales of their work for Capricorn. In 1984, Toy Caldwell, Paul Riddle, and George McCorkle decided to break up the band, and Eubanks and Gray played on using the name "The Marshall Tucker Band." Some excellent musicians, including guitarist Rusty Milner, drummer Ace Allen and bass player Tim Lawter, have been a part of the post-breakup version of the group, but Joe McConnell's assertion that it is now just "The Partial Tucker Band" is right on the money. In late 1996, Doug Gray bought out Jerry Eubanks' share in the band, leaving only one original member in a group that still performs regularly at festivals, clubs, and amphitheaters.

The influence of the original Marshall Tucker Band on today's music scene can be heard pouring from stages, jukeboxes, and radios all over the country. Blue-grass bands do "Fire On The Mountain," performers in fern bars and smoky honky-tonks play "Can't You See," FM radio stations play "Another Cruel Love" and "Heard It In A Love Song," and young, alternative rock bands embrace the Tuckers' jam band values in concert festival settings like Lollapalooza and The H.O.R.D.E. tour. One reason for the band's widespread influence is that they never made musical distinctions between genres that most people believe to be incompatible. "When we quit judging what is country and what is jazz and what is rock and roll, then everything becomes a circle," says McCorkle. "Then you can play it all."

Nowhere is the Tucker sound heard to a greater extent than on today's country radio. Performers like Travis Tritt and Garth Brooks obviously spent time as teenagers with an eight-track of *Searchin' For A Rainbow* wedged inside their car stereos. "That kind of music is what everybody's doing now," says McCorkle. "Maybe that's why I have a job here. I'm not quite sure."

"Here" is Nashville, Tennessee, where George McCorkle writes songs for a living. Each weekday, he travels to an office located between West End Avenue and Music Row, sits down with a guitar, and writes something that he hopes will end up on an album by someone like Tritt or Brooks. So far, he has sold some songs to both American and European artists, though none of his Nashville songs have been hits. That says absolutely nothing about the merit of his current work, which is in some cases (such as a song called "Crazy Molly Monroe") better than much of what he wrote for The Marshall Tucker Band. "They're making me pay my dues here," he says.

The notion of someone who has been playing music professionally for over thirty years having to "pay dues" is perfectly normal in today's "What have you done for me lately?" Nashville. McCorkle is practically bursting with the South Carolina work ethic that worked so well for the Tucker band, though, and his energy seems somehow rejuvenated by each rejection. "It'll come around," he says. "I know what my goals are, and I know where I want to be. After a couple of

number 1 songs, I could readjust my goals. I have no doubt they will come; I'm a very patient person."

One of the McCorkle songs that has been recorded recently, the jazzy "Two Faces In The Texas Moon," is directly attributable to Toy Caldwell. "I steal a lot from Toy," he says. "I used the same chord structure on that song as Toy used on 'Desert Skies.' I learned a whole lot about writing songs from that man. For one thing, I learned to write honest from him. Take his song, 'Property Line,' where he says, 'I'll leave the ax in the tree.' That's a great line, and it's very simple."

Eight years after the breakup of Marshall Tucker, Toy Caldwell released a well-received solo album. A year later, the Tuckers' chief songwriter, lead guitarist, and musical leader was gone. A television appearance on Ralph Emery's "Nashville Now" show that was telecast a couple of months before Toy's death revealed a man who was still a charismatic and vital performer, but who was in very poor health. On that show, Caldwell played a song called "Midnight Promises" to great audience response, then walked to a chair for the obligatory interview. After only a short musical performance, he was so out of breath that it was difficult to make out his answers to Emery's questions. On February 25, 1993, Toy died of a heart attack.

Mark Olencki

George McCorkle (1996)

"All Toy had was a Gibson Les Paul and a thumb," says McCorkle. "All these other guys had all this fancy equipment, but Toy didn't need it. I'm in awe of his ability. No matter who came on stage with us, he could hold his own. Carlos Santana was one of my heroes, but I've seen Toy hold his own with Carlos. Freddie King, B.B. King . . . I've seen Toy play with all of them: he'd just jump in there and blow 'em away. It didn't make a damn difference to him."

There was a rough side to Caldwell, and it is remembered by many in Spartanburg. He had quite a temper, and refused to accept disrespect from anybody. A memorable and humorous excerpt from an interview that Toy did with writer Jon Marlowe touches on that aspect of his personality: "I don't got nothin' against nobody . . . If they just leave me alone, we get along fine. But there's times, like, what the hell's that guy's name, he's with Deep Purple now . . . Glenn Hughes. He used to be in a band called Trapeze. Shit, I put that kid in the circus. He just kept bothering the hell out of me and finally I knocked the daylights out of him. He don't say nothing more about cowboys and horses, at least not to me."

Cowboys, horses, and Marines were three subjects not to be joked about around Toy Caldwell. "Toy and Tommy both came from a family of ex-Marines," says McCorkle. "Toy lived with a lot of pain inside of him. He had a lot of demons. I think Vietnam was a bad, bad thing for Toy. He never got over Vietnam, and he also never talked about it seriously or in-depth. He'd get drunk and get into the weird things about it, but I think he probably needed to express it more than he ever did.

"Musically, he was possessed by every demon that ever lived inside a human being. I've sat and thought about this many, many times . . . about that man. Hell, he just *flowed* with talent. We don't know anything about talent compared to what that guy knew. I use his inspiration every day. Always will, I hope.

"Toy was a true friend to me. We didn't speak every day, nor did we always hang around together, but we always had that mutual respect for each other. I admired him for everything he did. I thought he was a great human being. He and Tommy both died sad deaths, considering what kind of human beings they were."

Toy Caldwell is not the only member of The Marshall Tucker Band to have known demons. George McCorkle has known some, too, and he has kicked them. For a while, it looked like he might not. "I don't think I handled success very well," he says. "You look at the thing of people chasing you, wanting autographs and all that stuff. I thought, 'What is this? This is real strange. I'm a country boy from a little ol' town called Spartanburg, and I don't know anything about this.'

"All that pried at me too hard, especially when it went away. I think losing it bothered me, because I wasn't ready to lose it."

There was a rapid succession of negatives for McCorkle in the mid-eighties. The band broke up, he went through a difficult divorce, and he lost a lot of money in an ill-fated business deal. By 1987, he was living at The Corners, an apartment complex on Fernwood Road in Spartanburg. "That was when I was single, and I was real drunk back then. I don't think I ever drew a sober breath at that place." By the time he went into rehab in January of 1988, he was drinking an average of a gallon and a half of liquor a day.

"How a man functions like that is really ridiculous," he says. "I say now, because I met Mary and got married again, that it was a blessing that I went through all that." At the time, few who knew him would have described George's problems in terms of blessings.

Later that year, he quit playing music entirely and moved to Conway, South Carolina, a coastal town adjacent to Myrtle Beach. "I felt like I had some bad problems and didn't know how to cure them, so I sold most of my guitars and put a few under the bed. I was using my amplifier for a coffee table. Maybe I had played too long and was just burnt out, I don't know."

McCorkle bought a commercial glass company in Conway and worked with stained glass on the side. While in Conway, he met an attorney named Mike Battle. "He walked in my shop one day and introduced himself," says George. "He said, 'You know, I'd like to play guitar with you someday.' I said, 'I haven't played in so long, I have no idea if I can even think about doing that.' Well, he came over to my house one day and we started playing. He's the one that got me back into it. There's times where you meet people that you know you were supposed to meet, and I guess Mike was just supposed to become a good friend."

The ex-musician and the Conway attorney began writing songs together, and eventually put together The George McCorkle Band. "Mike played bass, the drummer was a family practice physician, my keyboard player was a gynecologist, and my other guitar player was an English professor at Coastal. In the paper they called it 'Four Yuppies and a Redneck.' "

George played around town

with that band for a while, then began playing with some younger musicians who could push him back towards the musicianship of his glory days. A few years later, he traveled to Nashville with a few original songs and was offered a publishing deal. He now resides just outside of Music City in Peagram, Tennessee.

"I'm real happy just being at home now," he says. "I've never known this life before, but I think it suits me."

Most Nashville staff writers have a music room in their homes filled with CDs and guitars and various songwriting tools. Few, however, have eight gold or platinum record awards tucked away in the closet. McCorkle is shy about openly displaying the records, but admits that "there's a lot of guys uptown beating their heads against the wall to get one of these, and I don't take that lightly. I'm very proud of those records. There's a lot of sweat and blood in them things, a lot of work. It's just like a song: if I finish a song, I don't take it lightly, nor do I call it 'stupid' or 'a ditty.' Because that's a gift, man. Whether it's a ditty to somebody else or not, it's still a gift."

McCorkle seems to regard his music career with the mixture of humility and pride that he shows towards his gold records. "I'd stand on stage at Madison Square Garden when I was with The Marshall Tucker Band and wonder why people paid money to see

us do what we did," he says. "A couple of beers and a dinner and two concert tickets and that's $100 for a guy and his date to go to that show. I'd think, 'If these people only knew what we were . . . we were just a bunch of guys from Spartanburg that loved what we were doing. Highly uneducated musically, too.'"

George's tone changes abruptly, however, when asked if *he* would have paid good money to see that show.

"Hell yes! I would have paid in a heartbeat. There was something about that band: call it 'karma,' call it 'meant to be,' call it any damn thing you want, but it was magic more than anything." MM

8 WALTER HYATT

"We had an old player piano in our house," says Walter Hyatt's brother, George. "You could peddle the rollers and it'd play songs like 'St. Louis Blues' and 'Sugar Blues.' Our daddy would sit at that piano and sing 'Darkness on the Delta' and 'St. James Infirmary' and all kinds of other stuff."

There is a discernible gleam in George's eye as he sits at his kitchen table in Lexington, South Carolina, and talks about the early musical experiences that he shared with the kid brother that he called "Pee Wee." The recollections come fast, but not easily, as George's obvious pride in Walter's musical accomplishments is set against the impenetrable sadness of recent loss. In May of 1996, Walter Hyatt was one of 110 people who died when a ValuJet DC-9 airplane crashed into the Florida Everglades, fifteen miles northwest of Miami International Airport. An influence to performers such as Lyle Lovett,

Junior Brown, and Jimmie Dale Gilmore, Hyatt was mourned by his audience as a master musician and by George as a beloved brother.

Less than a month before the tragedy, Walter arrived fifteen minutes late for a scheduled lunchtime interview at Spartanburg's Main Street Cafe. In town from Nashville for a concert at Player's Club, Hyatt had misplaced his car keys at his mother's Calhoun Avenue home. The subsequent search was cause for the quarter-hour delay. Dressed casually in dark jeans and a black shirt, a switch from his dapper stage attire, a characteristically ruminative Hyatt spent two hours at the cafe talking about his Spartanburg upbringing, his life as a member of Uncle Walt's Band, and his

Mark Olencki

career as a solo artist. It was to be his last extensive interview. Though he spoke in words both measured and gentle, Walter was not too shy to smile and greet a fan who walked in for lunch, or to break into song to help the interviewer remember the tune to "This Old House."

It may have been the Hyatt family's player piano, the bicycle-like pumping of the rollers and the resultant perfectly-played, exquisitely-arranged sonic payoff, that first turned Walter's attention toward music. Playing the piano was like riding a giant music box, and a young boy could sit on a bench in a log cabin in the woods just behind Union Street in southeast Spartanburg and summon melodic settings from dusty Western saloons to Carnegie Hall.

A majority of the musical influences that would later become the foundation of Walter's songs could be heard in that log cabin during the earliest years of the boy who would later become known as "Uncle Walt." The styles that were not represented on the player piano were found on local radio.

"We listened to the radio a fair amount," Walter said. "WSPA was on every morning at our house. One of the first songs I can remember was a song called 'This Old House,' and I remember 'The Wayward Wind' by Gogi Grant. They used to play a mix-

ture of hillbilly stuff and whatever else was happening."

"That show that was on in the morning was 'The Farmer Gray Show.' He'd slurp his coffee and play music," says George. "We also listened at night to a lot of AM radio from other places. We'd hear The Drifters, The Temptations, Soloman Burke, Bobby Blue Bland, people like that. I had a Silvertone radio, and I could get WLAC from Nashville with John R."

WSPA's schizophrenic format provided a musical meeting ground for Walter's parents. "My dad knew the New Orleans jazz," said Walter. "He was a Louis Armstrong fan, and he loved big-band stuff. That was maybe the earliest influence: I think what we naturally had in our ears from babyhood was World War II-style big band music.

"My mother, though, was very much into highbrow music. She was an opera lover. Every Saturday, that opera would be on. To me, that's the sound of Saturday afternoon: opera. She also used to take us to concerts at Converse College when we were kids. It was sort of a required thing for us to go hear those symphonies."

Piano lessons were also required, and Walter took from First Baptist Church organist Tom Lyles. George describes Lyles as a man with "a presence, kind of a hawk-like face, and his hair was always swept back. I think Walter unconsciously used to do

George and his brother Walter

that hair business like Tom Lyles. That's where Walter got his basic music knowledge: from Tom. He learned about music and then applied it to guitar. Later on, when Uncle Walt's Band would write songs, Walter was the only one who could write the lead sheets."

A performer from the word "go," Walter would put on what he called "Funny Shows" for his brother. "He had that dramatic flair," says George, "and he could keep you in stitches for hours. I remember lying in bed one time when I had some childhood affliction. I felt bad and he felt great, and he decided he was gonna give me a show. He put up a bedspread or a blanket, and he'd pop out from that thing and talk junk. I couldn't tell you a bit what he said, but he'd just prance and cavort and dance and jump and holler.

"Our whole family likes to sing, but Walter was always the most theatrical. He had a sense of style with everything he did. When we played Cowboys and Indians, we practiced to see who could fall the best, or who could look like the guy on the movie screen. Walter had the flair for it: it had to be right and it had to be dramatic."

Walter was "eight or nine years old" when he received his first guitar. "We were out in my dad's field in front of the house," he said, "and this boy came walking across the street with his guitar. He had no case or anything, and he offered it to my dad, who bought it on the spot for five dollars. He gave it to my brother and me and said, 'Here you go.' I did the monkey thing: sort of circled around and poked it and sniffed it.

"I sat down with that guitar and learned a few chords. That particular guitar was hard to play, but for some reason I kept going. I'd sit for hours and hours, and once I got the concept of fretting the strings, I'd look for new combinations. That's how I discovered a lot of different chords. Little by little I picked it up, I guess sort of like learning to talk."

A neighbor kid's father played country-style guitar, and it was from watching him that Walter learned his first song, "The Wreck of the Old '97," a tune made popular in 1924 by Vernon Dalhardt (it was the first million-selling country music record) and later recorded by Spartanburg blues musician Pink Anderson. The brothers would, George says, "pay attention to anybody who played a guitar. We'd watch the Grand Ole Opry on TV, and we'd watch our uncle, Clarence Spence. That man could play! I can remember him sitting on a stump in my Granny's backyard in Columbia, and all of us would be out there listening. Clarence would do a talking blues that was incredible, and I think he was one of our first inspirations."

Other early inspirations included Marty Robbins' *The Gunfighter Ballads* album ("That was the first record we bought together," says George) and a 78 record of Tex Ritter songs about Texas Rangers. The boys would study those records, figure out the chords, and play along. Having learned to play beyond their five-dollar instrument, Walter and George soon bought a Sears Silvertone arch-top for twenty dollars. Later, they scratched together eighty dollars of newspaper route money for their first "real" guitar, a Gibson flat top purchased from Alexander's Music House.

Walter and George played as equals for several years, but the musical pecking order was altered substantially one summer. "I was in high school, working at Scout Camp," says George. "While I was at camp, Pee Wee carried my paper route on the motor scooter. Well, a dog ran out in

front of him and they collided. The scooter fell over and tore his leg all to pieces. They had to graft skin on his heel. For that summer, he lay in bed, read a lot, and started playing *seriously*. He was probably twelve or thirteen then, and that summer was the turning point—he played so much. He left me then!"

In junior high school, Walter played with a group suspiciously similar to the line-up that later comprised Uncle Walt's Band. "In my early teens, I had a trio," he said. "One of the guys played stand-up bass and sang high tenor: his name is Barry Cabin. The other guy was a good baritone singer. It's funny; I've always gravitated towards having a group of some kind, and even back in junior high it was a trio. I remember the first time we got together was the day that Kennedy was shot.

"I just wanted to play music and perform for people. I've always loved music, but I also liked *playing* music. That's two different things. I wanted to be the one doing it."

Hyatt's flair for artistry extended beyond the realms of music. "He could paint very well," says George, "and he was a good actor. Later on, he played in *The Crime of Miss Jean Brody* at Converse College. Also, he went through a period of time where he did magic shows. He read a lot about Houdini. Walter was a voracious reader, even as a kid."

In Walter's early high school years, he and George were becoming more and more influenced by the then-current folk boom. They bought records by Sonny Boy Williamson, The New Christy Minstrels, Dave Van Ronk, Ian and Sylvia, and Greenville, South Carolina, native Josh White. "We'd listen to those mournful Irish and Celtic songs, too," says George. "Man, that's some terrible, soulful stuff. Tales of terror and jealousy and killing. Walter just dug deep and listened and learned."

The brothers' interest in folk music manifested itself in a group called The Lamplighter Minstrels, modeled after The New Christy Minstrels, a band that the brothers had seen play in Charlotte. "The main idea was just to get a bunch of people singing together," Walter said. "We had a couple of girls in the group. We would play at people's company banquets or church get-togethers."

The final major influence on Walter's later music was The Beatles. "The Beatles hit about the time I graduated high school," says George. "At first when I heard them, I said, 'Man, I could play as good as that.' Pee Wee said, 'Man, you better *listen*. It's great.' When 'Eleanor Rigby' came out, he said, 'Listen to this. I'll bet you can't sing it.'

"Later, when I got back from the service, he put *Abbey Road* on, put the headphones on my head, and played 'Here Comes the Sun.' I have a tender spot in my heart for that song because of that. The Beatles were innovators. It's amazing that four guys from Liverpool could come up with stuff like that. I guess it's like three boys from Spartanburg forming Uncle Walt's Band and coming up with the stuff that they did."

In the late 1960s, George left for the Army and Walter graduated from high school and began studies at Wofford College in Spartanburg. "That was a lazy sort of thing, really," Walter said. "My folks wanted me to go to college, and I let myself be nudged into going there. I didn't care about college; I was too much into enjoying life."

While in college, Walter formed a rock and roll band with friend Rick Lee called The Floorboards. "It was Walter going toward a rock and roll thing," says Champ Hood. "I remember we did a show together, Washington Subway and The Floorboards, at the American Legion Hall. Walter knew all these Beatles songs. He played a gut-string, wide-neck, Spanish guitar and played 'Blackbird.' That really impressed me,

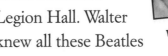

Wofford College sophomore (1969)

and after that we would talk to each other and exchange records."

The teenage Hyatt was already devoted to music, and he already possessed the gently peculiar manner that drew others to him throughout his life. "You talk about unique people . . . it was never a persona for him, it was just Walter," says Rick Lee. "As hard as everyone else tried to be different back then, Walter was already there. We all thought he was cool, but he was also acceptable to adults. Walter was nineteen when I was sixteen, and he was one of the few friends of mine that my parents would allow in the house.

"There was always an aura about him, and he had a very calming effect on whatever the situation was. You'd come to him with a problem and he'd nod and ponder on it and finally say, 'There's a song about this.' There was always a song, and he always knew what it was. He could hand-pick it and it'd be right on the money. Later on, he began writing the songs that I now lean on when I have one of those problems."

After two years at Wofford, Walter dropped out of college and began playing acoustic gigs at Spartanburg venues like The Italian Village and The Peddler. A couple of those shows at The Italian Village included a young guitarist named Champ Hood. Their musical alliance was seemingly short-lived, though, as Walter made the decision to leave Spartanburg.

"As far as I knew, he was on his way to Canada," says Champ, reflecting on the Vietnam era. "I went to the Atlanta Pop Festival in 1969, and I happened to run into Walter there. He had hitch-hiked to Atlanta and was a volunteer worker for the festival. He had an armband that said 'Friend' on it. We ended up hanging out a bunch and listening to a lot of music together. There were performers like Janis Joplin, Johnny Winter, and Creedence Clearwater Revival. That was where we first kind of bonded, because we had all this music in common."

"I left and went back to Spartanburg and assumed that Walter was going to Canada. He made it up to Montreal, and he liked it a lot. He had fond memories of Montreal, but he got mono and had to come back home! He was just out of it for a month or two with mono, and he had to hang out in his house with his bathrobe. I'd take records over there and play him my newest finds. We'd hang out and talk. After he recovered from all that, he eventually got out of the draft on a medical deferment: he had a big scar on his heel from that scooter accident."

Back on his feet, Hyatt began again to play music in Spartanburg. Champ recalls playing what he jokingly calls "The First Spartanburg International Pop Festival" at Duncan Park in front of an audience of about twenty people. The band that played that gig was comprised of Walter, Champ, bass player Steve Gore, and Walter's sister, Kathy, on drums. They played songs like "Sgt. Pepper's Lonely Hearts Club Band" and "With a Little Help From My Friends." "I think that's when we first impressed David Ball," says Champ. "He started kind of hanging out with us after that. He saw that we might could use a stand-up bass."

In the autumn of 1970, Walter began playing shows at the Wofford College Coffeehouse in a large group that included Hood, Ball, Kathy Hyatt, violin/piano player Jimmy Hilton, and cellist Nancy McElvee. "I kind of gathered up these different people," said Walter. "We put together a loose, big group of different instruments, and we started out by trying to reproduce some of the things we heard on records. We did some original stuff, but we weren't writing much."

The group was dubbed "The Walter Hyatt Consort," and it was a conglomerate of styles and songs. A surviving tape from one of the Wofford shows reveals several art/folk epics (like Walter's

"The Road to Montreal"), some stabs at popular material of the day, and one gem: an early version of Champ Hood's "So Long Baby," which would later become an Uncle Walt's Band favorite.

By the time that brother George returned from military duty, Walter was known around town as a musical force. "For a long time, Pee Wee was *my* brother," says George. "When I got back from the Army, boy, I was *his* brother."

The Consort was eventually

Courtesy of George Hyatt

The Walter Hyatt Consort

reduced to a group of four: Walter, Kathy, Champ, and David, and they wanted a new name for the band. "Walter was older," says Champ, "and it seemed like everybody who was involved in those coffeehouse shows were *Walter's* friends: people that *he* knew. He was a little older (Hyatt was three years older than Champ and four years older than David), and his sister was playing drums. We learned that Grateful Dead song, 'Uncle John's Band,' and so we jokingly began to call ourselves 'Uncle Walt's Band.' That just seemed like the natural thing, because Walter was definitely the wisest and most worldly figure in the band."

After a few more Wofford Coffeehouse shows and some gigs at the New China restaurant, the band had whittled itself down to an acoustic trio of Champ, David, and Walter, and

writer David Ezell remembers one coffeehouse gig in which Walter politely asked that the crowd not applaud until the completion of the hour-long set. The band then proceeded to meld Gaelic folk songs, Professor Longhair tunes, monastic chants, and original tunes into a stylistic whole that astounded those in attendance. "Who knows what this music was or where it came from? I had never heard any of it," says Ezell. "At the end, Walter just said, 'Thank you,' and the place just exploded with applause.

"I was already trying to write music at that time," Ezell continues, "and seeing that show had a real effect on me as a developing songwriter." Though Ezell was awed by what he heard, the effect was not necessarily a positive one. "For me, it was almost a curse. No matter what I wrote or tried to do, in my mind there was always

Uncle Walt's Band   (c) Allen McDavid Stoddard

the accumulated hours of performances and rehearsals resulted in a tighter, more focused sound. Uncle Walt's Band was not, however, above throwing a few curve balls at the audience. Spartanburg-raised song-

Uncle Walt's Band. I guess I was humbled at a very young age. Years later, I remember Walter asking me, 'David, why don't you have more self-confidence?' I couldn't say, 'Well, Walter, you're the reason.' Walter was a wonderful person, and he was always very helpful and encouraging to me, but he was just so good that it could be intimidating."

At some shows, Walter would recite poetry to the crowd. "The first time he ever pulled that trick was at the Wofford Coffeehouse," says George. "Ball and Champ were off-stage talking to somebody or getting a drink, and Walter looked out at the audience and launched into this poetry. Directly, the clinking of glasses stopped, and everybody in the room had shut up. They were thinking, 'He's crazy. What is he doing?' Well, he was reciting Dylan Thomas poetry with a Welsh accent. See, he loved Dylan Thomas."

"Yeah, I remember that," says David Ball. "We would take a break and Walter would recite a Dylan Thomas poem (adapts affected English accent): 'Through throats where many rivers meet/ The curlews cry.' I never could make sense out of what it was. To me, it was just words. But the gals in the audience would just *melt*. It was just a . . . who knows, man? It was cool."

The trio rehearsed sometimes at Champ's house, but mostly downstairs at the Hyatts' log cabin. "Each of us lived in the basement of our parents' homes, and that was also where we practiced," said Walter. "So Uncle Walt's Band came out of the basement."

In the band's early days, Walter, though viewed by his audience as the trio's leader, felt somewhat intimidated by Ball's and Hood's abilities. "David was the best singer," Walter said, "and Champ was a great guitar player, a really inspired, natural musician. It took me a while to figure out what my thing was. Their songs were better, also. I had a lot of unfocused stuff back then."

Hood remembers things a little differently. Told of Walter's statement, he says, "Walter . . . he was crazy. He was the one that pretty much taught us how to write songs. He had the best songs, but he was always making us do *our* tunes. He was really the true artist, and he cared so much about it."

The year 1972 saw the band's first move out of town: they left for Nashville and stayed there for nine months. In Nashville, they placed small-money gigs and concentrated on songwriting. At one performance, Texas songwriter Willis Alan Ramsey showed up to listen and was impressed enough to invite the group to Austin to record an album.

"We were looking straight ahead," said Walter. "I grew up in the same house for twenty years, and I was ready to go west a little bit, to go down to Texas. I was like, 'Man, it's gonna be a long way's away.' We already felt like Citizens of the World or something, though. It never occurred to me that it was going to be hard to

down to the Saxon Pub in Austin and saw Uncle Walt's, and they just totally blew my mind. Those guys were jaw-dropping great. Uncle Walt's Band is the greatest band I've ever heard. Listening was like going to heaven: there was no one else that entertained and sang like that. I asked them if I could manage them, and they said, 'Yes.' They wanted a record deal, but they didn't know how to get one. I thought I could help."

Marylou and her three musical charges were nearly able to secure a record deal, coming close with Elektra and Warner Brothers, but nothing was ever finalized. Uncle Walt's then returned to Spartanburg for a period in 1974 that included a trip to Arthur Smith Studios in Charlotte. It was there that the band first committed their songs to vinyl, printing 1,000 copies of the first album, called *Blame It On The Bossa Nova*. Walter handwrote and then mimeographed the song list on the back cover.

"Walter carved a design out of a piece of wood and made a stamp," says Marylou. "The carvings were of two angels blowing bugles. We ran the

get away. I've always taken life one day at a time. Really, I've taken some parts too much so."

In retrospect, it was a long way to go to be let down: the sessions proved fruitless. "Willis gets bogged down in the details of little things that he wants to hear, and it (the recording process) gets stuck in the sand and never gets out," said Hyatt. Uncle Walt's stayed in Texas long enough to further the members' interest in Western Swing music, and long enough to come into contact with a woman who would soon manage the band, and who would become Mrs. Walter Hyatt:

"I had been playing bass for Keith Sykes," says Marylou Hyatt, "and I left that band in 1972. I went

Uncle Walt's Band

BLAME IT ON THE BOSSA NOVA

Aloha
Four Til Late
High Hill
In the Night
Don't You Think I
Feel It Too

Seat of Logic
Dish Wiped Clean
Ruby
Little Sadie
Undecided
Gimme Some Skin

Recorded Arthur Smith Studios Charlotte, N.C., Sept. 1974
Photo, Bill Matthews
Cover Design, Jan Sundeen

cording sessions, Walter and Marylou, who were now married, and Uncle Walt's Band took the new album with them to Austin, Texas. When the first printing of the record sold out, they immediately reissued it with a slightly altered cover and a new song sequence, calling the new pressing *Uncle Walt's Band*.

The album was well-received in Texas, but Uncle Walt's was still unable to secure a record deal. "We were just bumming around together," said Walter. "There was nobody to make us brush our teeth or anything. We were looking for a record company or producer to offer us a contract, but somehow it just wasn't happening."

Uncle Walt's Band broke up in 1975 and Walter and Marylou moved to Nashville. Daughter Haley was born that same year. 1976 brought more changes, as Walter joined forces with Champ, ex-Pritchard Avenue Band member Tommy Goldsmith, Steve Runkel, and Jimbeau Walsh to form a Nashville-based group called The Contenders. That band can be very loosely described as electric folk/rock, but that doesn't begin to describe the strange amalgam of vocal and instrumental styles found in the quintet's music. "The Contenders were sort of like a songwriters-in-the-round thing, except it was a band," said Walter. "I don't really know what to say about The Contenders. Our style was all over the place, and we never achieved a real

record covers through a silk screening process at Converse College and then we would stamp the angels on."

The record was, said Walter, "a chance for people to listen to the songs a few times. When you play a live gig, there's a lot of distractions and it's hard for people to focus on the music with so many other things going on. It's liable to be a whole scene, with girls and all that."

Soon after the Charlotte re-

consistent sound."

"The Contenders were a great band," says Rick Lee. "Everybody was a fine songwriter, and Walter was able to just be part of a group instead of being a real focus. Getting that pressure off of him was something I think he needed at the time." Regardless of their musical merit, The Contenders were defunct by the time Moonlight Records released their one album in 1978. Walter left Nashville to go back to Austin, and the record languished in obscurity and soon fell out of print. Unavailable to this day, the album remains one of the lost treasures of the 1970s. *The Contenders* was not ahead of its time so much as out-of-time. Nothing even remotely like it has since been attempted.

"I started working as Waylon Jennings' manager in Nashville in April

of 1977," says Marylou Hyatt. "Two months after I started working for Waylon, Walter went back to Austin and we drifted apart. I stayed doing what I was doing out of financial need, and Walter's heart was still in bringing about his own music, which I totally believed in, too."

In 1978, Uncle Walt's Band regrouped in Austin and began what is now remembered as their popular heyday. Playing weekly gigs at Steve Clark's Waterloo Ice House, the trio became the band most respected and listened to by the Austin songwriting and performing community. "Uncle Walt's was the most popular band among musicians in Austin," says Clark. "I would have some friend in from out of town, and they would invariably look out at the audience with Lyle and Nanci Griffith and Tish

Uncle Walt's Band performing at the Waterloo Ice House (1978)

Hinojosa and Marcia Ball and Jerry Jeff Walker and say, 'What are all these people doing here?' I'd say, 'This is their favorite band.' There was something in the air that, even with all the great music out there, was completely unique and absolutely special. There was nothing like an Uncle Walt's show at the Waterloo.

"It was the most magic of all possible times. Uncle Walt's was playing purely acoustically, with no sound system at all. The crowd was quiet as a mouse during the songs and uproariously appreciative between numbers. They played the Waterloo every weekend for a year, never without a full house."

Elektra recording artist Jimmie Dale Gilmore remembers the first time he heard Uncle Walt's Band. "I had been living in Denver, and I was moving back to Austin. I stopped over in Lubbock for a while, and some friends of mine there had a record called *Uncle Walt's Band*. The first time I heard it, I just couldn't believe it. It still ranks among my favorite records in the world. Walter and David and Champ made what to me is perfect music."

The year 1980 saw the release of *An American In Texas* on the band's own Lespedeza Records. That album fully embraced the group's country and bluegrass influences, and included four songs written or co-written by Hyatt. In concert, Uncle Walt's was

playing country, western swing, big-band, soul, and bluegrass styles with equal vigor and feel.

In the aftermath of *An American In Texas*, the band played crowded halls across the Lone Star State. One of their regular gigs was at the Texas A&M coffeehouse, where a student named Lyle Lovett often opened shows for them. Lovett, already a rabid follower of Texas guitar poets Willis Alan Ramsey and Eric Taylor, was instantly intrigued by Uncle Walt's swing-inflected sound and by Walter Hyatt's easy-going, off-beat personality. "Lyle has told me that he never liked that kind of music—the big-band-influenced kind of stuff—until he heard us," said Hyatt.

Another now-famous performer who came into contact with Walter Hyatt and Uncle Walt's Band in the early 1980s was Junior Brown, whose honky-tonk country songs are bolstered by the "chunk-style" rhythm guitar of his wife, Tanya Rae. Brown is now known for his inventive guitar work and for songs such as "My Wife Thinks You're Dead," but in 1980 he was a struggling Austin musician who played for a time as an unofficial fourth member of Uncle Walt's. "I was a big fan of theirs," says Brown. "Walter saw a way of 'countrying' the sound up with my steel, and so we booked some gigs at VFW halls and country bars. Uncle Walt's could do all that country stuff: that's another example of how versatile those boys were."

"Uncle Walt's had an almost innate sense of the entire history of music," says Steve Clark. "They had an incredible ability to cover a song and make you think that they had written it. 'Ruby' is an example of that."

"Ruby," made famous by Ray Charles, was a staple of Walter's concerts (both solo and with Uncle Walt's Band) for twenty-five years. "He was always able to take music, dig out the treasure in it, present it to an audience and have them be amazed," says Marylou. Rick Lee is less academic in his analysis: "Ray Charles? Who's that? My pal sings that song! I've heard him do it since I was ten years old. He had the soul and the feel. Always."

The second life of Uncle Walt's Band was both financially and artistically fruitful, with the trio making good money, winning

(c) Allen McDavid Stoddard

numerous fans, and appearing on the nationally televised *Austin City Limits* show. A live album, recorded at the Waterloo Ice House, was released in 1982. Uncle Walt's second incarnation is remembered by most observers as nothing less than a triumphant return,

but it is with some regret that Walter recalled that period in the band's existence:

"If I had it to do all over again, which is a foolish way of thinking, I don't know if I would try to go back to something that had broken up. That's what we did, and we made some good music after we got back together, but it wasn't ever really the same. It became a much more work-a-day thing to me. I mean, we still did a lot of good songs after that, but, ultimately, Uncle Walt's Band did not really achieve what we were trying to achieve. I still don't know what that was, exactly."

After breaking up for the second time, Uncle Walt's Band continued to hold reunion gigs every now and then, playing a number of shows together through the late 1980s. Those shows, including an appearance at Dawg Gone in Spartanburg that is remembered as one of the greatest musical performances in the city's history, were marked by the same tight harmonies and satisfying eclecticism of the band's 1970s incarnations.

"It will always mean a lot for me to get together with those guys and play," said Walter. "It's always a great thing. I express a little disappointment with the albums of Uncle Walt's Band, but really what that band was about was getting up and playing for people. We were performance art: a thing of the moment. It's there and hopefully it puts a better feeling in the atmosphere than was there before, and then it's gone. It's a very ecologically-sound activity."

After Uncle Walt's Band's second break-up in 1983, Hyatt stayed in Austin and attempted to begin a solo career. He used Champ Hood as a lead guitarist, but found that the audience that had always supported the trio was not nearly as interested in listening to him play his own songs in his own way. In 1985, he released an independent cassette EP, *Fall Thru To You*, which featured four well-crafted original songs in instrumentally busy, less than sympathetic musical settings.

Throughout his career, Walter was forced to augment his musical income by taking other, less glamorous jobs. "One time he ran Webb's Cue Room in Austin," says George Hyatt. "I talked to him on the phone one night while he was working there. He said, 'I've improved my pool game a lot, and right now I've got my Lone Star beer and I'm just kicked back.' Then he said, 'Excuse me, George, I've got to get this fellow a beer.'

"He did whatever it took to

provide for his family, pay the rent, whatever. Lots of times he didn't have money, but I never heard Walter say, 'Oh, poor me. Man, I've got it tough.' We could commiserate about hard times, but he didn't whine."

It was in 1987 that Walter returned to Nashville with his second wife, Heidi, and began working toward a solo record deal. In 1989, he was asked, along with Ball and Hood, to sing on "Once Is Enough," a song that was included on the *Lyle Lovett and His Large Band* album. Within another year, he and Heidi had given birth to a son, Taylor, and Walter had secured a one-album recording contract with MCA records. That album, *King Tears*,

was produced by Lyle Lovett and Lovett's arranger Billy Williams, and was a part of MCA's Master Series. Following its release, Hyatt toured for a while as the opening act for Lovett.

King Tears was a soft, jazzy album, and the songs were centered on Hyatt's rich baritone. Made up of eight original songs and two standards, "Ruby" and "Que Reste-T-Il De Nos Amours?," the record included a song co-written with David Ball ("This Time, Lucille") and one co-written with Champ ("Situe"). Two Uncle Walt's Band songs, "Outside Looking Out" and "Aloha," were reprised, the latter a vocal reunion with Ball and Hood.

"In a way, it was a producer's album," said Hyatt. "I really wanted to know what Lyle pictured as being my thing. We consulted together about that album and came up with material, and Lyle had certain things that were favorites of his that he wanted on there. 'Outside Looking Out' was one, and it came out neat. It was a very atmospheric sort of album: not one of those records that is going to bowl you over when you first hear it, because it's very laidback."

One of *King Tears'* laidback song offerings was a lament called "In November," co-written with Walter's friend Tom Mit-

chell, who soon became involved in the marketing of the album. "The record company was not about, nor did they know how, to market Walter. They're being paid to market country music, and this was *not* country," Mitchell says.

"It was hard figuring out what I was supposed to do after I made that album," said Walter. "It was hard figuring out how it fit into a career, and it was hard getting gigs."

Mitchell and Hyatt convinced MCA to allow them some operating space in the company's Nashville office and use of a record company telephone (the "long dime," as Walter

called it). They called radio stations that might be receptive to *King Tears*, and they also set up a Northern tour where they could play co-billed shows and sell some copies of the record. The pair was unable, however, to stir up much of a commercial storm, and Walter was soon dropped from the MCA roster.

Texas musician David Halley, who later toured with Walter, recalls Hyatt's lingering frustrations about *King Tears'* lack of popular success. "He told me that he felt uncomfortable in Nashville to some extent, because he felt like he was the guy that people viewed as having been given a chance with the Lyle Lovett record and who did *that* instead of something more mainstream. He felt he was viewed as someone who ruined a really good chance because he didn't take an easy shot at broad appeal."

David Ezell was living in Nashville in the early 1990s, and he would often see Walter at a Nashville sandwich shop. David would drop by the shop to eat lunch, and Hyatt was there to deliver other people's lunches. "That was a place called Stage Deli," says Ezell. "I'd be in there eating and Walter would be behind the counter. He'd get his orders together and get in his car or on his bike and go deliver the food."

George Hyatt confirms the story: "Yes, Walter had a job at that shop for a good while. He delivered sandwiches on a bicycle, but I think he actually had fun at it. He never spoke of it in a bitter fashion."

Though he was still struggling financially, the years following *King Tears* found Hyatt enjoying fatherhood and writing songs at a faster rate than ever before. He had begun to embrace the Nashville co-writing ethic, although even Walter's co-writes tended to be artful and, with few exceptions, commercially hopeless. "The kind of music that is the lowest common denominator is not the stuff that Walter was interested in," says David Halley. "Very amiably, he made all the decisions to embrace the life of an artist. He knew that his music had a grasp and a depth, and knew that he was making a choice to do what he loved rather than what there was a market for."

A conversation between Gene Berger, owner of Greenville, South Carolina's Horizon Records store, and Barry Poss, president of Sugar Hill Records, led to the 1991 reissue on Sugar Hill of the original songs from Uncle Walt's Band's long out-of-print records. Though cover songs such as "Gimme Some Skin" and "Four 'Til Late" were omitted, the two-volume series stirred popular interest in the band. "Walter laughed about how we got a record contract ten years after we broke up," says Champ. The Sugar Hill CDs were the first nationally distributed collections of Uncle Walt's material.

In 1993, Sugar Hill released a new solo album from Walter, *Music Town*. "*Music Town* was supposed to be a country album," Walter said, before admitting that it, like the rest of his work, didn't really fall into the parameters of what most people consider "country." Produced by Hyatt and multi-instrumentalist Jim Hoke, the album is, in Hyatt's words, "slicker" than *King Tears*, but it retains an organic, acoustic soul. It was for the song "Are We There Yet Momma" that Walter starred in his first music video, enlisting the help of his kindergarten classmate Marshall Chapman to fill the roll of "Momma."

A critical success, *Music Town* nonetheless did little in the way of expanding Hyatt's audience. A 1994 show at Greenville's Handlebar, a club located no more than forty-five minutes from Hyatt's childhood home, drew only thirty people. Ever the professional, Walter played the show as if it were Carnegie Hall, filling his set with energy and vocal nuance, and displaying surprising skill on guitar. His instrumental prowess had obviously improved since Walter's days with Uncle Walt's Band, when Hyatt was known as a rock-steady but unspectacular rhythm guitarist.

"Walter was always trying to improve," says friend and fellow Nashville songwriter David Olney. "I think

he had a vision of what you're supposed to do to be a real musician. You're supposed to be able to sing good and to write good, you're supposed to know all those chords, and you're supposed to know the history of songwriting. The way he figured it should go was ten times more demanding than most songwriters would ever think about. There was a TV interview with Walter that I saw where the interviewer asked, 'How long do you think you'll be playing music?' Walter said, 'Until I learn how to do it well.'"

Hyatt's commitment to improvement is evidenced by George's remembrance that Walter committed the entire *Mel Bay Book of Chords* to memory in the late 1980s. Walter was not, however, ignorant of his exceptional musical talent. It may have been the knowledge of that talent that made his lack of commercial success difficult to accept.

"I think he knew how good he was, and that was part of his frustration," says Victor Mecyssne, a follower of Uncle Walt's Band since the mid-1970s and Walter's friend and unofficial protégé in the mid-1990s. "Someone who is on the level of Walter Hyatt knows the good stuff when they hear it, even when it's coming from themselves."

"Walter's music was coming from a very eclectic, stylized, hybrid place," says Tom Mitchell. "He wasn't so left-field that he didn't have an audience—he had his pocket of support—but your everyday Joe on the street is not going to get the nuance in that kind of music. Part of Walt's frustration may have been in thinking, 'Why doesn't everybody get this? It makes perfect sense to me.'"

Hyatt's dilemma was compounded by the fact that he could see

major-label recording contracts and national touring schedules. Less commercially successful artists such as Mecyssne, Olney, and Halley also revered Hyatt's music, and it must have felt to Walter like the only true connection being made with his music was to other performers.

"You know what Walter said?" asks Mecyssne. "He was talking about

Mark Olencki

Uncle Walt's Band at Clancy's, Spartanburg (1989)

his mark on so many performers who were experiencing far greater success than he. In the mid-1990s, Lyle Lovett, David Ball, Jimmie Dale Gilmore, Marshall Chapman, Hal Ketchum, and Junior Brown all claimed Hyatt as an influence, and each of them had

how audiences reacted differently to him solo than they did when he was with Uncle Walt's Band. I told him that I was elated to be hearing him in any incarnation, and he said, 'Yeah, but you're a musician.'

"One time, Walt and I were

playing a twin-bill together, and there was a Canadian TV crew there to do interviews. Walter was on stage in the back of the club doing sound check, and I was being interviewed up by the door. The interviewer was asking me about influences, and he asked, 'If you could play with anybody, who would it be?' I said, 'Living or dead? Because the Glen Miller Orchestra would be pretty cool and it'd be okay to hang with Robert Johnson. As far as alive goes, that guy standing up on that stage in the back is as good as it gets.'"

Though his friends could see Hyatt's frustration about his lack of commercial success, Walter displayed a much more positive energy to the rest of the world. At Christmas, he would put on a top hat, walk the main floor of the Nashville airport, and sing carols. At other times, also, he radiated a decency and empathy that could be instructive to those around him.

"Walter was a kind man," says Tom Mitchell. "We were out on my back porch one day, spinning through the country channels on the radio. When you listen to those stations, there are an awful lot of hat acts with a lot less talent than Walter Hyatt. They're on the radio getting to do their thing, and we're sitting on the porch trying to figure out how to stretch a can of soup. I remember asking about one particular artist. I said, 'What do you think of this guy?' After a long pause, Walter said, 'I'll bet he's having

a great time.' When it's easy for so many of us to write off a negative reaction as an honest answer, Walter had a way of showing that there was more than one honest answer."

In 1995, Walter put a band, "King Tears," together, and began playing each Monday night at a small but funky Nashville club called The Sutler. Tuesdays, he worked the sound board at The Sutler's Tuesday night Western Beat Barn Dance, which is not really a dance but rather a kind of high-level open mic night. "I used to just shake my head," says Mecyssne. "I mean, the best musician in the whole room was on the sound board. But he needed a gig."

Hyatt toured a good deal in 1996, playing both with and without King Tears. He also performed regularly in Nashville and planned for a third solo record. "I want to have a new record out by the fall, or by Christmas at the latest," he said. "I have a few feelers out right now, and I'm gonna have to make a choice soon and start going in a direction with somebody."

Mark Montgomery's Chelsea Studio comped Walter and King Tears a day in the recording studio, where they cut three new songs: "Going to New Orleans," "Houston Town," and "Foolin' Round." "They did those three songs complete in one day," says Mecyssne. "Also, right before he left for Florida, Walter gave Mark a seven-song tape that he may have done at (King Tears band member) Rick Plant's studio: that tape was just guitar and vocals. Those songs plus the three that were already cut were going to be the nucleus of another record."

At home, a daughter, Rose, was born, and Walter continued to dote on six-year-old Taylor and on his grown daughter, Haley. "Walter was trying to help Haley get through her senior year in college," says Marylou Hyatt. "He was reading *Treasure Island* to her one chapter at a time. He would send her a cassette tape every week, and it was a nice break time for Haley. That was Walter in his true form, just reading away."

In February of 1996, Marylou, in the midst of relocating, was stuck without a place to stay while she waited for a room to open up at her new apartment building. "Walter and Heidi invited me to stay with them," she says. "Looking back on it now, it was such a blessing. I fell in love with those two kids, I got to know Heidi a lot better, and I was able to babysit the children and give Walter and Heidi some quiet time together. I treasure that month.

"Walter was a breakfast cooker. He would get up early and walk the dogs, and then he'd make breakfast. Heidi and Taylor would be in the kitchen, and little Rose would be in her high chair that was bolted to the table. Walter would cook eggs or tortillas and make sure that everybody ate. It was a great time, and then my apartment came open and Walter helped me move into it. It wasn't three months later that he was gone."

Walter played in Key West, Florida, with King Tears in May of 1996. "He did the Dylan Thomas thing again at Key West," says Marylou. "Walter had standing ovations at that little place where he did that last gig. (King Tears bandmember) Rick Plant said that Walter played several encores there, and then he just burst into Dylan Thomas."

The next day, Hyatt boarded the airplane, intending to travel to Virginia for his daughter's college graduation. "Haley had a graduation dinner that Walter was trying to get to," says Marylou. "She was graduating the next morning. Walter's mother, brother, sister, sister-in-law, and aunt were all there. There were more Hyatts there than anything. We just waited and waited, and he never came."

Since Hyatt's passing, all-star tribute shows featuring such musicians as Brown, Lyle Lovett, Victor Mecyssne, David Olney, Shawn Colvin, David Halley, Jimmie Dale Gilmore, David Ball, Champ Hood, Willis Alan Ramsey and Jerry Jeff Walker have been held at Nashville's Ryman Auditorium and Austin's Paramount Theatre. A third tribute was taped for an episode of *PBS's*

Austin City Limits. In addition, MCA Records has reissued *King Tears*, and Walter's song catalogue, long ignored by commercially successful artists (B.J. Thomas and Jerry Jeff Walker are among the very few musicians to cut Hyatt's songs), is beginning to attract attention. Jimmie Dale Gilmore, for instance, wants to record a version of Walter's "Georgia Rose" on a future album. There are also rumors that Lovett will include "I'm Calling" on an upcoming project.

"I just wish that Walter had gotten the recognition in life that he's gotten in death," says Marylou. "I wish I could be certain that he knew how much people loved him and loved his music." Indeed, many in the Nashville community who paid concert ticket prices to attend Hyatt's tribute show at the Ryman ignored Walter's weekly

performances only a few miles away at The Sutler.

Television shows and celebrity tributes are a step towards preserving a legacy and extending an audience, though, and if people attend these functions for less than the purest reasons, they will surely be won over by the beauty and integrity of the music. Crowds may come to gawk, but they'll stay to listen, and in the process of listening they will learn something about Walter Hyatt. When the words have been spoken, Hyatt's songs can be a proxy.

Marylou Hyatt surmises that it was the very things that attracted people to Walter—his gentility, respect, and lack of pretense—that ruined his chances at greater success in the Nashville music industry. If that is the case, then it is a trade-off that Walter made with his eyes open: a conscious decision to prioritize decency and an artful humanity over business and money.

"Walter was a very giving, generous person," says Junior Brown. "He was like a storybook person to me. He had a lot of drive, but he tread softly and never got the thorns stuck in his feet."

Hyatt's influence is in the music of his many devotees, in the elliptical stage patter of Lyle Lovett, and in the lives of those who knew him well enough to be touched by more than his music. "My daughter reflects a lot of Walter's wonderful personality

A TRIBUTE TO WALTER HYATT

AN EVENING TO BENEFIT THE FAMILY OF THIS NOTED SONGWRITER AND FRIEND

LYLE LOVETT

DAVID BALL   CHAMP HOOD
JEFF HANNA HAL KETCHUM
WILLIS ALAN RAMSEY
MARSHALL CHAPMAN   SHELBY LYNNE
MATRACA BERG   DAVID OLNEY
AND OTHER MUSICAL FRIENDS

SUNDAY - JUNE 23 8 PM
RYMAN AUDITORIUM
TICKETS - TICKET MASTER   255-9600
HATCH SHOW PRINT CO.

traits," says Marylou. "You know, children imitate things they respect."

Extraordinary talent, diligent work, and unswerving artistic principles made Walter Hyatt a unique and influential musician. Airport Christmas carols, *Treasure Island* cassettes, and childhood Funny Shows point to a higher honor. ⓂⓂ

(c) Allen McDavid Stoddard

Mark Olencki

9 DARYLE RYCE

"I was born a poor black child," says Daryle Ryce, laughing but not lying. A civil rights "Bubble Child" who attended both segregated and integrated public schools, Ryce's recollections of Spartanburg are not the stuff of Chamber of Commerce pamphlets or old-money dinner conversations. If her status as a native of the town has helped her career in any way, it is only from the most perverse sort of angle: the struggle for musical success became for her a way to leave and never have to come back. In the many years since she moved away, her opinions of the town have mellowed, but only from bad to ambivalent: "It's not that I hate it," she says, "but there's not a whole lot of love in me for Spartanburg."

That lack of love is perhaps nothing but a reciprocation of the attitude shown to Ryce by her original hometown and its populace. Despite an international fan base (bolstered by two successful European CDs), a smart and beautiful American debut album on Rounder Records, a list of industry friends and admirers that includes Chet Atkins, Dizzy Gillespie, Buddy Rich and Pat Boone (yes, Pat Boone), a formidable guitar style and a stunning voice, Ryce is still practically unknown by the listening public in Spartanburg. "I have some fans in Spartanburg, but I don't have many," she says.

The greatest conglomeration of Ryce fans exists in Charlotte, North Carolina, the city that Ryce has called home since 1991. Ryce plays several shows each week in Charlotte and also records personalized lullabies for children through her Lady Lullaby business. An interview with Daryle in her Charlotte house is only interrupted by her dog Bear's occasional bids for attention. Our discussion centers on the hows and whys of a career that has until quite recently been marked by constant shifts in locale and strategy and also on her memories of her often tumultuous early years in a Spartanburg that she is both glad and proud to have left behind.

Daryle Rice (she changed the spelling of her last name to "Ryce" in the early 1980s) was born in Dr. Bull's clinic on South Liberty Street on September 29, 1953. Her older brother and sister each played and sang, and Daryle was left to hang from their musical coattails for some time. Her interest in sound and performance was bolstered in preschool years by forays into her mother's and father's record collections. "I would go in and play my mother's hi-fi," she says. "I remember songs like 'Green Door,' 'Canadian Sunset,' and then some classical music. We listened to some spirituals, but we didn't listen to gospel, because we were Methodists."

One of the defining moments in her musical upbringing came about

Daryle (front, center) and the "Dean Street Gang"

through the same singer who altered the social and artistic course of fellow Spartan Marshall Chapman: "It changed when I heard Elvis Presley," says Ryce. "I went through kindergarten *being* Elvis! My mother was a hairdresser and she'd give me a little curl. I'd walk around with my leg shaking and my lips curling up."

Daryle began piano lessons from her godmother before beginning first grade at Cummings Street School, an all-black primary school that held grades 1-9. "My first grade teacher was great," she says. "She was the one who discovered I could sing. In my family, my sister was considered the singer, but now I was getting support from somewhere else."

By the fourth grade, Rice had progressed on piano to the point where she was ready for a professional teacher. "I took from a lady called Beatrice Cleveland. She was the course teacher at Carver High School. After four years of teaching me, she kindly asked me not to come back to her house because I was the most obnoxious child she had ever met. It was a class, not private lessons, and I would do things to sabotage classmates who were having better lessons. Sometimes I would erase notes out of their books and write in other notes so they would play them wrong.

"I had a little mischief in me. I was a temper tantrum kid. See, I had trouble getting people to listen to me sometimes. When they didn't listen to me the first time, I had to yell. I was very direct as a kid. If you were wrong and I knew it, I'd let you know I knew. I would correct a teacher in a heartbeat."

While Rice was still at Cummings, a music teacher entered her seventh-grade class and asked if any of the students would like to play violin. "My hand shot up," she says. "I think I was the only person in the class who really knew what a violin was. I started taking violin and became a totally different child about music. By my third year, I made Junior All-State."

Learning the violin was not the only new thing in Daryle's life. Ninth grade brought with it a shift from segregated Cummings Street to newly integrated Evans Junior High School. Evans pulled most of its student population from such white, high-income neighborhoods as Hillcrest and Converse Heights. "The other junior highs, Jenkins and Cleveland, had the poor kids," says Ryce. "Our family just happened to live on North Dean Street, near Evans, so I ended up going there. I don't remember exactly how many black kids were there, but there probably weren't more than seven or eight. There weren't any other black kids in my classes.

"No one would sit down with me at lunch, and nobody would talk to me. It wasn't like the other kids hated me, but they didn't know what to do.

Courtesy of Daryle Ryce

It was very new for all of us. Finally, music became the common denominator that broke some of those barriers."

Rice had orchestra class right after lunch, and she would often escape the staring eyes of her lunchroom peers by eating quickly and going straight to the orchestra room. Right next to the orchestra room was the chorus room, and in the chorus room there was a white student named Terri Cashion sitting alone, playing piano or guitar. "I'd sit outside the chorus room door and listen," says Daryle. "One day, she popped her head outside the door and said, 'Come on in.' She would let me play her guitar, and would show me a chord every day. She also showed me some fingerpicking styles, and I'd take the guitar and go sit in the hall and practice. Sometimes, she would let me take the guitar home on the weekends. Terri was just the kindest person in the world."

Terri and Daryle were soon joined in their chorus room jam sessions by another white student, Margaret Kennedy (Kennedy now writes for public radio's "Thistle and Shamrock" show). The three would remain friends throughout high school, and Daryle recalls that their relationship was not looked kindly upon by white or black students. "Among my black friends, it was not acceptable to have white friends for some reason. It was like I was doing the Oreo thing, which they let me know in high school when they crushed Oreo cookies and put them on my head."

In truth, the Rice family was more involved than most Spartanburg residents in the struggle for racial progress. "My family was into the NAACP, very quietly, because at the time it was a thing to be quiet about. We were followers of Dr. Martin Luther King: everything done peacefully and in the right way. I was taught that you can get what you want and you don't have to kiss butt."

Ejected from her piano lessons with Beatrice Cleveland, Rice still wanted to learn from a private instructor. "It was like, 'Who's going to teach me?' The lady who was teaching at our school was white, but my mom finally talked her into it. The teacher was a little nervous, and she had a right to be, about what her neighbors

were going to say about me coming over. So, occasionally I would babysit for her so it would appear that I was the babysitter. That helped her cover up, and I didn't care as long as she didn't treat me badly."

White contemporaries of Rice's (like David Ball) took lessons at Alexander's Music House. Asked why she didn't follow suit, Daryle says, "You could shop there, but blacks couldn't take lessons. My sister actually managed to take lessons there, but not in the daytime when people would know about it. She had to take a night class from a guy who was kind of sleazy. Eventually, she had to stop that."

A "pretty decent" (her words) violinist in her high school years, Rice was also working hard to become a good guitar player. "The violin and the guitar were neck and neck there," she says. "One was the classical side of me, and one was the pop side." At fourteen, she wrote a political tune called "Hang on, Humphrey" and played it in the ninth-grade talent show, and she began spending time with a group of Spartanburg High students who would sit on the school's lawn and play music.

One person who proved inspirational to Daryle at the time was Walter Hyatt. Hyatt would visit the Rice house to play music with her brother, Don. "Sometimes Walter and Don would play up at Wofford, also, and I'd come and listen to them doing old tunes." Later in life, Hyatt would prove a help to Ryce when she was trying to get a foothold in Nashville. Another string-playing friend was future country star David Ball, who played bass in the orchestra with Daryle. "When I think of David, I think of pranks," she says. "We were always pulling pranks in orchestra on Mrs. Gignilliat. One time, David egged me on to put a tack in her chair. She may have thought that David did it, because he did a lot of things like that."

Her senior year in high school brought a music scholarship to Converse College, an invitation to attend a summer strings camp at Furman University, and the news that her father was dying of cancer. Daryle was extremely close to her father, and though she tried to maintain her equilibrium in the face of his death (she even starred in a Kellogg's Rice Krispies television commercial that summer), she entered her freshman year at Converse College frazzled and emotionally raw. "A lot of my first year is kind of a blur, because my dad died in November," she says. The memories of that year that are not blurred are mostly unpleasant.

"I was the first black freshman at Converse, and there was a big thing in the paper about me going there. I was a day student, but I had to stay on campus during orientation, and they gave me a white roommate. My room-mate was from England: they wouldn't have put me in there with a little Southern girl."

During orientation, the incoming freshmen were brought in for a private sitting with faculty members. "I remember one of them telling me that she realized I had been deprived and that Converse would build my standards up as a woman. I went home and told my mother this. My mother said, 'If you see this woman again, you tell her that she can take care of the education and *we'll* take care of the morals.' My mother said, 'I don't think any Converse girl is going to have the morals we want you to have.' See, at that time Spartanburg was notorious for its protection of the elite: rich kids could get away with anything."

The hard words did not end with Converse's faculty. "At orientation, one girl told me that I reminded her of her maid. She said, 'I had a black woman that raised me.' I said, 'Well, that's good. I did, too.' Then I went to the dinner table and someone else made a derogatory statement about what black people could do for her. She told me to get up and go get her some milk. I said, 'Get your own milk,' and then I shoved my soup into her lap. That weekend was hell."

When her father died in November, Rice felt that she needed a way to get out of the house. She auditioned to perform three nights a week at a Hillcrest restaurant called The

Buccaneer Inn. Owner Christ Christ paid her ten dollars plus food and tips, a package that resulted in Daryle taking home "twenty to twenty-five dollars a night." She was also receiving royalty checks from her Rice Krispies commercial. "I made over $10,000," she says. "I made twice as much as my mother that year."

Soon after taking the job at The Buccaneer, Rice asked for a position on the "Carolina Country Music Time" television program broadcast on Spartanburg's WSPA. "I asked Dave Craig if I could be on the show, and he kind of laughed. I said, 'I don't want to hear that I can't be on the show because I'm black.' He said, 'No, I wouldn't do that. What I was

going to say was, you're going to have to play country music.' I said, 'I like country music.' He said, 'Oh, you'd say anything to be on a television show.'" The charge was partly true, but Daryle did have an appreciation for some country music. She, like Walter Hyatt and George McCorkle, cites Marty Robbins as a favorite singer. Certainly, she loved acoustic music, having been fully won over by the early albums of James Taylor. Ryce says it was her perceived vocal resemblance to then-popular Anne Murray that caused Craig to award her the job.

The "Carolina Country Music Time" show featured guest performers Dolly Parton, Buck Owens, Marty Robbins, and Billy "Crash" Craddock, and the cast also traveled for the weekend shows. Mark and Phil Lister, who later became part of country music one-hit wonder Dixiana, were also on the show, and Daryle became friends with them. Still, Rice felt herself to be an outsider in the show's mostly white male world, and this time race had very little to do with the problem. "The fact that I was female and played the guitar bugged the hell out of some of those people. I knew how to deal with the black stuff, but I didn't know what do with them not being able to accept my being female."

Back at Converse, an all-women's school, there was no problem with being female. Still, things weren't working well. "I was kind of a case for

Daryle performs on "Carolina Country Music Time"

Converse from the beginning. They didn't know how to deal with me, and after my dad died, I was just kind of weird. I lost my temper a lot, and I would sometimes get up and just walk out of class. Might come back, might not. I was kind of a blank page."

College remained a struggle for Ryce. She received support from Dean of Music Dr. Henry Janiec, but little help from her violin instructor and large doses of vaguely hostile ambivalence from her classmates. Her musical successes at this point were confined largely to the guitar, and her songwriting was spurred onwards by meetings with Nashville legend John Hartford and singer/songwriter Harry Chapin, both of whom came to Wofford College for concerts. In the summers, she began working at Charlotte, North Carolina's Carowinds amusement park in a group called Merlin's Overland Express Progressive Bluegrass Band. "I didn't know a lot about bluegrass," she says, "but bluegrass is so close to jazz and be-bop. It's just the rhythm that's a little different. Bluegrass, jazz and baroque music all sound alike to me."

After three years at Converse, just a week before her twenty-first birthday, Daryle left Spartanburg to tour the country as a solo performer. "I got in the car and drove to Toledo and started playing that night at nine o'clock. I played piano and guitar, and I sang. I went on the road not really

knowing how to play very well, but I was a good enough musician by ear that I could get by." Rice was by this time writing a lot of original material, but people in the Midwestern fern bars where she made her living were unwilling to listen to songs that weren't written by "real" artists. "When I did an original song, I'd say, 'This is a new song by Linda Rondstadt' or 'This is a lost Patsy Cline tune.' That way, people would listen."

Three years of touring brought little income and no record deal, and Rice returned to Spartanburg for a brief time in 1977. She played for a while at a place called Mickey's at Hillcrest Mall, which she remembers as a nice room. "The guys from the Marshall Tucker Band used to come in and shoot pool in the back, and I also met the guys from Garfeel Ruff there. We used to all hang out at Joy Nanny's farmhouse, where we'd have jam sessions on weekends.

"But coming back made me see how much I really hated living in Spartanburg. I always felt that it was such a racist town, and that there was just nothing that could be done about it. I knew they didn't like outsiders, and I knew I was an outsider."

The year 1978 was when things began to turn around for Daryle Rice. She moved to Charlotte and began working at a place called The Roadway Inn, which later became The Registry Inn. At The Registry, she sang solo and with a big band called The Sunday Night Jazz Band. Her performances with that band resulted in her coming to the attention of famed Charlotte composer-pianist Loonis McGlohon. In January 1980, she went into the studio with McGlohon and recorded an album called *I Walk With Music*, which was released on the Audiophile label. The record featured Rice singing standards by Hoagy Carmichael, Paul Williams, Rodgers and Hart, and George and Ira Gershwin, as well as two original songs, with a backing that included McGlohon, former Brubeck Clan bassist David Powell, and alto saxophonist Don McClure. The album played to Rice's vocal strengths, and Owen Cordle's liner notes praised her "deep mahogany tones, her flowing diction, her tapered, expansive-to-barely discernible vibrato, her rhythmic suppleness and climactic curve of dynamics."

Mahogany-toned or not, Daryle's voice received its first real national exposure through *I Walk With Music*, even garnering a positive write-up in *Stereo Review* magazine. By the time she read the review, she was in Chile performing shows with Pat Boone and The Village People. "Yeah, I hung out with Pat Boone for about ten days," she says. "I had a blast; he's an interesting guy. We played tennis on the top of the hotel building. The

man is in great shape, and he just killed me."

The Pat Boone connection was only the beginning of a spree of celebrity attention that Daryle received. Rice's most memorable Chilean gig was a solo acoustic show that she did at Pinochet's presidential palace. "I was doing a lot of television down there, and I guess Pinochet's people saw me doing that. They came to pick me up in a limousine, but they took my guitar in another car because it had a battery in it, and they were curious as to why the guitar had electronics. They pulled the wires out. We changed cars a couple of times before we reached our destination.

"I was introduced to Pinochet, but it took me a while to figure out who he was. I got paid a huge amount, probably the most I've ever been paid for a gig. The money was in a little case. I had a friend in Chile from America, and I would tell him stuff about that gig and he would tell me not to talk about it, not to even tell anybody I was there."

Rice then came back to Charlotte for a few months, then moved a few hours' drive up I-85 to Durham, North Carolina. She stayed there for seven months, and got to play for "a lot of people who came there on the Rice Diet." One of those people was comedian Buddy Hackett. "I used to eat pizza with him every night. He would pay me $50 to bring it to his room. He got to the point where he said, 'They're going to smell this pizza in my room,' so he came in my room and ate pizza and drank beer!"

The most incredible coincidental superstar meeting was with a group of scruffy Irish boys who met Daryle while she was playing in a hotel lounge. "They were these little ragamuffins sitting on the couch listening to me," she says. "They were in t-shirts: very skinny. I finally said, 'So who are you guys?' They said, 'We're a band called U2. We're on tour with Todd Rundgren. We're playing at the university at Chapel Hill.' I asked one guy if he wanted to play my guitar, and he said, 'No, I'm just a singer.' Of course, that was Bono. Then Adam Clayton said, 'I'm a bass player. I would love for you to show me how you play those bass runs on your guitar.'

"We had pizza and hung out the next day, and I gave Adam Clayton a bass lesson. He knew the strings, but he knew nothing about the bass. I was sitting there thinking, 'They have an album out?' We started with just basics, like key signatures. I wrote all of that down for him. We sat there drinking cognac. He was in his smok-

Daryle
Ryce

161

Courtesy of Daryle Ryce

ing jacket, and Bono was jumping across from bed to bed like a trampoline. I was thinking, 'Who *are* these guys?' I guess we sat up until four in the morning, and then they gave me a tape. Two months after that, they were on the front of major magazines." U2 went on to become arguably the best-known rock band of the 1980s.

Separated from her now-famous Irish buddies, Daryle returned to Charlotte as "Daryle Ryce." The mid-eighties were a time of personal difficulty and professional renewal, as she released a semi-autobiographical cassette of what she calls "let's slit the wrists" music titled *Lonely Days*. The tape sold two hundred copies on New Year's Eve alone, and eventually Ryce sold out of the thousand copies that she had dubbed. Daryle released *Hold Me*, a tape that she dedicated to her father, in 1988, and soon after was offered a recording contract with Rounder Records. She accepted.

The *Carolina Blue* CD was released to the national public in 1989. *Rolling Stone* magazine's Fred Goodman wrote the liner notes, calling Daryle "a distinctive and uniquely American artist . . . an outstanding pianist and guitarist, equally comfortable playing bluegrass, country, swing, jazz, bossa nova and folk." Indeed, *Carolina Blue* shifts freely among those styles but somehow retains a coherency and focus. The album's strongest cut may be "Put Me In the Movies," a song that draws blood with edgy humor: "They're gonna put me in the movies/ Soon as I clear my face/ Dye my hair blond/ Maybe change my race."

The packaging of the album was interesting in light of Ryce's ambivalent relationship with her homeplace. The cover featured a close-up of Ryce's smiling face adjacent to a white quarter moon. The moon was on a deep blue background, a reference to the South Carolina state flag.

Ryce remembers the time of *Carolina Blue*'s release as an understandably exciting one. "I had a whole band, and the album was released at birthday time. I had a big concert at Spirit Square in Charlotte, which was my first headliner concert."

The problem was when it came time to figure out how to sell the album to radio programmers and music consumers in places where Ryce's name was not known. The many musical influences that came through in the songs were a selling point in the liner notes, but in the real world they became a blockade to any kind of breakthrough. The acoustic funk of "Chain It Up" would appeal to certain listeners, but if they bought the album hoping for more of the same they would be rebuffed. Likewise, there were plenty of blue notes in the tunes, but there was nothing that could truly be called "blues music." The advice on the bottom of the front cover said, "File under folk/pop," but it may as well have said, "File under musically adventurous, but commercially obscure."

To make matters worse, Ryce was unwilling to go on the coffeehouse tours that would have better enabled listeners to understand where the music was coming from. "They wanted me to come to the Boston area and play for $150 a night, and that was hard, especially considering that I was making $2000 a week in Charlotte. I think now that if I would have gone up there and played those places that I would have built an audience faster than I realized, but I didn't have that kind of confidence then. Emotionally, I was not at a very confident place back then."

Rounder Records didn't take particularly kindly to Daryle's Get-Rich-At-Home plan. "It was kind of like, 'If you don't do this, then we don't know what else to suggest.'

down some doors for me."

Hurricane Hugo also knocked down doors for Ryce in 1989. Blown out of her Charlotte apartment by the storm, she decided to move to Nashville. Just prior to *Carolina Blue*, Daryle had met legendary guitarist/producer Chet Atkins, and he had been impressed enough to stay in contact. "After Hugo, I called Chet and said, 'Hey, what's going on?' He said, 'Hey girl, when ya comin' to town?' I said,

Courtesy of Daryle Ryce

Daryle with Chet Atkins

Eventually, there was no contact at all, or I would contact them and they wouldn't take my call. Still, it did me a lot of good to have the album on Rounder. I could call other people and say, 'Well, I'm on Rounder Records,' and they would talk to me. It knocked

'Sooner than you think!'

"I moved to Nashville in January of 1990, and I figured I'd give it a year. I'd go to Chet's office and he'd send me out to different publishers. He'd call 'em up on the phone. It was funny, because you'd figure that he would have a Rolodex or something, but he'd look up the publishers in the phone book. One time, Chet got up to go to the bathroom or somewhere, and I was walking around his office looking at all his stuff. I picked up one of his Grammy awards. Holding that thing was a really cool feeling. If I never get one, I still know what one feels like. I was holding it with my eyes closed, getting the feel, and I could feel this presence behind me. It was Chet: he caught me. He said, 'You can hold it if you like.'"

Atkins proved a valuable ally in Nashville, and he arranged for Daryle to take part in a guitar-picking session that included Jerry Reed, Glen Campbell, Roy Clark and Johnny Cash, introduced her to numerous other celebrities, and helped her find people with whom to co-write. Atkins was, however, unable to help Ryce secure a publishing deal that would have allowed her to make money writing songs for other people. "They turned all my tapes down flat," says Daryle. "It became difficult to make money and difficult to pay for my apartment, so I kept driving to Charlotte fairly regularly to work a couple of gigs for real money. Finally, I decided, 'This Nashville thing sucks,' and I returned to Charlotte at the end of 1990."

A 1991 National Public Radio interview with Linda Wortheimer led to an offer for Ryce to tour overseas. On Labor Day, she found herself in Sweden for the Blues to Bach Festival, and she met an Italian record company owner named Franco Ratti. Ratti gave the green light for a CD release on his Appaloosa Records, and Daryle went back to Charlotte to record *Rosa's Grandchild*. The album was similar in musical scope and artistry to *Carolina Blue*, but the European audience proved more receptive than American listeners. The success of *Rosa's Grandchild* opened the door to another Appaloosa album, but in between foreign projects, Ryce released *Unless It's You*, a record of standards with old friend Loonis McGlohon.

Today, Daryle spends much of her time playing music in the Charlotte area or making personalized tapes of songs for children through her Lady Lullaby company. She is not satisfied with her lack of popular success, but she is not embittered, either. "Getting compliments from people I've admired a lot: that's meant more to me than a Grammy could mean," she says.

"Dizzy Gillespie told me that he liked my stuff. I opened for Buddy Rich, the great jazz drummer, and he told me that I was a really good singer. I haven't made a lot of money, like Madonna

SOON YOU WILL BE SITTING ON TOP OF THE WORLD.

A fortune Daryle has kept with her from the early 1980s

or somebody, but I can take those compliments to the grave."

Daryle's most recent record is *From Now On*, an Appaloosa release that Daryle considers her "country album." "*Carolina Blue* was a sampling of everything I'd done to that point," she says, "but *From Now On* is much more focused. I wanted it to be the way that I see country music, since everything I'd written had been turned down in Nashville."

In truth, the way that Ryce sees country music is quite unlike the way that anyone else sees it. Sure, there are fiddles and a steel guitar on the album, but *From Now On* is no more in the tradition of Ernest Tubbs or Hank Williams or even, God forbid, Garth Brooks, than it is in the tradition of Ella Fitzgerald or Billie Holiday or Pat Boone or U2.

It would seem that Daryle Ryce is not a traditionalist or a revisionist: she exists, for better or for worse, completely outside the lines, as she has since childhood. "I don't know too many people that I sound like," she says, and she is most certainly correct.

Mark Olencki

Daryle on stage
at Converse College's
Dexter Auditorium (1997)

10

DAVID BALL

T
V personality Bob Eubanks smiles and says that David Ball has a "nineties approach to fifties honky-tonk," then proceeds to shuffle papers around and stare off into space while the tall, hatted Spartan-bred singer looks into the camera and delivers his newest single, "Circle of Friends." Ball sings hard and strong, and the audience looking on at this taping of The Nashville Network's "Prime Time Country" show applauds loudly and remains attentive through-out the song's two minutes and fifty seconds. At the tune's conclusion, Eubanks appears startled, as if shaken from a deep meditative state, but he recovers nicely, shakes Ball's hand, and says, "I *love* your kind of music."

The next few minutes of TV time are killed with talk not of "Circle of Friends" or of David's new album, *Starlite Lounge*, but of the song that has become David Ball's calling card, "Thinkin' Problem." That tune, which

features the most immediately memo-rable first six beats of any country song of the decade, seems both a blessing and a burden to Ball's career. On the one hand, the tune's 1994 release shot David's name into the upper reaches of the charts, allowing him the popular and financial success for which he had worked more than twenty years. Still, it must be frustrating that even on the day before his new album is released, he must spend valuable on-camera minutes talking about a song whose chart run is over instead of publicizing *Starlite Lounge*, the CD whose sales will

Mark Olencki

either mark Ball as a consistently marketable force in the industry or tear at the considerable progress that has been made towards that end.

Mark Olencki

Besides the release of the new album, there are other issues playing on David Ball's mind as we sit and talk in The Nashville Network dressing trailer at Opryland, USA. Just last night, June 21, 1996, Ball took part in a musical tribute to his friend and long-time Uncle Walt's bandmate, Walter Hyatt. Walter's ValuJet plane crashed in Florida just as Ball was due to begin an extensive North American tour opening for neo-hillbilly Dwight Yoakam.

The tribute show, and today's television appearance, fall squarely in the middle of the Yoakam tour, and it is obvious in talking with David that the miles and stress have worn him thin. It is also obvious that, although Ball has been maligned by some Uncle Walt's fans who perceive that he turned his back on that band's acoustic swing sound in favor of a

more obviously commercial mix, Walter Hyatt and Uncle Walt's Band are very much on the mind of the man in the tall, black hat.

David Ball's first years were spent in Rock Hill, South Carolina. His father was the preacher at Oakland Baptist Church, and Ball's recollection of a poem that his mother taught him as a small child points to an early infatuation with rhyme and meter: "Ebeneezer, Lemon Squeezer/ I fell in love with an ice cream freezer." That cryptic couplet was taught to young David in hopes that he might remember that he lived on Ebeneezer Road. There was always music in the house, as both parents played instruments. "My mother played piano," David says. "She'd play all kinds of stuff. She'd play Sousa marches, and my brothers and I would get out our little pistols and rifles and march around the house. My dad sang a lot, and he also played fiddle when he was a kid."

It was while living in Rock Hill that Ball encountered his first musical influence. "We'd go up to Charlotte to buy shoes, and I must have been about five years old when I saw a guy up there named Fred Kirby. He was under a spotlight in a red shirt with white fringe on it, and he was wearing a cowboy hat and singing 'Big Rock Candy Mountain.' That was pretty much it for me. I was hooked. I started out playing ukulele, doing 'Five Foot Two' and 'Little Brown Jug' and that kind of stuff."

Before the end of his first decade, Ball's family moved to the Fernwood section of Spartanburg, and he began taking lessons from Judy Hill, whom he describes as a "great finger-picker and flat-picker." It wasn't long before his mother began shuttling him around town to play with other young musicians. "She used to have to drag me around. I'd take my guitar and play with some of the wildest characters all over Spartanburg. I mixed it up with a bunch of 'em. My mother, bless her heart, she'd take me way over on the other side of Howard Street to play. It got kind of rough over there, but there'd be some boy that I knew who played guitar and we'd get together."

Ball's life-long friend, Chip Smith, remembers a trip to the downtown Woolworth's with David when they were both in the eighth grade. "We were standing there in the store and David pointed out another kid," recalls Smith. "David pointed at the kid, looked at me and said, 'Do you see that guy? That's Paul Riddle. He's a great drummer. I'm gonna get that guy to be in a band with me.' I said, 'That guy? That guy's a *seventh* grader. I wouldn't *ever* be in a band with a seventh grader.'"

Ball remembers the seventh-grade Paul Riddle not as a future

member of The Marshall Tucker Band but as a then-member of the improbably named Stanley and the Stardusters. "Paul was already taken, so I got the next best drummer, Benny Littlejohn, to be in my band.

"There were a lot of bands in Spartanburg back then. We would all hook up and do those March of Dimes Battle of the Bands shows that Mrs. Jane Hughes would put on. Me and Benny, Bill Brannon, and Heyward Hodges had a band when I was in the eighth grade. Heyward's dad played in the Rupert Hodges Sextet, and they played jazz music. These guys were playing big-band jazz out at the country club, and Heyward and I were playing rock songs like 'Love Potion #9.' All these different kinds of music were being heard in Spartanburg at the time."

As much as he played guitar, Ball never felt himself to be accomplished at the instrument. "I never got very good on guitar. I used it just as accompaniment for writing songs and singing. I wasn't near as good as Champ or Walter at guitar. That was the main reason I switched to bass. As far back as the eighth grade, I knew Champ Hood was *the* guy on guitar. Him and his cousin, George Blackford, they could both really get it. I was in eleventh grade when I saw Champ and Walter play together. I knew right then that I couldn't compete with them on guitar, but I wanted to sing with them. I thought, 'The perfect thing is to play string bass.' And, lo and behold, Walter had one at his house. So I started immediately playing that bass and bugging them to let me play with them.

"I ended up playing bass with the Spartanburg Symphony as a high schooler, but my heart wasn't in it. You know why I did it? I liked playing music at Twichell Auditorium over at Converse. I loved that hall. The bass gave me a lot of opportunities, though. I played with Ben Ballenger, who was a sax player who'd played with Charlie Mingus and other popular jazz musicians. Ben and Mike Johnson and David Haddox, a big Spartanburg drummer, and I worked quite a few gigs together.

"I wasn't all that good back then. Champ knew me, and he wouldn't hardly give me the time of day. But Walter let me get up with them and sing, and I *could* sing. To say that I was bored at school at that time would be an understatement, I mean I flat *hated* it. But when I found the music and was able to get into it with them, it got me going in the right direction. We'd go over to Walter's house and sit around singing. It was work, but it was also a whole lot of fun."

By this point, Ball had developed an interest in classic country music. He became a record-hound, scouring Mercury News and Music for bargain-bin Webb Pierce records from the fifties or hounding antique store clerks for 78s of Jimmie Rodgers. David's love of honky-tonk and country records had a noticeable effect on the early Uncle Walt's Band sound.

Champ Hood, David Ball and Walter Hyatt (Uncle Walt's Band, 1980)

"Uncle Walt's Band at that time did some Doc Watson-type music. It was like Doc Watson with harmonies, lots of vocals.

"We were very influenced by country and bluegrass. We used to have a guy who would sit in with us named Jimmy Pruitt: he had played some with Don Reno and Red Smiley, famous bluegrass musicians. We were different than other acoustic roots music bands, though, because of our singing. We really put out a wall of sound."

Uncle Walt's Band gigged around the Southeast for a few years, then entered Arthur Smith Studio in Charlotte in 1974 to cut what would become their first record. "I think our best shot was that first album," Ball says. "We walked into that studio in Charlotte, that guy set us up and turned us loose and BAM! Best acoustic guitar sound I had ever heard. From there it just gets kind of bitter, to tell you the truth, man."

The bitter part has to do with the mastering of the album. This is the process by which a recorded tape is transferred to a vinyl record (or, today, a CD). "When you take a tape and have a pressing done of it, the amount that they squash (compress) on the

signal alters the sound of it. We grabbed the tape from the Smith studio, took it to Austin, where we were living and working at the time, and had one of the rattiest-sounding pressings done that I have ever heard." As a result of that inferior pressing, the vocals sound somewhat thin and the acoustic guitars sound almost one-dimensional. As Ball succinctly puts it, "We were better live."

While Ball's assertion that the mastering of that album was substandard is supported by the recorded evidence, the album, *Uncle Walt's Band*, is still a strikingly original and highly accomplished effort. In addition to nifty covers of songs learned from Robert Johnson, Doc Watson, and Professor Longhair, the record features five original tunes that rank among their most memorable. Ball's prime songwriting contribution to the album is "Don't You Think I Feel It Too," a song that has since been performed by

David Ball

171

luminaries such as Shawn Colvin and Lyle Lovett. "That song just fell out of the air on me," he says. "I don't know where it came from. I knew it was good, though. The lyrics were a little vague, but I like it a lot. I knew what I was trying to say."

Uncle Walt's Band failed to earn the trio a big-time record deal, David, Walter and Champ couldn't agree on musical or business matters, and Ball left the band to pursue other interests. The mid-to late-seventies found him playing music in Charleston with friend David Siebring, working some with Ballenger, Johnson, and Haddox in Spartanburg, and opening up his own Spartanburg music bar, Hooley's. That bar was favored not only by Ball and his band, but also by The Contenders, a Nashville folk/rock act that included Champ Hood and Walter Hyatt. Eventually, Ball removed himself from Hooley's and went back down to Austin. It was there that he met up with Steve Clark, owner of the Waterloo Icehouse, who gave David a place to play. Finding that the town was still more interested in Uncle Walt's Band than in any combination of Ball, Hood, and Hyatt by themselves, Ball began considering an Uncle Walt's reunion. Six months later, Walter and Champ were back in Austin, and Uncle Walt's Band was back together.

The second incarnation of Uncle Walt's Band was quite success-ful, playing on "Austin City Limits" in 1980 and selling out the Waterloo Ice House every week for an entire year. There were a few offers from record companies, but the band couldn't agree on a direction in which to go. "The first major offer was from some guy at Elektra Records who wanted to sign us. The catch was that he wanted us to concentrate on one lead singer: he wanted me to sing all the songs. My reaction was that I wouldn't even consider it. I figured that the guy obviously did not get what we were doing."

The band stayed together for some time and released *An American In Texas*, a more country-flavored album than *Uncle Walt's Band*. "I was pushing for that album to be country," says Ball. "Champ was playing real good fiddle, and Walter had written some great country songs: "Deeper Than Love" and "Green Tree" were two of them. But the band would change directions a lot. It was real hard for us to come together on any particular point. Real difficult."

When the band broke up for the second time, David began to seriously pursue a solo career. Nashville record producer Mark Wright, a fan of Uncle Walt's Band, helped secure Ball a solo record deal with RCA. That record, *Steppin' Out*, was shrink-wrapped and ready for release when it was shelved by the record company. It seems that RCA wanted

David performing in an Uncle Walt's Band reunion concert (Champ in foreground) at Clancy's Pub, Spartanburg (1990)

of freedom in playing his music his way, Ball slowly says, "Hell yes. I didn't do it for the freedom, though. I did it because the opportunity was right there. That's where I wanted to go: that was my direction. I started writing a bunch in Nashville, too, and going down there and playing the music live. Then I landed a publishing deal in Nashville where they shopped *my* versions of *my* songs.

"When Champ and I started playing on a street level in Austin, I didn't book us into the old clubs where Uncle Walt's used to play. I knew better than that. I'd find a real dump out on the interstate and we'd go in and play 'Your Cheatin' Heart' and old Bob Wills Texas swing music. There was nobody there screaming, 'Sing "Undecided." Nobody was yelling 'Why don't you have Walter with you?!!'

"We cut a four-song demo in Nashville of 'Thinkin' Problem,' 'Honky-Tonk Healin','' 'Look What Followed Me Home,' and 'Don't Think Twice.' A good buzz started happening around town about that tape, Warner Brothers heard it, and the next thing I knew we were in the studio with (producer) Blake Chancey and then we had a record out. It happened real quick."

When it happened—when David Ball suddenly hit the big time—

to put its promotional muscle behind a young singer named Clint Black. Ball dismisses that aborted album: "I didn't have the right musicians to do what I was trying to do," he says—but it contains two of his best recorded performances: "Texas Echo," a beautiful western song that was often performed at Uncle Walt's reunion gigs, and "Message in a Bottle," a co-write with Walter Hyatt.

With *Steppin' Out* pronounced DOA by the record company, Ball began touring Texas honky-tonks with Champ as his fiddle player. "We'd just go out and book dance halls," says David. "I told Champ that I wanted to play *country* music for these people to *dance* to. Champ did it for a little bit. I don't know if his heart was really in it, but Hood can do anything."

Asked if there was an element

he was simultaneously embraced by country fans and sneered at by many Uncle Walt's Band fans who felt that he'd sold his jazzy, acoustic soul to commercial country radio. Some of the old fans thought that he'd changed. Others offered the more damning accusation that he hadn't changed, he was only "acting." Ball points to his childhood obsession with country music as evidence that his music today is a legitimate, heart-felt amalgam of his influences. And, he says, he frankly doesn't agree that his newer material is much different than the songs he wrote in the seventies:

"It's true that I shifted and went to a completely different audience, and I'm not sure what that old audience thinks. If they can't see the connection in the *Thinkin' Problem* album and Uncle Walt's Band, then . . . a lot of the elements of Uncle Walt's are things that I still carry. I mean, 'The Thought of You' is basically an Uncle Walt's song. 'Down at the Bottom of a Broken Heart,' too: it's that bouncy, chug-a-lug, boogie music. It's what I did and it's what I do."

As soon as Warner Brothers released "Thinkin' Problem" to radio, David's life changed. It became busier, more lucrative, and, to hear him tell it, much more fulfilling. "'Thinkin' Problem' was the first single, then we hit the road and went to work," he says. "It was real fun. We played every-

where: fairs, music festivals, did a tour with Brooks and Dunn and the Tractors. It was paradise. I hear talk about country musicians having to play the game. There's no *game* out there. People come, they sit down, and they want you to sing to them. It's just *real*."

At this point in the interview, David's voice grows wearier. His responses begin to pull away from the solo career that has brought him here, to a Nashville Network dressing room with a star on the door. The events of last night's tribute concert still fresh in his mind, he stares at his boots, lowers his vocal pitch, and releases a little bit of the pressure that he is so obviously feeling.

"It was frustrating for me in Uncle Walt's Band because we never got our due. Walter never got his due. There was so much good music. There were so many songs that Walter wrote, so many sides to Walter. Those songs of his need to be on record and they need to be done *right*. Stuff like 'Sheik of Shaboom.' I never really heard that song until after he died. What a song. Brand new. Walter wrote all the time. It's terrible. This is just terrible."

Two months later, I catch David's show at Atlanta's Lakewood Amphitheater, where he is performing the next-to-last gig of his tour with Dwight Yoakam. Ball's tour manager, Jeff Jackson, walks on stage and speaks into the microphone: "Ladies and Gentlemen, the man with the Thinkin' Problem . . . David Ball!"

Since our last meeting, "Circle of Friends," the first single off *Starlite Lounge*, has collapsed, making nary a dent on the country charts. The second scheduled single from the album, "Hangin' In, Hangin' On," was not released to radio. "I don't know," he will say to me after the show. "It just didn't happen with that song. I don't know if it's too country for country radio or just not . . . it just didn't happen."

The theater is a flurry of activity as Ball takes the stage with his band. It is not yet dark outside, and only about half of the ticket holders have found their seats. Ball's band plays on the stage's front portion, just in front of a giant gray screen that covers the bulk of the stage. The musicians are wedged between an army of electric guitars, multiple stage lights, and

other ominous-looking devices that will be a part of Yoakam's high-tech stage show. The sound is boomy, bass-heavy, and many decibels below the volume of the Yoakam show. There is little opportunity for Ball's group to steal any of the thunder from the headline act. This is Dwight's show put on by Dwight's people with the money made from Dwight's music. David Ball is, to most of the people who file towards their seats as he plays and sings, both a precursor and an afterthought.

David in a backstage trailer of "Prime Time Country" (1996)

Mark Olencki

Still, David sings awfully well for an afterthought, and he's touring with a tight little honky-tonk group. A small contingent in the crowd claps in recognition as the band plays the first bar of "Look What Followed Me Home," a minor radio hit from the *Thinkin' Problem* album. No one applauds in recognition of "Circle of Friends," the critically acclaimed but popularly ignored first single from *Starlite Lounge*.

A particularly awkward moment occurs at the end of the ballad, "When the Thought of You Catches Up With Me." As Ball sings the last lines of the song, a crew member standing off-stage right (but still in view of at least a third of the audience) lifts up a cow-

boy hat to cue David to wave his own hat to the crowd. As steady applause rises, Ball smiles and somewhat stiffly doffs his white hat to the audience.

Thankfully, the moment passes quickly. As he puts the hat back on his head, the evening's energy level goes up several notches. The band breaks quickly into the Texas swing of "Honky-Tonk Healin'" just as the guy on the mixing board finally fixes the amphitheater's sound so that the bass doesn't sound like it's coming from the maxed-out stereo system of a 1978 Firebird. As the mix of instruments through the huge speakers levels out, Ball's voice is, for the first time this evening, clearly audible and richly textured.

The sky darkens, the crowd fills in the remaining empty seats, interest in the opening act's performance grows, and David romps through a hopped-up version of "Heartbreak Hotel" before bringing the tempo back down for one more ballad, "I'll Never Make It Through This Fall." Then the band shifts into a protracted teaser which ends with an abrupt staccato thud. Ball is able to sing only the words "Yes, I admit" before his voice is joined by nearly everyone in attendance for the rest of the chorus:

I've got a thinking problem
She's always on my mind
Her memory goes round and round
I've tried to quit a thousand times
Yes, I admit I've got a thinking problem

Mark Olencki

David performing at the Walter Hyatt tribute (June 1996)

Fill the glass up to the top
I'll start with loving her
But I don't know when to stop

What was to most in the audience a distant spectacle has suddenly become a giant block party. Western-attired couples line dance in the aisles. The entire crowd claps along to the rhythm. A pre-kindergarten girl in a pink dress jumps up and down on the seat in front of me and sings along at the top of her lungs. "Daddy," she says, "that's the man from the radio."

Ball leaves the stage to healthy applause as his band reprises the song's instrumental hook. The same audience that sat, smoked, talked, and mingled through most of David's set is now on its feet. It is unclear whether they are applauding the singer or the song.

Backstage, the "man from the radio" is in good spirits. This is the last road gig of the Yoakam tour, which winds up tomorrow night in Nashville. Ball lights up a cigar, greets a couple from a Georgia radio station, and sits down to chat with me for a few minutes before the bus is loaded and ready for the trip back to Nashville, where he now lives.

"I was dog-tired last time we talked," he says. "Walter's death just knocked me for a loop. The first part of this Dwight Yoakam tour I was really in a daze."

We talk about the tour, and then about old days in Spartanburg. I ask if he can think of any parallels between Uncle Walt's Band and The Marshall Tucker Band, two groups who were popular at the same time but seemed to attract very different followings. "Uncle Walt's had many influences," he says, "but Southern Rock was not one of them.

"We didn't do anything that was even close to that. I understood it; I knew exactly what they were trying to do, and we shared certain influences. Certainly, both bands were very influenced by the blues. We came from the same place, but we did different things with it. People in South Carolina at that time were just embracing music across the board."

When I ask if there is an element of freedom to leading the band instead of working in a trio, Ball does not hesitate with this answer. "Hell yes," he says. "This isn't really about freedom, though, it's about doing what I do. If you had to boil it down to a couple of songs, 'Don't Think Twice' and 'Thinkin' Problem' is what I do. I'm working right now, and the work ethic is 'Stand right up there and sing to the people.' I'm trying to reveal parts of my experience in a poetic form. That's a job, you know? I've done it right a couple of times."

Mark Olencki

Dorothy Chapman

11 MARSHALL CHAPMAN

Back in 1956, I was seven
And the second grade was going real slow
I could read, I could write
But learning to be white was nothin' that I needed to know

— from "Why Can't I Be Like Other Girls?"
(M. Chapman, D. Hickey, J. Wahl)
Enoree Music (BMI)

"I came from privilege," says Marshall Chapman. "It was a beautiful way of life for some, but stifling for somebody like me. I had to get out of there. My spirit was suffocating, so I turned wild . . . *deeply* wild. Rock 'n' roll was my ticket."

Inman Mills owner James Chapman was not intending to foster an inclination towards unbridled willfulness when he presented his fourteen-year-old daughter with a Martin D-28 guitar. The gift was well intended yet essentially misunderstood, an honest-to-God smoking gun mistaken for a water pistol. Within the instrument lay the rebellion, self-destruction, and eventual redemption that would mark the daughter's life as a rock and roller.

Nowadays, as she sits and talks in her luxury high-rise apartment or drives the streets of Nashville in a new BMW, Marshall Chapman appears to have settled into a domestic world not altogether different from the upper-crust Spartanburg into which she was born. If life is comprised of a series of revolutions, then Marshall has completed her first swing around. What makes Chapman's story an interesting one is the astonishing height of the apex of her circle, and the harrowing lows at the nadir. She hung on for the ride, cursing and spitting part of the way, cowering in other parts, and clinging to the battered but beautiful Martin guitar that today sits on a stand in her music room.

Even before receiving her father's six-stringed present, Marshall was singing and playing a borrowed guitar in a teenage folk group led by future Uncle Walt's Band guitarist Champ Hood and his cousin George Blackford, but her hobby seemed to her parents a harmless diversion. Her mother would often ask Marshall to play a song or two at cocktail hour in front of the assembled adults. "It was a

Steve Canaday

novelty to my parents, nothing that anybody would take seriously. They thought it was cute," says Marshall.

Really, they should have known better. Signs of the depth of Marshall's spiritual connection with rock and roll flash through her childhood memories in red neon, clashing sharply with the soft whites and muted blues of an old-money upbringing. The first indicator should have been the day that she was sent home from Pine Street Elementary School for singing Elvis Presley's "Too Much" too loud in the hallway. Then there was all that time she spent in the basement with the hired help:

"I used to go down while our maid, Lula Mae Moore, was ironing," she says. "We'd listen to the radio, to stuff like Big Joe Turner. Sometimes I'd slick my hair back and imitate Elvis—it was always Elvis—and she'd laugh and scream and applaud. See, I didn't get that kind of response from upstairs, so I'd go get it in the basement."

Marshall says that the big blow came when Elvis himself appeared in Spartanburg on a package show at the Carolina Theater. "It was February 4, 1956, and I was seven years old. My parents were out of town, and our family's cook took me out there. We sat up in the colored balcony. It was a hillbilly show, with the Carter sisters, Justin Tubb, and The Louvin Brothers. I guess it was like all the other hillbilly shows, but then this *cat* came out. It

wasn't that big a deal to most of the crowd, but the people up in the balcony were going crazy: they were already hip to him."

Though the details of Marshall's "Elvis Story" have been called into question by some childhood friends, the fundamental truth of the story—that rock and roll was the vehicle through which Marshall Chapman and others like her began to seek a different reality than the one with which they were raised—is unquestionable. The acceptance and popularity of Presley was both a starting point and a breaking point for the first rock generation.

Before puberty, Chapman remembers herself as a typical, if somewhat Elvis-fixated, tomboy. She

Elvis left his mark at Spartanburg's Piedmont Cafe.

Mark Olencki

played football, field hockey, and a mean game of basketball (still does), and she connected deeply with music. "There weren't many women role models that I had in music, but I liked some of the girl groups of the sixties. I liked The Shirelles, and I was always trying to get my sisters to sing harmony with me. When one of them would get off key I'd go crazy!"

Adolescence brought with it not only the normal angst and confusion, but a different set of cultural restraints that are experienced most harshly by the daughters of the very rich. "That was when all the Southern lady stuff started. You know, 'You've got to sit like this,' the gloves, the whole lady-like upbringing. It didn't fit me very well. I wanted to be in the NBA or be Elvis, but they told me that I wasn't the right gender for either one."

She refers to her teenage years

The Assembly Ball, Spartanburg Memorial Auditorium (December 1967)

as her "dead period," though she looks happy in pictures like the one taken at her debutante "coming out" party. The problem wasn't in what she lacked (Marshall had the grace, charm, and beauty to match any Spartanburg belle); the problem was that there were fundamental and insurmountable differences between who she was and the way that she was expected to be. "It wasn't like I had this dirt-poor existence that I wanted to get away from," she says. "As far as the *soul* goes, though, the forces at work were just as strong as that.

"When people met me later in life, they'd all say, 'I'll bet you were a real rebel!' Actually, my mom will tell you that I was pretty good. I took piano lessons, made great grades in school, and went to Vanderbilt. I never planned escape or anything, because I really wanted to fit in. The pain was in the fact that I didn't fit in. I wanted to marry some guy that my parents thought was cool and that would take good care of me, have kids, and live that kind of life. For the longest time, I was in some super denial about who I was. I had to find my own values.

"I was very well-provided for, but, and this is not saying anything negative or critical about my family, I was suffering from emotional poverty. My parents grew up in the Depression, and so providing for their kids became top priority. I went to the best schools, I never had to worry about clothes,

Backstage with Marshall and Andy Warhol

hand!" she says). Her parents, along with her grandmother, Martha Marshall Chapman, arrived from Spartanburg with a U-Haul, ready to take the graduate back to South Carolina. Marshall told her father that she already had a job, and then took the family down to the saloon to see her new place of employment. "My family walked in and met the owner, and my grandmother burst into tears," she says. "I told my father, 'I like all these musicians out here, and I'm just going to hang out for a while. I'll come back in two years.'" After two years, her father called and told her it was time to come home, but Marshall was not to be swayed from her intended course.

By early 1974, Marshall was playing music at clubs like The Jolly Ox and hanging out with musicians Cowboy Jack Clement, Kris Kristofferson, and Willie Nelson. She had not yet begun to write songs, instead filling her sets with personal favorites such as "July, You're a Woman" by John Stewart, "To Be Alone With You" by Bob Dylan (which later showed up on her album *Take It On Home*), "Sister's Comin' Home" by Willie Nelson and "Let's All Help the Cowboy Sing the Blues" by Jack Clement. It was her rendition of the latter song that caused her to be abducted by Waylon Jennings:

"Waylon and his wife, Jessie Colter, came down to The Jolly Ox at

but there weren't really many hugs. I never went hungry, but I just had this *hunger*."

After high school graduation, Marshall moved to Nashville, where she would major in French at Vanderbilt. "My parents always said, 'Get your degree; after that you can do anything you want.' I believed them."

The day that Marshall received her diploma from Vanderbilt, she got a job waiting tables at a Nashville joint called The Red Dog Saloon ("I was the only waitress who could hold six beer mugs in one

two in the morning. Waylon had all that leather on and he was all hopped up: we *all* were back then. I was just about to finish playing, and I sang 'Let's All Help the Cowboy Sing the Blues.' Right when I finished, Waylon got up and left. Later, I was packing up out in the parking lot and here comes this black Cadillac. Waylon said, 'Where is Cowboy?' I said, 'Well, he lives over . . .' and they abducted me. Waylon said, 'Come on, we've gotta talk to him about this song.'

"I put my guitar in my trunk and they pulled me into their car. Jack's house was at Hobbs Road and Hillsboro, about a block away. Waylon pushed me up to Cowboy's door, hid behind me, and said, 'Knock.' I knocked. He said 'Louder!' and I knocked louder. Then he said 'Hit it!' and I'm just banging on the door. Cowboy had been in the club earlier and I knew he was sleeping soundly, 'cause he was lit up by eleven o'clock.

"Finally, the door opens and there's Cowboy, sleep falling out of his eyes, looking like he's gonna kill me. Then Waylon pushes me aside and says, 'Look here Hoss, I gotta cut that song. I gotta cut it right now!' That was the best album Waylon ever did: *Dreaming My Dreams.* I was there for all those sessions. You know, Nashville was electric then. Stories like that don't happen anymore."

In the fall of 1974, twenty-five-year-old Marshall began co-writing

songs with Jim Rushing, a regular at The Jolly Ox. One of their first songs was called, "Somewhere South of Macon," which was actually about Enoree, South Carolina, a town located somewhat north of Macon ("We changed the names to protect the guilty"). That song, as well as the Chapman-Rushing effort "Know My Needs" would appear on 1977's *Me, I'm Feelin' Free,* Marshall's debut album for CBS Records.

The year 1974 also found Marshall touring Australia with Roger Miller and being mentioned from the stage by Willie Nelson during a concert at the Troubadour club in Los Angeles. "I thought, 'I've arrived now!,'" says Chapman. "I didn't know my you-know-what from a hole in the ground, but I thought, 'This is it!'" Before long, Crystal Gayle cut Marshall's "A Woman's Heart (Is A Handy Place To Be)" on her debut album, and Chapman really *had* arrived.

A threatening letter from Orkin regarding an unpaid bug bill reveals the financial reality of Marshall's mid-seventies Nashville situation, but the social reality was much more intriguing. Chapman was making the Nashville rounds, playing around town with her own backing group, The Lost Love Band, living fast, and running free. By now an unofficial member of Waylon and Willie's "Outlaw" crowd, she was signed to Epic/CBS

Records imme-
diately follow-
ing a gig at a
club called Mis-
sissippi Whiskers.
Much of
1976 was
spent in
preparation
for that
initial re-
lease.

The cover
of *Me, I'm
Feelin' Free*,
which hit stores in 1977, depicted a
bare-shouldered Marshall wearing
a battered hat (borrowed from Donnie
Fritts). The reverse side's photo was
Marshall's uncovered back, with Chapman's arms outstretched towards a
blue sky. The back cover also featured
blurbs from press clippings and established industry friends like Waylon
Jennings, who said, "Marshall's a good
ole boy. She can come on the bus."
Critics immediately hailed the album
as an original and accomplished work,
and Marshall Chapman's star was
officially on the rise, though some
aspects of her life were on the decline.
"It was heady stuff back then, and I
didn't handle it very well," she says.
"I was getting deeper into valium and
cocaine, and my parents were like,
'What have we raised?'"

While critics were impressed,
FM programmers were less so. The

frank sexuality of some of the songs
was not what country radio was looking for. The line, "I first made love in
a cotton mill town/ Somewhere south
of Macon" caused the initial single to
be yanked from many radio stations'
play lists.

Chapman is to this day a little
peeved by radio's attitude towards the
song. "At that same time, Charlie
McClain came out with a song called
'Lay Something on the Bed Besides
a Blanket.' That was the title of the
song, and it went way up the charts!
Radio liked that kind of snickering-
behind-the-barn sexuality: that
'Nudge, nudge, get it?' kind of thing.
My music was more direct, and they
wouldn't accept that. That's why me
and country music had to part ways."

There was another reason why
Marshall's relationship with country
music was not longer lived, and that
is that while Chapman had a love and
appreciation for country music, she
was, like Elvis, a rocker at heart.
When she signed on with CBS, the
label tried steering her towards the
Tammy Wynette side of what country
radio would deem acceptable, discour-
aging her rock leanings. "They wanted
the ballads," Chapman says. "I had
all these rock and roll songs that I
couldn't get recorded until three
albums later. They only wanted the
safe stuff. I had to fight real hard to
get even one rocker on the record."
That one rocker, "Rode Hard and Put

Up Wet," is certainly the most memorable song on *Me, I'm Feelin' Free*.

The honesty that radio deemed unsuitable was the very quality that critics picked up on, and Chapman garnered an impressive music industry reputation through her album's mostly positive reviews. The Waylon comparisons were both flattering and frustrating, as Marshall's press notices often included remarks such as "Destined to be the female Waylon Jennings." "Back then, you couldn't just be who you are," says Chapman. "They all thought you had to be the female version of some guy. The same thing happened later when I was out really rocking: they called me 'The female Mick Jagger.'

"That's one of the great things about getting older. You become so much who you are that they can't compare you to anybody else."

Nashville was, Chapman says, "getting crazy," and Marshall made a temporary getaway with songwriter/novelist/music critic Dave Hickey. The pair went down to Texas, and Chapman hooked up with a band, tuned up, turned up, and dropped out of country music all together. When she went back in the studio to cut her sophomore effort for Epic/CBS, Marshall abandoned the country music mother ship for what promised at first to be a chance to fulfill her rock and roll destiny.

Al Kooper, who produced Lynard Skynard's "Sweet Home Alabama" and played the organ part on Bob Dylan's "Like A Rolling Stone," seemed a dream choice to produce Chapman's second record, *Jaded Virgin*. He had a proven track record as a producer of radio hits and an encyclopedic knowledge of rock music. Unfortunately, he was also enamored at the time with ridiculous synthesized-drum sounds (*"swoosh,"* "ba*dooob*"), the likes of which are only heard today via forty-dollar Radio Shack electronic kiddie drum kits. The finished album had soul-stirring songs in stomach-turning musical settings, and Chapman knew it was all wrong before it ever hit the stores.

"It was a bad time. There was a lot of cocaine going around, and I had no control at all over how that album sounded. *Jaded Virgin* was really an Al Kooper record, and it just broke my heart. I left Los Angeles before the record was even finished, and I was so upset that I wrecked my car driving in from the Nashville airport. They were really just trying to get me on the radio, and they did." The record made Chapman some in-roads where rock radio was concerned, although it failed to produce any real hits.

As odd as *Jaded Virgin*'s musical mix sounds today, it was on many of the critics' Top Ten lists for 1978 (*Stereo Review,* for one). The album contained an eerie, slowed-down version of Johnny Cash's "I Walk the Line," the first recorded rendition of "Why Can't I Be Like Other Girls?" and a brilliant Hank Williams tribute/Nashville music industry kiss-off called "A Thank You Note." Kooper opposed the inclusion of "A Thank You Note" on the album, and he left his regrettable mark (*"Swoosh,"* "B*adooob"*) on its production, but the power of the song's lyrics remained intact: "If Hank Williams was alive today/ I can tell you where he wouldn't be/ Hangin' around the Hall of Fame in Nashville, Tennessee."

Just after the album came out, Marshall met up with her dad in New York City. James Chapman was in town on business and Marshall was there to play a gig. The two met for dinner at a supper club called The Cookery, where legendary jazz singer Alberta Hunter was performing. Hunter was in her eighties at the time, and her performance that night was transcendent, stunning both Marshall and her father. After Hunter's performance, Marshall turned to her dad and asked how he enjoyed the show. "That's the greatest thing I've ever seen," he said. "Well," said Marshall, "I just want you to know that if I'm lucky that's what I'm gonna be doing when I'm eighty years old." James Chapman never again questioned his daughter's choice to be a musician.

Marshall's live shows of this time period featured *real* drums, loud guitars, and a frontwoman who seemed alluringly on the verge of losing control. Watching a particularly magical Rolling Stones gig at the Fox Theater in Atlanta provided Marshall with the inspiration for a couple of new songs and a no-holds-barred on-stage attitude. "I looked at the Stones and I felt just like I did when I was seven and saw Elvis. When I came back to Nashville after that concert, everything changed with our show. I was like, 'Why hold back? Why not let out everything you're feeling?' I just went nuts."

A third Epic/CBS release, this one called *Marshall,* came closer to Chapman's stage sound, but still fell short. *Marshall* contained Stones-induced songs "Running Out in the Night," "Don't Leave This Girl Alone," and "Rock and Roll Clothes," as well as a re-worked and improved "Why Can't I Be Like Other Girls?" The album's second side opened with "Rock and Roll Girl," a song that paints a disturbingly accurate picture of what life was becoming for Chapman in the late seventies:

Down at the club they're still screaming for more
You know, they don't give a damn what they're
*   screaming for*
I'm already at the hotel in my black silk hose
Listening to Lou Reed and cleaning out my nose
Lookin' in the mirror by the light of dawn
I'm countin' all my bruises and it's turning me on
I'm a rock and roll girl

—from "Rock and Roll Girl"(Marshall
Chapman) Enoree Music (BMI)

"It can get ugly when you start rocking like that, knocking up real hard against everything out there," she says. "Back in those days, I could never sleep after a show. That's when I started taking a lot of downs. I think, again, that it relates back to growing up like I did. Everything had been squelched for so long that it was like I was just exploding with energy.

"Word gets out about your drug of choice. I'd take the stage and, all of a sudden, there's hundreds of Placidil pills being thrown up there. Later, my manager gave me this little necklace that had a gold Quaalude on it, and I

Courtesy of Marshall Chapman

Marshall and fan Willie Nelson

started wearing it. I walked on stage one night in Bloomington, Indiana, and it looked like it had just hailed. There were Quaaludes all over the stage!

"I think about those times, and I don't have any shame about them at all, 'cause I understand now why I was doing all that. I'm just glad it didn't kill me."

It almost did. By the turn of the decade, Marshall was out of gas. Depressed, anorexic, bankrupt, and dropped from the roster of CBS Records, she went a full year without writing a song. That dry spell, the first of her career, upset her even more, and she began to feel that she would never write again. Just after her thirtieth birthday, she picked up the Martin guitar given to her by her father and felt something inside of her change. In a few moment's time, a fully-developed song had arrived.

And like a fine spirit
That mellows with time
This guitar's a full-bodied
   Burgundy wine
That never runs dry
She pours out the songs
While I play along
And I hope to heaven
My soul goes to her when I die

— from "Guitar Song"
  (Marshall Chapman)
  Tall Girl Music (BMI)

Chapman still held the smoking gun given to her so many years ago, and a number of songs followed in short order. Regaining her confidence ("If I get a batch of new songs, I'll go talk to anybody"), she met with representatives from Rounder Records and signed a new recording contract. The resulting album, *Take It On Home*, still ranks with her finest work, although Rounder has yet to issue it on CD.

During the tour for *Take It On Home*, Marshall found that although her creativity had been revitalized, her personal problems had not gone away. "I booked that Rounder tour myself, made all the calls, sent out the press kits, and drove the van. It was getting ugly out there on tour, though, and I was real skinny. I've got pictures of that time: I made Hank Williams look like Johnny Russell. Right after that tour, I had a complete breakdown. My mother put me in a mental hospital in January of 1983."

Her stay at Marshall Pickens Hospital in Greenville was not a cure-all, and Chapman left for Nashville feeling better rested but still not quite healthy. She went back to touring, but she describes the latter part of 1983 as the worst time in her career. Back home in Spartanburg, her father was dying of cancer, and Marshall knew that he was concerned about her even as he got sicker. "When my dad died, he knew what kind of shape I was in," she says. "He didn't tell me I should be doing something else, he just said, 'I'm worried about you.' After he died, I was totally lost."

On a freezing day in early 1984, Chapman was sitting in a Nashville pancake house, talking with someone who had an idea for her. "This guy told me about this town in Belize," she says. "He said, 'I know this family

down there that owns a restaurant. They have a house with rooms upstairs that they rent. Here's the telephone number.'"

Within a week, Marshall Chapman was in Belize. "I got so healthy down there. The men all fished for a living, so we ate great food, and all the women had gardens with fresh vegetables. I woke up that first morning hearing children laughing in the street."

It was not music for which Chapman earned a reputation in Belize; it was basketball. The whole town would watch as the tall, blond American woman played with and against the native hoopsters on a court right next to the ocean. In the conservative, Catholic town, it was highly unusual for a woman to be traveling alone, much less sweating, shooting, and winning on the basketball court. "We played full-court every evening at dusk," she says. "I'd play so hard and get so tired and drenched in sweat that after the games I would just fall into the ocean and steam would come off my body. It was the most purifying thing." Marshall stayed in Central America for months before returning to Nashville, where she found plenty of opportunities to lose what had so recently been found.

Upon her return to Music City, Marshall put a band together and played such clubs as The

Bluebird Cafe and Bogie's. Still in shaky financial shape, she had no money to put together the kind of song demos that would enable her to sell some tunes and earn some royalty checks. In Nashville, as in most places, it takes money to make money. Chapman's financial salvation came from a most unlikely place: Ralph Emery's "Nashville Now" television show.

"Ralph Emery loved me," she explains, a bit incredulous about the situation even to this day. He must have, for the nationally televised show, not known for its support of acts outside of the mainstream (and Marshall has never been anywhere near the mainstream), kept asking Chapman back for return appearances. Marshall not only played her music, she became sort of a conversational sparring partner for Emery during the interview portion of the telecast.

"We would just insult each other," she remembers. "He'd say, 'Why aren't you married?' I'd say, 'I'm just waiting to catch you in-between wives. Which one are you on now, Ralph?'"

Chapman was getting good exposure from the show and making good money from her appearances, but the best part of the deal was that it enabled her to make free, full-band demo tapes. "Instead of doing songs that I was already known for, I'd go on the show and do songs that I'd just written," she explains. "I would work

Courtesy of Marshall Chapman

Marshall and fellow performer Delbert McClinton

the songs up with the Nashville Now band, perform them on the show that afternoon, then tape the show when it aired that evening. That way, I had demos with background vocals, drums, keyboard, everything. I was actually being paid to do this! It was this little scam I had going, and I was the only one that knew it. That's how I demo'd my songs in 1984."

While her career was back on the upswing, Marshall's personal life was not without turmoil. "I got involved with this married guy: the last really unhealthy relationship I was in," she says. "He told me he was going to leave his wife, and I believed him . . . for five years. I was qualifying for the emotional Special Olympics! I believe now that in relationships, you don't get what you want: you get who you are. Well, I was a mess."

Mess or no mess, Chapman's career as a songwriter was taking off again. In January of 1985, she was invited down to Key West to write with Jimmy Buffett. "Jimmy had this rule: we never spent more than two hours on a song," she says. Chapman and Buffett wrote three songs on the trip, and Marshall spent the rest of the time on a large yacht complete with maid service provided by Buffett.

The year 1985 turned out to be the most lucrative year of Marshall's career. Jimmy Buffett recorded her "The Perfect Partner" and then guest-hosted "Nashville Now" himself. His hand-picked guests for the evening were John D. Loudermilk (who wrote "Tobacco Road"), Dan Fogelberg, and Marshall Chapman. A Capitol Records employee was in the audience that night as Marshall played a new song called "Betty's Bein' Bad." After the show, he requested a tape of the song so he could play it for a band that was in the midst of selecting songs for an album. The name of the band was Sawyer Brown.

"Betty's Bein' Bad" was picked by the record company as Sawyer Brown's first single, and Marshall got the word via a phone call to her cinder-block apartment near Vanderbilt University. "My knees buckled, I hit the floor, and I started crying, 'Thank you, Jesus,' because I knew then that I was gonna get out of that apartment," she says. The song was a huge

country hit.

Next, Tanya Tucker cut a Chapman song called "Daddy Long Legs." After that, Marshall's friend Doc Pomus (who wrote, among other songs, "Save the Last Dance For Me" and "Sweets For My Sweet") found out that a pro wrestler named Hillbilly Jim needed a theme song to record on an album. Fifteen minutes later, Chapman and Pomus had written him one. Believe it or not, *that* record sold a million copies.

Despite her financial turn-around, Marshall spent much of 1986 depressed and musically inactive. "1986 was a 'missing year' for me," she says. "I knew this relationship was over with this guy, but I was having a hard time letting go. I didn't know what to do. I finally had money of my own, and I was still miserable. I couldn't believe it."

Chapman used the five-figure checks that were arriving regularly in her mailbox to buy a beautiful, high-rise apartment near Music Row in Nashville. It was there that she began to slowly piece her life back together, partly by adopting a monk-like attitude towards alcohol, drugs, and boyfriends. She was, as she wrote later in a song, "A girl in a bubble/ Stayin' out of trouble." A long-distance, platonic but emotionally intense relationship with Doc Pomus helped to get her through what she remembers as "a very lonely period."

Wanting to record music but lacking a record company, Chapman decided to start her own: Tall Girl Records. The first Tall Girl release, 1987's *Dirty Linen*, was also distributed in Europe through Line Records. That album contained "attitude songs" like "Great Big Crush," "Daddy Long Legs," "Bad Debt," and the wry "Hollywood Here I Come."

Slowly, Chapman began making the musical rounds again in Nashville, playing more often at The Bluebird Cafe, co-writing, and singing backing vocals on Emmylou Harris' version of Chapman's "Better Off Without You." The turn of the decade signaled a period of personal growth for Chapman, one in which she still finds herself today.

"I was scared to change for a long time," she says. "I had always written songs to survive, and then all of a sudden I was at a point where everything I'd needed to *survive* wasn't what I needed to *live*. For a while there, I was ready to sign up for the Mother Teresa Training School and quit writing music altogether. That phase didn't last. It ended when I wrote 'Happy Childhood.'"

Some never make it
Some never try
Some try to fake it
Some barely get by
Survival is easy
It's living that's hard
It takes lots of courage
Just to be who you are
So do what you love
Not what they say you should
It's never too late to have a happy childhood

— from "Happy Childhood"
(Marshall Chapman, Terri Sharp)
Tall Girl Music (BMI)

Marshall celebrates the release of <u>Love Slave</u> with Beth Nielsen Chapman (left) and Emmylou Harris (1996).

"Before 'Happy Childhood,' I had always felt ambivalent about being a songwriter," Chapman says. "I knew when I would write something that was good, but I had my doubts that music was what I was supposed to be doing. My dad once said, 'You'll get this music out of your system, and you'll come back to the real world.' Well, this *is* the real world. I feel it so strong. Now I don't have to write to get out of trouble or to stay sane. I'm just a *writer*. Whatever changes I go through, I'm going to write about them."

"Happy Childhood" was first released on 1991's *Inside Job*, a Tall Girl Records production that also included "Better Off Without You" and a lovely piece of semi-autobiography called "Good-Bye Little Rock and Roller." Marshall dedicated *Inside Job* to the memory of Doc Pomus, who died in February 1991 after a brief illness. "I was devastated when he died," she says. "But the thing about loss is that if you just feel everything and *then* let go, something good can come along. It was the fall of 1991 that I met Chris."

Marshall Chapman is talking: "It's like I was saying earlier about how you don't get what you want, you get who you are. You go around saying, 'I wish I had a good boyfriend that understood me; I wish I had a producer that wouldn't clobber my records; I wish I had a drummer that wouldn't play too loud and mess up my songs.' If I had that stuff in my life it's because that's who I was at the time. I was making too much noise in my head or something. I'm at the point in my life now, at age forty-seven, where I feel like I'm down to the absolute essence of who I am. There's very little noise now."

The clatter is further reduced

Courtesy of Marshall Chapman

these days by Marshall's beau, Nashville doctor Chris Fletcher. They live together in the high-rise (she calls it "The Sky Palace") that Chapman bought after 1985's windfall of royalty checks. The years since they've met have been good ones: Marshall now has a record deal with Jimmy Buffett's Margaritaville label, and her two most recent albums, *It's About Time . . .* and *Love Slave*, have been met with greater critical fanfare even than *Me, I'm Feelin' Free*. *Love Slave* is probably the finest set of songs she's ever re-corded, a fact that strikes many people as highly unusual: most musicians hit their stride well before their late forties.

Chapman's recent years have been well lived, though not without tragedy. May of 1996 brought the death of her friend and kindergarten classmate, Walter Hyatt, and in the same year she has watched her own brother, Jamie, dying from an AIDS-related illness. "For years, I was just in a room by myself," she says. "Now I choose to live life fully, with all the horror and beauty that goes along with it. I'm learning that I can be really sad and happy at the same time. I can feel all these things at once."

Marshall is trying to make a point about her new approach to writing. She pulls out her guitar and plays a song that she has just written:

> *Call the lamas!*
> *I saw little Buddha*
> *in the checkout line*
> *at the grocery store*
> *today*
> *Call the lamas!*
> *He was sittin' like a prince*
> *in his grocery cart*
> *with a perfect smile*
> *on his face*
>
> *His mom and dad*
> *preoccupied*
> *with paying for their food*
> *They could not see*
> *him smile at me*
> *with calm beatitude*
>
> *Call the lamas!*
> *I saw little Buddha*
> *in the checkout line*

> *at the grocery store*
> *today*
> *Call the lamas!*
> *He was sittin' like a prince*
> *in his grocery cart*
> *with a perfect smile*
> *on his face*
>
> *Then suddenly*
> *in front of me*
> *I saw three little girls*
> *Their mother*
> *bagging groceries*
> *while around her feet they swirled*
> *Their peals of laughter*
> *silenced when they*
> *all looked up to see*
> *Little Buddha*
> *smiling at them*
> *beatifically*
> *He leaned down towards them*
> *holding all them*
> *in a state of bliss*
> *Then one by one*
> *they each received*
> *his transcendental kiss*
>
> *Call the lamas!*
> *Om...*
> *I saw little Buddha*
> *in the checkout line*
> *at the grocery store...*

— from "Call the Lamas!" (Marshall Chapman) Tall Girl Music (BMI)

"This *thing*, this *song*, came out and I was thinking, 'What the hell is *this*?' Three days later, it hit me—little Buddha is Jamie, the only boy in our family. He's the baby and he's got three sisters: 'I saw little Buddha in the checkout line at the grocery store.' It's me and my sisters telling Jamie good-bye. Sometimes it blows my mind how my songs are so much smarter than I am. They *know*. My job's just to keep my dumb ass out of the way.

"It used to be that it would scare me so bad when I would write a good song, because I didn't know where they came from. Now I just know that they come from somewhere else, and that's mind-boggling but it's okay. It used to scare me so bad that I'd have to go get drunk, put out the fire with alcohol or drugs or something. Now, I'll write a song and get through and write another one. I don't have to go out and try and kill myself. All that is just a difference in perspective. I didn't have it then, but I have it now.

"Perspective's a wonderful thing. I'll take tendinitis, a bum knee, loose skin on my neck, and perspective over firm flesh and piss and vinegar any day."

With that, Marshall Chapman puts up her guitar. We talk for hours more, but the important things have already been said. 𝕄𝕄

Mark Olencki

Mark Olencki

ANDRE KERR

"My mother's dream was for me to be some type of musician or entertainer," says Andre Kerr. This Friday and Saturday, just as he has on more than 4,500 other nights, Andre will honor his mother's wish, though perhaps she wasn't thinking of The Boar's Head Lounge on Church Street in Spartanburg as the proper stage from which to publicly display her boy's talents.

The Boar's Head is not what you would call a "listening room." It's a bar, a place where people come to drink and maybe dance a little. The crowd appreciates the immediacy and sheer volume of a live band, but they also want the danceable familiarity of the latest country and pop hits. For Andre's Trik Alley Band, entertaining a crowd involves a type of advanced mimicry as the musicians attempt to reproduce as closely as possible the songs that the Boar's Head patrons know from the radio. It's Kerr's show,

but it's not his vision.

Andre's story has to do with hard work, talent, perseverance, and what happens when none of those turn out to be a ticket to the musical promised land of record deals and royalty checks. "I guess I'll be in the 'Failure,' chapter," he jokes when told of his inclusion in this book, although Andre Kerr is far from a failure. His abilities have allowed him to travel the country and work in bands with performers such as Percy Sledge, Billy Joe Royal, and Paul Revere and the Raiders. Further, he has spent the past thirty years as a professional musician and a fine fellow, qualifying as a rousing success on either count.

At the same time, Kerr is a symbol for all the guys who almost made it—who would have done *anything* to make it—out of Spartanburg and into a position in which they could make the radio hits that local cover bands play on Friday nights. There are

I'm nearly famous

hundreds of people in town, and hundreds of thousands of people across the country, who throw their lives into music and end up back in towns like Spartanburg at bars like The Boar's Head.

Those guys are often awfully good musicians, and many, like Andre, genuinely enjoy their weekends on stage. Some learned enough in their attempts at stardom to know now exactly what they would do differently if only they had the chance. For Andre Kerr, the music industry must seem like a particularly difficult school exam, the answer key for which he was given ten minutes after he'd turned in his paper. Interviewed at his home in Spartanburg, Andre is quick to emphasize that he is happy in his current situation, and honest enough to admit that he might be happier somewhere else.

Raised mostly in Jonesville, the home of blues harmonica man Peg Leg Pete, Kerr began playing the piano at the age of four. Jonesville is quite rural and somewhat isolated from larger towns in the area such as Spartanburg and Gaffney. It's the kind of place where blue-collar work usually takes a precedent over more frivolous pursuits like rock and roll, but Andre's parents were adamant that he would receive a proper musical education. As a child, he took formal piano lessons from Spartanburg's

Grace Hoddell, and also began playing guitar, drums, and other instruments that were "just around the house." His father would purchase the instruments from the Sears Catalogue for Andre and his siblings to play. As a pre-teen, he and his brothers formed a family garage band called The Wanderers. Meanwhile, Kerr's mother was shuttling him all over the county for "guitar lessons, voice lessons, dancing lessons, you name it," he says. "She really wanted me to do something with music."

Kerr's fourteenth summer brought with it the opportunity to take

Courtesy of Andre Kerr

Andre performing with the group Flash at a live radio broadcast at Union's WBCU (1971)

lessons at Converse College, and it was there that he learned the music theory that would allow him to pick apart the chord structures of hundreds of popular songs that he heard on the radio. The music theory also helped him with the saxophone, an instrument he played in the junior high and high school bands in Jonesville.

It was in the tenth grade that Andre became a member of The Change of Times, an eleven-member dance band that was managed by Ron Weathers of Buffalo, South Carolina. "Ron organized us, got us clothing, picked us up for practice, and helped us open a charge account so we could get equipment," says Kerr. "We had a full horn section, and I was playing saxophone. We'd play 'Hold On, I'm Coming,' 'Knock on Wood,' stuff like that." The band included trumpet player Todd Logan, who went on to play on albums by the Allman Brothers and The Marshall Tucker Band.

The Change of Times was a yearly participant in Spartanburg's Battle of the Bands, an event sponsored by the Jaycees. Andre has a program from the 1968 competition, and the featured bands included The Endless Tyme, whose drummer was future Marshall Tucker Band percussionist Paul Riddle, and Washington Subway, which featured Champ Hood, later of Uncle Walt's Band.

"The Battle of the Bands was a lot of exposure," says Kerr. "Those were held at the Spartanburg Memorial Auditorium, down in the arena. We usually placed pretty well because we practiced and we tried to be real professional about things. Back then we used to rehearse at the West Springs School House, which we shared with Tommy Caldwell back before he was in the Toy Factory or The New Generation or Marshall Tucker. He was in a band called The Inspirations. They tore that old schoolhouse down. There's a brick building down there now, and they have the West Springs Haunted House there every Halloween."

As contemporaries Champ Hood and Toy and Tommy Caldwell were beginning to forge their own musical visions, scratching out a few dollars playing clubs once in a while, Andre was playing cover tunes in one of the most popular and busiest bands in town. History knows Spartanburg's Sitar club as the place where The Caldwells' Marshall Tucker Band and The Allman Brothers used to hold court, but few remember that years before Marshall Tucker, Kerr's Change of Times band was the first group ever to play the Sitar.

"Yeah, we played opening night," says Kerr. "We were on as the warm-up act for The Platters, so we were the first group on that stage."

The fact that a teenage cover band was given such a prestigious slot on the club's opening night bill speaks

to the musicianship and professional-
ism of the young players. It also speaks
to the nature of music audiences at the
time. While it is advantageous for
bands today to play their own songs, it
was difficult for musicians to get gigs
in the late sixties unless they played
the songs that were on the radio.

Thus, a band playing original
material (like Marshall Tucker) might
stand a better chance of landing a
record deal, but they would make far
less money on the local club circuit
unless they played cover tunes of songs
that were already popular. The Change
of Times played note-for-note recre-
ations of radio hits, enabling listeners
to sing along and to dance: that was
what club owners preferred because
that was what local audiences wanted.

In 1970, The Change of Times
was interested in playing more gigs at
college fraternities. When a band
called "Fraternity, Incorporated"
disbanded, Kerr's band adopted their
name. "We were managed now by a
guy named Jim Woods, and he would
put us in a practice building and assign
us a song by, say, Chicago. When we
had learned all the horn parts and
everything then we were allowed to
take a break. Jim was sort of a slave-
driver, but it really did us a lot of good.
We took things seriously, and we knew
if we didn't show up on time with our
uniform pressed that somebody else
would have our job. That paid off
later on."

Fraternity, Incorporated played
dances and parties all over the deep
South, from Florida to Tennessee. A
promotional letter from their booking
agent describes the band like this:
"Showmanship plus the big sound of
brass equals the number-one horn
group in the South. Eight members
coming from South Carolina lean
towards soul music but include enough
Chicago and Blood, Sweat and Tears
music to please any crowd. College-
aged."

The sixties hit South Carolina's
Upstate in the early seventies, and
"Fraternity, Inc." soon changed its
image and name to fit the times. "We
started getting a little hippie-fied,"
says Andre. "We painted peace signs
on the bus, started wearing bell-bot-
toms, and changed the name of the
band to Circus." By this time, Andre
was playing keyboard, saxophone, and
guitar in the group, as well as singing
lead or harmony vocals.

A picture of Circus reveals a
complete change from the conservative uniforms of The Change of Times.
In the snapshot, Andre has shoulder-
length hair, a big, white, Peter Brady-
style belt, and a Captain America
t-shirt. "This is in 1971, right after
high school," says Kerr.

"We were doing Santana songs
and that sort of thing, and we were
starting to grow our hair out. I had
some problems with this band, because some of these guys decided to

Andre (bottom left) with the band Hocus Pocus

try some things I didn't want to try, like drinking lots of wine and smoking a little wacky-weed once in a while. That wasn't for me: I'm a straight guy, and I got out of that band."

Kerr's insistence on a drug-and alcohol-free environment stems not only from a personal code, but also from a family promise. "I made a promise to my mother when she was dying that I would keep straight and act right and try to be a good person," he says. "I made that promise and I've tried to keep it. So far, I've been able to. I've seen a lot of good people have a lot of problems because of drugs and alcohol, and I just never wanted that for myself."

Andre left Circus and immedi-ately joined a band called Flash. Flash played in the same style as Cir-cus, but they were substance-free and had t-shirts with lightning bolts and stars. The booking agency rag boasted "Satisfaction guaranteed. Flash gets it on!" while *Fast Beat*, a paper in Lau-rens, South Carolina, described a typical Flash concert this way: "Light-hearted, young people sat or stood in a giant horseshoe as other couples in the middle were freaking out. In the darkening shadows beyond the horse-shoe, other couples were sitting on the floor listening to the ear-splitting tones."

Flash was short-lived: the band made some personnel changes and became Hocus Pocus, a band perhaps best remembered for its unique promotional photograph. Next, Andre got back together with Ronnie Hayes from The Change of Times, and Pickle Eaves from Flash, along with Flash's original drummer. This group was called, interestingly enough, Circus. This edition of Circus played mostly cover tunes, but they did release one original 45:

"That was when we decided to try and put a real record out," says Andre. "We went to a guy named Sherwood Burton in Laurens. He had a two-track recorder and some bailing wire, and we thought we had hit the big-time. The first side of the record was a goofy thing that we opened our set with called 'Hello, Hello.' The other side was the real song: 'Love Is What We Share.'" The record, which never charted, was released in 1972, with Kerr receiving at least partial writer's credit on each song.

Throughout all the changes in musical styles and band names and affiliations, Andre had been making a living as a touring musician since graduating high school. Still, Circus' failed single served as a reminder of the drudgery of the road and the financially beneficial yet musically uninspiring tyranny of the fraternity and dance-lounge circuit. A change in scenery would soon come in the form of million-selling soul singer Percy Sledge.

"Percy used to call me Fats Domino," says Kerr. "The guys in Circus met him through our talent agency, and we became his backup group, The Sledgehammer Band. That was kind of a star position, and it gave us all a real good boost in salary. When we went to the motel, we each got a room instead of having to sleep four people in one room. We thought we were moving up in the world, and I was glad because I had a wife and a daughter to support."

Andre with Percy Sledge and the band

As a Sledgehammer, Andre played concert halls and listening rooms as Sledge's keyboard player. A few years past his 1966 smash, "When a Man Loves a Woman," Sledge was still a good concert draw, and Kerr remembers that souvenir-seekers would often break into the dressing room while the band was on stage in hopes of acquiring a small piece of soul music history. One hopes that the band members' street clothes were never stolen, because that would mean that they would have had to leave the building still dressed in a stage outfit that Andre says included "big shoes, satin pants, big ol' oversized bow ties and pink tuxedos."

The Kerr-Sledge partnership might have lasted longer had it not been for Percy's difficulties with sobriety. "For about a year, Percy did great," says Kerr. "But he had some problems before, and he got a little messed up again." Andre remembers that the key of "When a Man Loves a Woman" would change depending on the sobriety status of the lead singer. The classic song could be in "A" one night, "E" the next.

"We could be in Raleigh, North Carolina, and Percy would want to get something. If he couldn't get it in Raleigh, he'd jump on a plane and go to New York. I wouldn't even know that he was gone, and I'd be up on stage introducing him. We'd travel four or five hours, set up, play four hours, and not get paid because Percy wouldn't show up. People in the crowd would be angry because they'd paid ten bucks apiece to get in, and that was a lot of money in 1973. After a few times of that, the band just had to get

away from the situation."

Despite the circumstances behind the parting, Kerr looks fondly on his time with Sledge. "We got to go to Muscle Shoals with him and record with Quinn Ivy, who produced all of Percy's records. Quinn cut some records of just our band, without Percy. We also got to see more of the country, and we'd established a better name for ourselves by being Percy's band. That helped us to move into some of the other things we did."

When the group left Percy Sledge, they kept the name The Sledgehammer Band and went back to playing smaller, less prestigious venues. As The Marshall Tucker Band continued to climb the charts, Kerr found himself back in Spartanburg playing other people's music. "Yeah, we'd copy a Marshall Tucker record if they had one out.

"We were basically a cover band: I guess we had the wrong idea of how to get out. We should have been writing and doing our own stuff, but we were making a living the way we knew how. When the music on the radio would change, we changed with it. When disco got popular, we'd play disco. If it was commercial rock, we'd do that."

In 1975, The Sledgehammer Band got another break; this time it was a chance to back up Billy Joe Royal, the singer of the 1960s hit

Courtesy of Andre Kerr

Andre (center) with the Raiders portion of Paul Revere and the Raiders

"Down in the Boondocks." Royal was coming east from his home in California for a series of shows and he needed a backing band. Tapes were forwarded, songs were learned, and The Sledgehammer Band spent an evening as The Royal Family. "The agent also put a couple of horn players in there with us," says Kerr. "Then Billy Joe went back to California and we were right back in the clubs.

"Later on, Billy Joe decided he couldn't get enough gigs on the West Coast, and he was still real popular over here. So when he came back, he had to have a band. He wasn't crazy about the horn players that he used before, but he liked the rhythm section

he'd used: well, that was us. That's how we got tangled up with Billy Joe Royal."

In addition to what emerged as an ongoing gig with Royal, Andre was at this time playing occasionally as one of Paul Revere's Raiders. Revere was another ex-hit singer from the sixties, known for his song "Kicks." "I was beginning to play a little better and bumping into people that needed musicians. The Paul Revere stuff was just when he needed somebody, but I played piano with him a number of times. I've still got my pirate suit and three-cornered hat and all that. The front of his piano was an Edsel car grill, and that was always fun to play."

Now officially The Royal Family, Andre's band was booked with Billy Joe around the country, playing such rooms as The Golden Nugget in Las Vegas and appearing on television and in large concerts (Kerr remembers an outdoor package show in Alabama where there were 15,000 people in attendance). Kerr not only played keyboards, he also served as road manager, keeping up with bookings and taking care of the organizational aspects of the tours.

In the mid-seventies, Kerr used the Billy Joe Royal connection to try to garner a record deal for The Royal Family Band. "We did a session in Atlanta that was produced by Steve Clark, who had produced 'Wendy' by The Association and who produced Joe South, The Tams, and Billy Joe. We got that record placed on 4-Star Music out of Nashville. It was released, and two weeks later the company went bankrupt. See, we bumped around and scraped the surface a couple of times, but we were always back down before we could think about going up to stay.

"A lot of times when we'd send out demos, the record companies would say, 'The lead singing is a little weak.' So on one of the records we cut, we had Billy Joe singing lead. I've got a record of Billy Joe Royal singing on our song! (After saying this, Andre gets up, goes to the stereo, and plays me the 45. Sure enough, the unmistak-able warble of Billy Joe Royal is right up front.) His name is nowhere on the record, and we were just waiting for somebody to say something about *that* lead singer."

A 1976 article from *The Charlotte Observer* documents one of the nights when Las Vegas glamour was far from the reality of The Royal Family:

Billy Joe Royal's band shuffles onto the stage at Charlotte's Atlantis Club and stares out over an audience of twelve people. "Welcome to Shoney's," says keyboard player Andre Kerr in a thick Southern drawl. There is no response. Standing behind his electric piano, which is draped with a bicentennial flag, Kerr tries again. "I've never seen so many dead people sittin' up." No one laughs. No one is paying attention. Kerr and the Royal Family Band break into their first set, running through some warm-up disco numbers before they introduce the star of the evening. "And now, a big hand for Billy . . . Joe . . . Royal."

Although that night was among the worst that Kerr remembers with Billy Joe, the road was surely beginning to wear on The Royal Family. Royal was not the big draw that he once had been, and he was thinking at the time of changing his musical direction. "He kept saying, 'I'm gonna start singing country music,' and we kept encouraging him to do that," says Andre. "He never did try it back then. After we left, he came back with a bunch of country hits (among them "Love Has No Right"). I guess my timing was bad on that one, too."

In the late 1980s, during the time that Royal was on the country

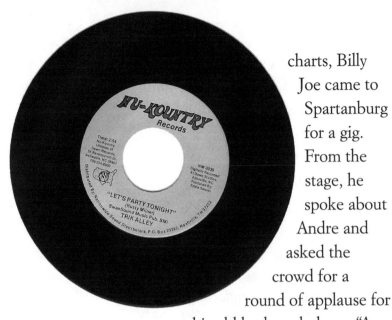

charts, Billy Joe came to Spartanburg for a gig. From the stage, he spoke about Andre and asked the crowd for a round of applause for his old keyboard player. "A lot of people were there that knew me from playing around Spartanburg. They couldn't believe I really knew Billy Joe Royal," says Kerr.

The road was also taking a toll on Andre's home life. "I'd be on the road with Billy Joe for ten weeks at a time sometimes," he says. "My family put up with that for a while, and then it got too old, I guess."

In 1979, Andre quit The Royal Family, came back to Spartanburg, got a divorce, and took a job as a public safety officer at Wofford College. He attempted to cut music completely out of his life, and he did so for close to a year. Itching to play again, he was tipped by a keyboard-playing friend that there was an opening in a local band for a keyboard man. The friend intended to audition for the spot, but Andre beat him to The Boar's Head, the Church Street club where the band was playing. Kerr was given the job on the spot.

For the past fourteen years, Andre Kerr has led several bands through two- to three-year stays as the house band at one of several Spartanburg area clubs. His current band, Trik Alley, plays every weekend night (excluding Christmas Eve) at The Boar's Head. "I've got Ronnie Hayes from The Change of Times playing guitar, and Mandale 'Pickle' Eaves from Flash as my bass player," he says. Drummer Allen "Tank" Shetley ("He's a big guy, but he's lost about 200 pounds") and pianist Scott Moss round out the group.

Today, Kerr works in the daytime as director of public safety at Spartanburg Technical College, overseeing security operations, inspecting buildings, and checking out fire equipment. Music is a serious hobby now, a second job, although it is clearly the

job with which he is most comfortable: "It's been instilled in me my whole life to perform, and I guess that's the best thing I do. I love to do it, and I feel best when I'm having a good night up there. I can't help it, I guess it's like a disease. But what I do now is for fun, and it kind of gets things out of my system. We have fun and meet a lot of nice people.

"Really, the Trik Alley Band is a lot like Circus or The Change of Times or any of those others. We are more country music than those other groups, but we're a dance band, and we play what people request. Whatever's the number five song on the charts, we'll play it. We go buy the music charts, learn the song, and play them when people call them out. I really make more money now than I used to, because the equipment stays in one place and there's no traveling costs."

Asked if he has any lingering regrets about his life in music, Kerr is quick to name several. "I wish I'd concentrated on songwriting. That's the way to do it if you want to get somewhere: original material. Also, I wish I'd gone on to Nashville or New York or Los Angeles when I was young. One thing about Spartanburg, you don't ever have to worry about getting discovered here.

"There's a lot of things I'd do different. Hindsight's 20/20. We never did go out and beg and aggravate the other people who *had* made a little

something. Every time I turned around, I guess I could've been sending a tape to Marshall Tucker or somebody, trying to get them to do something for me. We just tried to go out there and earn it. We felt like if we stayed with it and really gave it our all that it would get there, but it just doesn't always work that way.

"Ronnie and I joined The Change of Times in August of 1967, so we'll be celebrating our thirty-year anniversary this summer. I spent more time on the road with him than I did at home with my wife. We traveled together, ate together every day, saw the country together, and now we're back together in Spartanburg. Thirty years is a long time, and I guess everything changed except us." MM

Andre performing at The Boar's Head, Spartanburg (1997)

Mark Olencki

Mark Olencki

13   CHAMP HOOD

"I think magic is just a big part of Champ's whole thing," says David Ball. "He walks through life in a state of grace. There's an angel looking out for him. He's a lot like Walter Hyatt. They were two . . . they're very similar. They touch an awful lot of people and yet they're just who they are. Champ is a natural player. I've played with the schooled musicians, and I'll take a natural musician any day."

DesChamps "Champ" Hood would laugh at that assessment, with a cigarette-hollowed chuckle that is the vocal equivalent of a roll of the eyes. The part about being a natural player would, after the over-100,000 hours that he's spent honing his craft, seem especially ridiculous to him. It's true, though. Knowledge and rehearsal—self-schooling, if you will— in no way disguise or alter the inherent, essential naturalness of his rolling, tumbling fiddle lines and casually masterful guitar-work.

The "state of grace" allusion is also correct. Performing in auditoriums with Lyle Lovett or downing a Rolling Rock at his parents' kitchen table, Hood is unfailingly and somehow almost unwillingly graceful. Walter Hyatt's mother recalls Champ playing guitar on small Spartanburg stages during the first years of Uncle Walt's Band, long hair bathed in a cheap spotlight shine. She says he "looked like a Renaissance angel up there," and he probably did. Probably played like it, too, then hung around after the show to smoke a few cigarettes, drink some beer, and laugh about how funny David Ball looked singing with his eyes closed, playing that bass fiddle with his butt sticking out.

"Walter Hyatt lived in this neighborhood," says Champ, talking about the Duncan Park area of Spartanburg. "Even though we didn't hang around together until we were teenagers, I knew of the Hyatt family and I knew of Walter. They had this field where you could play baseball. I'd go over there to play ball every once in a while."

The first memorable encounter that Champ had with Walter Hyatt involved the purchase of a baritone ukulele. "I had a neighborhood friend named Rob Hicklin, and Rob got me interested in guitar," Hood says. "I was about eleven years old. Rob played guitar, and he offered to give me lessons for fifty cents per session. He said since my hands were small that I should get a baritone ukulele, and he knew where one was. It turned out that it was Walter who had the ukulele. We went over to Walter's house one day, and I bought it from Walter for thirteen dollars: thirteen dollars of my own money that I had saved!

"At the time, I knew two chords: a G and an E minor. Rob had me play those chords in front of Walter, and he gave me a look that I always thought of

Champ's fiddle and Walter's guitar   Mark Olencki

as kind of a smirk. I gave Walter a lot of grief about that over the years. I mean, he *smirked* at me the first time I ever played for him. Of course, he always denied that it was a smirk. He says he hardly even remembers it, anyway."

Upon purchasing the instrument, Hood set to work. The first song he learned was "Puff the Magic Dragon," and from there it was off to the races. "It got to be quite an obsession for me," he says. The obsession was multiplied by the excitement of competition, which was provided in spades by Champ's cousin, George Blackford.

"George had been taking piano at the house right across the street. He was pretty good at piano, and he was also a Beatles fanatic. After he saw me playing guitar, he started playing guitar. He learned it *way* too quickly. I tended, even back then, to be a little bit lazy sometimes, and I would have to credit George with inspiring me to keep up with him. It became a real competition. All in all, it was very good, but sometimes it could get kind of painful."

Accounts of the rivalry confirm that George Blackford was at least every bit as good as Champ. Had they not been cousins, the situation might have escalated into ugly rivalry. As it stood, they chose to join forces, and their first foray into the semi-organized musical world included another future professional musician:

"Our very first group was with Marshall Chapman. We called ourselves 'The Townships,' mostly because we really liked The Villagers. The Townships probably did about two gigs: we didn't last too long. I think I was in sixth grade, and Marshall was a little older. She was going to private school. We were doing folk stuff like Peter, Paul and Mary, The Kingston Trio, The Christy Minstrels, that kind of stuff. I was trying to convert George to the folk thing. He was into the Beatles, but I was way above that music."

Folk and rock music were battling for control of the national airwaves, but there were at least two other early influences on Champ Hood that would later appear in his writing and playing styles. Hood's father, who had played clarinet in the L.S.U. band, was a fan of big-band jazz and owned records by such artists as Glen Miller, Lawrence Welk, and Les Paul. Champ was not a fan of that music, but admits

to "absorbing" it from an early age. In addition, his brother, Robin, belonged to the Columbia Record Club and ordered albums by country artists Johnny Horton and Ray Stevens.

"I had the folk records," says Champ. "I could do a mean Barry McGuire at one time. I used to sing the hell out of 'Green, Green.' I sang that at a boy scout jamboree one time and brought the house down. Of course, that was before I started smoking."

Already, Champ had a reputation around town for being a gifted player. "I knew Champ Hood," says David Ball, "and I knew he was a great guitar player. As far back as eighth grade, he was *the* guy. Him and his cousin, George Blackford, they could really get it."

After much trepidation, Hood began to experiment with rock and roll guitar syles. "Eventually, George converted me to the Beatles after I heard *Rubber Soul,*" he says. "The Byrds came out with 'Mr. Tambourine Man' and after that I could see it: the folk and the rock gettin' together. That's when I wanted an electric guitar. That same summer, the Rolling Stones came out with 'Satisfaction.' George's mom had given me a Stones record, but I was still kind of a snob towards rock and roll. I put it on the first track, which was 'Around and Around' that Chuck Berry wrote, and I really liked it. So that helped to convert me, and then, too, I was entering junior high and I wanted to impress girls and be in a rock and roll band."

There were several rock and roll bands for Champ and George (an early group sported the distinctly un-Spartanburg monicker "The Mod"), but the best-known was certainly Washington Subway. "George knew these guys at Spartanburg Day School (the local private high school) that were older than us. Jody Paul was a charismatic eleventh grader who sang Rolling Stones songs and played harmonica and was pretty cool. Jody could do some blues stuff on harmonica, Paul Butterfield stuff. His brother, Charlie, played keyboards, and they lived in Tryon, North Carolina. We got together and Washington Subway got going. We did the Stones and the Beatles, and then all of that San Francisco stuff started coming out and we did some of that, too. Every now and then we'd let the amps feed back and we'd get real loud. We called the Subway a psychedelic band, but it really wasn't."

If it wasn't psychedelic, it was at least very different from any other bands in town. Washington Subway appeared at the yearly talent shows at the auditorium, and they are remembered as being very good and a little bit arrogant about their musical mission. "We were pretty ambitious," says Hood. "We weren't doing what was popular in Spartanburg then, which

was the beach music. I love that stuff now, but at the time I had an attitude against it. We would try to be different from anybody else."

The Subway practiced at drummer Penny Hodges' house. Penny's father, Dr. Rupert Hodges, led a jazz sextet that played at the Spartanburg Country Club, and brother Hayward was in a band with David Ball. "They had a nice basement with all these amps set up, and we liked to practice there," says Champ. "Sometimes we'd have to fight with David's band over who got the basement to rehearse. Most of our guys were older, so we usually won. I had met David playing childhood football with the Fernbrook Tigers, but that was our first musical experience together." According to both Ball and Hood, it was not a particularly positive experience.

The late 1960s were a time of enormous activity in Spartanburg's local music scene, with musicians Toy and Tommy Caldwell, Walter Hyatt, Andre Kerr, David Ezell, Alvin "Little Pink" Anderson, Paul Riddle, Doug Gray, and George McCorkle all attempting to make names for themselves. Champ attributes the increase in involvement to several factors. "I think the folk groups like The Christy Minstrels had something to do with it, and the Beach Boys did, too. It was the Beatles, though, that started the real band thing. All of a sudden, everybody wanted to be in a group. We

Champ Hood, David Ball, and Walter Hyatt relaxing before a sound check

all wanted to be big stars like the Beatles."

Comprised mostly of members who had college educations in their future, Washington Subway was doomed from the start. The band understood this, and they celebrated the ending of their existence with the same oddness that characterized their sound. "I was the youngest, so I was still in high school, but the other guys were going off to college," says Champ. "We planned out a big funeral, and had a tombstone carved for the band. It was a big event, and we had a real nice funeral. There's a box buried in a yard in Spartanburg with a bunch of artifacts like guitar strings and a history of the band. I think there are some photos, and maybe even a tape in there."

In Champ's senior year at Spartanburg High School, the Beatles started their Apple label and Hood became intrigued by the acoustic music of the first Apple artist, James Taylor. "His music hit home with me in some way, and I found myself drifting back to an acoustic thing," says Champ. Hood's revitalized interest in acoustic and folk music was a factor in cementing a friendship with Walter Hyatt, by now a student at Wofford College, to whom Champ had been reintroduced at one of the Subway's last performances.

"This friend of mine, Rick Lee, he got Walter and me together,"

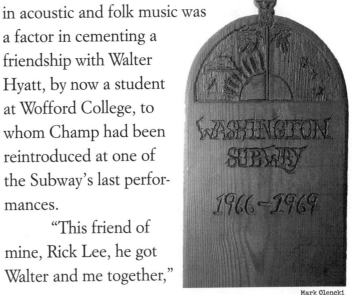
Mark Olencki

says Champ. "Yeah," says Lee, "I brought Walter over to Champ's parents' basement one day. I thought those two would hit it off."

Hyatt and Hood found that, while their public efforts at music-making had to this point been fairly incongruent, they shared immense knowledge and passion for music. Both were record collectors, though Hyatt gave Champ credit for a superior knowledge. "Champ in particular was a very eclectic listener," said Hyatt. "He had a good record collection and listened to all kinds of stuff. He was the one to try to keep up with what was going on, with whatever was the new, hip thing."

It was not easy to keep up with the new, hip thing when you lived in a town that was typically at least a year behind the music, fashion, and social trends of the day. Luckily for Champ Hood, there was Sky City, the sixties equivalent of a more regionalized Wal-Mart. "In Spartanburg, you had to really search for records," says Champ. "I'd find all that psychedelia stuff out at Sky City. Really, that was the only place I could find it. They had a record section there, and, at one point, I would buy just about any record that had a weird name or a psychedelic cover. When I think back, I was buying all that San Francisco stuff, and right behind me in the country section were all these George Jones and Buck Owens records that I wish I'd gotten.

I'd look at those records and think, 'These guys are doofballs.' I had nothing to do with country music back then, but I realize now that a lot of people I was listening to actually listened to all that stuff.

"I bought a lot of records, but I wouldn't say that I was really knowledgeable back then. I'd get music I thought I liked, and it was a long time before I realized where it was all coming from. You dig back and realize that it goes *way* back. When I'd listen to Eric Clapton or his band, I didn't know that they were getting that stuff from Robert Johnson. We were all just hungry back then, and we were trying to find out as much as we could."

While Champ and Walter were becoming friends, Hood was attempting to make a local name for himself as a solo musician. "I played with Walter as a duo a few times around town, and he introduced me to some of the places to play acoustic music. I remember going out and trying to get a gig at The Peddler. I was gonna do a solo thing. The guy auditioned me and said, 'Well, I like the picking, but you can't sing worth a shit. I'll hire you to come in and do some picking.' I went and showed up for the gig, and he'd hired someone else. That really hurt me, and pissed me off, too. I went straight to the Italian Village and asked that guy for a gig. He didn't like my singing, either, but he let me play. I ended up getting this female singer,

Donna Green, and he liked that. I just backed her up on guitar, and then I also played solo there a few times."

Walter Hyatt left Spartanburg briefly and traveled to Georgia and Canada. After Hyatt returned to Spartanburg, he and Champ went back to trading records and playing music together in a shifting cluster of musicians called The Walter Hyatt Consort. The two made a duet demo to send to Apple Records (they never got a response), and began delving into musical forms that they had previously shunned. "Walter had already dropped out of Wofford," says Champ. "He was a great influence on me; I used to skip high school and go over to his house. We were always listening to music. One time, I picked up a Flatt and Scruggs record, *Live at Vanderbilt*, because Rick Lee told me how much he liked Flatt and Scruggs. I had never liked bluegrass, but this just blew my mind. I knew Walter would like it because of all the harmony. We were over at my house one night, and I made him listen to it. He was trying to leave, and I said, 'Just listen to one song.' He was like, 'No, I promised my parents I'd be home.' I said, 'Just one song,' and I played him the first song on the record. Then, of course, he stayed to listen to the whole thing."

Figuring he would have to go to college, Hood began practicing classical guitar in order to become skillfull enough to study music at the North Carolina School of the Arts. His admission was turned down, though, and he ended up going to Spartanburg Junior College for two semesters before dropping out. By this time, the Walter Hyatt Consort had become Uncle Walt's Band, featuring Hood on lead guitar, Walter on rhythm guitar, David Ball on string bass and, at first, Kathy Hyatt on drums. The quartet soon lost the drums and became a trio, and the line-up was solidified. The three members shared lead and harmony vocal duties, and it was those harmonies that first signaled the potential excellence of the combo. "We knew early on that we

Jim Wilson

had created a monster," says Champ.

Just as George Blackford's guitar prowess had pushed Champ to a higher level, Ball and Hood developed a competitive attitude toward record collecting. "Once we got old enough for our parents to let us leave for the night, we would make special trips up to Raleigh or Chapel Hill to the Record Bar store," says Champ. "David and I would see who could get a particular record first."

It seems the boys in Uncle Walt's Band were looking everywhere *except* their hometown for inspiration. "Toy Caldwell was kind of the king in Spartanburg," Champ says. "He was somebody that everybody respected, but I don't remember any major influences locally on my music. It was after I left Spartanburg that I began to find out that there were actual musical people from here. When we got to Texas, I'd tell someone that I'm from Spartanburg and they'd say, 'Oh, that's where Pink Anderson is from.' I'd say 'Who?'"

By this time, Champ was heavily into songwriting, a third area of his musicianship that was bolstered by a need to keep up with or better his peers. "I think I was always making up music, but Walter and I went through some healthy competition where he inspired me to keep trying to one-up him. I think a lot of the fun in Uncle Walt's Band was in blowing each others' minds. Walter would write

something new and show it to me, and I'd think, 'Wow, I've gotta go write me one to top that.'

"Even though each person wrote his own songs, we always collaborated on the arrangements. Everybody would put in their two cents, and we'd try different harmonies and different vocal parts. Those rehearsals could be just nuts, and we were good at beating a dead horse into the ground sometimes. We'd finally get something worked up after spending days on it, and then somebody would say, 'I want to change the arrangement.' But I go back and listen to some of that stuff now, and I'm truly amazed at how *arranged* these songs were."

"I remember driving back to Spartanburg from Myrtle Beach with Walter, David and Champ in the early 1970s," says Spartanburg musician David Ezell. "Champ was driving, I was in the front seat, and it started snowing about the time we hit Columbia. We were going twenty miles an hour at the most up I-26 in the snow, but somebody had a bottle of whiskey. It took us about six hours to get from Columbia to Spartanburg. We started singing, and I'll never forget Walter and Ball leaning up towards Champ in the front seat, singing 'As the Crow Flies,' which I'd never heard before. I was sitting there listening, thinking, 'My God, this is great.' Champ said, 'Walter wrote that.' Then they did

Champ's song 'Seat of Logic,' and it was the same thing. The harmonies were just incredible. That's when I really knew: I knew I was hearing the real thing."

As the reputation of Uncle Walt's Band grew, they began to move out of their Spartanburg base. A trip to Nashville in 1971 preceeded a relocation to Music City in 1972. Uncle Walt's was playing at a Nashville club called Our Place, where they were seen by Texas singer/songwriter Willis Alan Ramsey. Ramsey arranged some gigs for the band in Texas, after which the band moved *back* to Spartanburg and considered a move to Winston-Salem, North Carolina.

"Then Willis called us up and said, 'Ya'll come down and record an album with me in Austin,'" says Champ. "We were just going to go down there and record an album, but we ended up helping to build Willis' studio and spending a lot more time in Austin than we had originally thought."

No material from those 1973 recording sessions has ever surfaced to the public, but Hood's account of the resulting tapes points to some Beatles-esque studio experimentation. "We recorded a lot of stuff with Willis, but he would never play it for us. Just recently, he gave me a tape of that stuff, and some of it sounds pretty good. It had Walter playing piano a

bunch, and there was stuff with electric guitars, too. It sounded like listening to out-takes from *Let It Be* or something. You could hear us working up songs and experimenting with things, but none of it was really finished product."

In 1974, the frustrated trio left Austin without any recorded product to show for their Texas efforts, returned to Spartanburg, and drove to Arthur Smith Studios in Charlotte to cut a self-released album called *Blame It On The Bossa Nova* (in a second printing, the title changed to *Uncle Walt's Band*). The album was recorded live in the studio, with each member of the trio playing acoustic instruments and sharing singing duties. Champ's two songwriting credits on the record, "High Hill" and "Seat of Logic" each became among the most requested and remembered of the band's songs. Introducing "High Hill" at an April 1996 show at Spartanburg's Players' Club, Hyatt called it "the greatest 'hit' of Uncle Walt's Band."

Just after recording *Blame It On The Bossa Nova*, Uncle Walt's had their closest brush with stardom. The trio was now managed by Walter's first wife, Marylou, and they had attracted the interest of Eddie Wilson, the proprietor of the famous Armadillo World Headquarters venue in Austin. Wilson had submitted the new record, along with a video of a live performance, to Warner Brothers Records.

Champ's description of the following turn of events is backed up by Marylou Hyatt.

"We played a gig in Chapel Hill, and we knew that (guitarist, Warner Brothers recording artist and significant Uncle Walt's influence) Ry Cooder and Randy Newman were doing a concert in Raleigh. Walter and I decided to go to the sound check and give Ry Cooder a copy of our record. Ry was real nice and cordial, and he let us into the sound check.

"At the time, the album didn't even have a cover on it; it just had a white jacket. He pulled the record out and said, 'Uncle Walt's Band! (Warner Brothers president) Lenny Waronker has been raving about you guys! He played me this record. You guys are signed, aren't you?' We were like, 'No, not that we know of.' He said, 'I could've sworn Lenny said you were signed.' We were scratching our heads, wondering what in the world was going on.

"Finally, we went back down to Texas and the Armadillo guys were having a big meeting with the Warner Brothers people. We had done a demo for Warners at Arthur Smith Studios—they gave us $2,000 and the Armadillo people produced it. The Warners people were looking kind of grim-faced in

Champ "picking" the fiddle mandolin style

the meeting, and when it came down to a final 'yes' or 'no,' they just said, 'no.'"

Warners never stated a specific reason for turning down the band, and Hood heard rumors that the artist and repertoire department at the record company had voted unanimously to sign the band. Marylou Hyatt, who worked in the music industry not only with Uncle Walt's Band but also with Waylon Jennings, says sources told her that Lenny Waronker decided that the trio was too close in image to California acoustic swing combo Dan Hicks and the Hot Licks. This is like saying that the Rolling Stones were too close in image to the Beatles since they were both electrified rock and roll bands with large followings, but a decision's a decision.

With their new album in tow, the band returned to Austin, played some gigs, and broke up in 1975. "We were burnt out at that point, and we didn't really see it going anywhere," says Hood. "David quit the band, but there was no big blow-up. I'm glad that we never got to the point of hating each other. Being in a band can be like being married, you can get real co-dependent."

The trio remained dissolved for three years, during which time David Ball moved back to South Carolina. Hood and Hyatt took a different path. In the early Nashville days of Uncle Walt's, when the band played at Our Place bar seven nights a week for three months, two musicians from Raleigh named Tommy Goldsmith and Steve Runkel would often get up and play music between sets. Goldsmith and Runkel had a duo in Raleigh called The Pritchard Avenue Band that was a favorite of Ball, Hood, and Hyatt. After the breakup of Uncle Walt's, Hood began calling Goldsmith, Runkel, and Hyatt to urge them to consider forming a different kind of band.

"We'd done the acoustic thing, and we were ready to get out the electrics," says Champ. "I was living in Nashville when we decided to give it a try. We got a great drummer named Jimbeau Walsh, Goldsmith managed to come up with some money to live on while we rehearsed, and we got together at my house in Nashville. Walter was the last holdout, then he decided to come up from Austin and give it a try. We all listened to groups like Moby Grape, Buffalo Springfield, and The Byrds in the sixties, and those bands were a big influence on our new band."

The quintet called themselves The Contenders. As to what type of music they played, no one can precisely say. The Contenders' one album, released in 1978 on Moonlight

The Contenders performing "Chain of Emotions" at P.B. Scott's

The Contenders opening for the Nitty Gritty Dirt Band

Records in Chapel Hill, North Carolina, melds electric and acoustic instrumentation, oddly structured harmonies, and enlightened pop music experimentation.

"I didn't think of it as being all that off-the-wall," says Hood. "It was basically a bunch of songwriters that wanted to play each others' music. We covered a lot of musical ground, because we knew a wealth of songs. Guys like Walter and Tommy were walking encyclopedias of songs, so there was never a shortage of songs to play.

"None of us was really a bass player. We passed the bass around at first, and I believe I was the first one to get fired from playing bass. Walter played it for a while. We finally made Steve Runkel be the bass player, even though he didn't particularly want to do that."

The band's one album has a cover with a picture of the band members' feet standing around a set list. The album's songs were written on the set list, but there was one song on the set list that was not included on the record. That song was "Getaway," which was the only song ever tri-written by David Ball, DesChamps Hood and Walter Hyatt. "We had intended to put that song on the record," says Champ, "but when we listened back to it, we noticed that everything was out of tune." The song later resurfaced in Uncle Walt's Band's performance on the *Austin City Limits* television show.

The Contenders played a number of performances in South Carolina, and Champ says that Hooley's, a Spartanburg club owned in part by David Ball, was the band's best spot to play. "That band never was really successful, but it was a major part of my career," says Hood. "It was a learning experience, and it was great to play with Tommy and Steve and Jimbeau. Those were people I'd always wanted to play with. Part of the problem with the group was that there was no focal point. We had too many chiefs and not enough Indians."

Walter Hyatt left The Contenders after a year, and Goldsmith, Hood, Runkel and Walsh played together as a quartet for another year. The album came out just after the band broke up. Ball then asked Hood and Hyatt to come to Texas for some reunion gigs that were quite well received by the Austin club-goers. "Those were real successful," says Champ. "I remember splitting $1,500 one night, and that was real surprising. I figured people in Austin had totally forgotten about us, and they probably would have if we hadn't put out that one record. We started playing gigs at the Waterloo Ice House and became a band again."

Champ had long since augmented his musical attack by learning to play fiddle. David Ball remembers that Champ picked up the instrument because "we decided that a fiddle player would add to our sound, and we didn't have one. Champ just *learned* the thing." The fiddle added another color to the trio's sound, and it opened up the soundscape of Hyatt's rhythm guitar to come through at full force. The instrument was also a last remnant of Carolina in a musical mix that could at times approximate Western Swing. Austin musician David Halley says, "I like the Appalachian flavor that Champ brings to the fiddle. It's more of a long bow approach than people normally use in Texas. I prefer him to any fiddle player around."

Champ had not laid his guitar to rest, however, and Waterloo Ice House owner Steve Clark recalls that many of the musicians who came to see Uncle Walt's looked to Hood as a musical model. "The guitarists, even

(c) Stephen L. Clark

Uncle Walt's Band in the studio above the Waterloo Ice House (1978)

the ones who were supposedly more 'accomplished' than Champ, would look at him and say, 'Champ is much more of a guitarist than I am. That guitar is a part of him.' Champ could go out there with those dangerous leads that made you think he was going to fall off the world, then he would somehow bring the lead back into the song and the guitarists would go crazy. There were a number of musicians who would actually cut their gigs early so that they could see Uncle Walt's at the Waterloo."

In their second incarnation, the trio went on to record some of Champ's more memorable songs, including "An American In Texas," "Sad As It Seems," and "Walking Angel." There were more near-miss record deals, such as an offer from an offshoot of legendary Stax Records that Ball, Hood, and Hyatt turned down on advice from their lawyer, who told them that the label was in financial trouble. "We had to pay our lawyer to negotiate the deal, and then pay him again for his advice not to take the deal. The label folded not long after that. They were trying to expand. Maybe they were looking for us to save 'em," laughs Champ.

"I think Uncle Walt's wanted to break out of Texas," says Steve Clark, "but they wanted to do it on their own terms. Champ's a road warrior, but David and Walter were a lot more genteel than that. They didn't want to go play a lot of crappy places when they could stay in Austin, play nice rooms, and make

Mark Olencki

more money. They wanted to get to the next success level, and I'm sure Champ would have gone whatever direction any of the others wanted to go, but you had two strong personalities in David and Walter. You had an all-star band that was very small, and they had a hard time agreeing on how to get to that next level.

"Maybe the comfort of the Waterloo hurt them in a way: they got one hundred percent of the door (the patrons' admission fee), had no traveling expenses, knew people would love them, and made a lot of money. It was fairly easy, and the song production was huge, because they had time for it."

In 1983, Uncle Walt's Band broke up again, though they continued to play a number of reunion gigs whenever the mood hit or the bank accounts cried out in hunger. Champ made the decision to stay in Texas after the breakup, where he played some solo gigs, performed as a duo with Hyatt, and, as he says, "hustled to get any work I could."

"Champ has about become a Texan," said Walter Hyatt in 1996. Really, there's not much "about" to it. Hood's most recent press biography reads, "Although David Ball and Walter Hyatt now reside in Nashville once again, Champ has never wanted to leave the vibrant music scene in Austin and it appears that Austin wouldn't let him if he tried." In the mid-eighties, he might have been able to make it out of town without too much of a fight. "I went through some lean times," he says. "Walter and I were playing some happy hour things together, and then I got a gig with Rusty Weir. The work with Rusty was my first decent-paying gig in that time period."

David Halley, himself a stellar guitarist and the author of two excellent albums, 1990's *Stray Dog Talk* and 1993's *Broken Spell*, was among the first to play with Champ in the post-Uncle Walt's Band period: "Champ and I would call each other to fill in or do a gig where we needed another guitar player or whatever. Eventually, we started calling ourselves, 'The Champ and Dave Show,' although it wasn't a real *show*. Neither one of us were outrageous performers."

Before long, Champ was playing with singer/songwriter Christine Albert and working solo shows at Gruene Hall, a small dance hall in the hill country outside of Austin that is also a favorite venue of David Ball. Gruene Hall was also the location for the recording of an album that would mark Hood's first recorded work as a sideman: Jerry Jeff Walker's exquisite *Live at Gruene Hall*, on which Champ played lead guitar.

Another door opened up for Champ in the late 1980s, and this one led straight into Austin's famed Threadgill's restaurant, home of the weekly Wednesday night "supper sessions" at which some of Texas' finest musicians play for hungry Austinites. It was through singer/songwriter Jimmie Dale Gilmore, now an Elektra Records recording artist, that Champ became involved in the Threadgill's scene. "Every Wednesday night I hosted these supper sessions," says Gilmore. "Then Champ became one of the guys that would come and play with me." In fact, Gilmore and Hood played for a time at the restaurant as a duo, before Jimmie Dale began putting a band together.

"Champ joined my touring band, and we even played a gig in Spartanburg at Dawg Gone. He played fiddle and guitar with me, and then, when I quit playing at Threadgill's, he took over as the M.C."

Threadgill's gave Champ the most exposure that he'd gotten in Austin since his time with Uncle Walt's Band. That exposure reached outside of the city when Watermelon Records agreed to distribute a recording of one of the Wednesday night sessions (*Threadgill's Supper Session*, 1991). On that CD, Hood duets with Jimmie Dale, sings lead and harmony vocals on a number of tracks, and plays fiddle and guitar behind Gilmore, Butch Hancock, Sarah Elizabeth Campbell,

Marcia Ball, and others.

A similar CD, *Threadgill's Supper Session: Second Helping*, was released in 1996. On *Second Helping*, Hood leads his Threadgill's Troubadors through an eclectic selection of tunes—everything from the public domain "The Beale Street Blues" to The Carter Family's "Gold Watch and Chain" to Janis Joplin's "Turtle Blues"—and shares the stage with guests Tish Hinojosa, Toni Price, and Walter Hyatt. The show was taped on Hyatt's 46th birthday, October 25, 1995, and at one point the musicians and audience sang "Happy Birthday" to Walter, who was killed the following May in the ValuJet plane crash.

Hood's two Threadgill's albums are only a part of his recorded output in the past ten years. He played and sang on Lyle Lovett's 1988 *Lyle Lovett and His Large Band* album, made large vocal and instrumental contributions to both of Walter Hyatt's solo albums, appeared on two CDs by one of his current employers, Toni Price, and recently laid down fiddle tracks for the major label debut of San Francisco

Champ and Lyle Lovett

singer/songwriter Richard Buckner.

There are other album credits, but the better part of Hood's living is earned as a live gun for hire. Since the late 1980s, he has toured with Jimmie Dale Gilmore, David Ball, Toni Price, Kelly Willis, Willis Alan Ramsey, and several others, and he spent 1993 and 1994 as a member of Lyle Lovett's Large Band. He even performed as part of Gaffney, South Carolina native Andie McDowell's backing band in a scene in John Travolta's angel movie, *Michael*.

The constant grind of performing has further sharpened Champ's fiddle and guitar skills, but it has done nothing positive for his songwriting. Though he wrote some of Uncle Walt's best songs, Champ's pen has been stilled for a long time. "Situe," a song he and Walter Hyatt co-wrote, appeared on Hyatt's *King Tears* album in 1990, but even that song was a holdover from The Contenders years.

"I can't remember the last song I finished," he says. "That's always in the back of my mind, but I get kind of lazy about it. I spend so much time learning everybody else's songs that my own writing really suffers. I've thought about going to Nashville and doing some co-writing, hooking up with a really good lyricist. The music comes easy to me, but the lyrics are something I labor over."

If the lack of recent writing credits is a disappointment to some

Uncle Walt's Band fans, it does not seem to have hurt his reputation as a player's player. In 1996, he was inducted into the Texas Music Hall of Fame and picked up another award for Best Strings Player. Both awards are testament not only to his musicianship, but also to his localized but very real star status in the Austin music community. It's not just what he plays, it's how he plays it, loping around the stage beneath the cheap spotlight glare with a slow but easy grin across his face. "A lot of professional musicians act like playing is such a pain," says David Halley. "Champ actually has fun on stage, and that makes it a better experience for everyone, players and audience."

Walter Hyatt summed up Hood's appeal with a return to an earlier theme: "Champ is an inspired, natural musician," Walter said, with a tone of authority born of over a quarter century spent listening to Hood's music. To Hyatt, it was a statement not of opinion but of stone fact, an irrefutable truth that Hood could no more laugh off than he could change it. Norman Vincent Peale used to tell a story, not worth repeating here in full, in which the hero of the tale (Peale, of course) admonishes some garden flowers to "lift up your heads and be what you are supposed to be."

Champ Hood is what he is supposed to be. ⚡

DOGS
NOT ALLOWED

Mark Olencki

74 MATTHEW KNIGHTS

Everybody comes back here to die
After spending their whole lives trying to get away

— from "Big World"
Matthew Knights

"That's Spartanburg," explains Matthew Knights. "It seems like everybody—musicians, artists, photographers, writers, whatever—they leave this town bound for somewhere else and then they always come back."

Knights himself has waged several attempts at an escape, but now he's back in Spartanburg, sitting out in his yard in a neighborhood located just behind Express Music, the store where he works. His job at Express involves salesmanship and public relations, two skill areas in which Matthew has often been found lacking. A greater measure of either one would probably have propelled him into the national spotlight back in the 1980s, and maybe his noticeable improvements in both will help to guide his presently stalled music career to a place where his visceral brand of rock and roll can be heard by a greater audience.

It's been a fishbowl existence for Matthew, with Spartanburg stages such as Arthur's, Dawg Gone, and Clancy's serving as exhibit areas for the anger, confusion, excess, self-absorption, and startling artistry that have marked his fifteen years in the localized public eye. He's been the next big thing, the teen darling, the reckless abuser, and the laughed-at self-parody. Most of all, he has been, and today remains, the Patron Sinner of Spartanburg Rock and Roll.

Matthew was born in Marion, South Carolina, but he didn't live there long. "Yeah, we had to move," he says. "My dad got tired of seeing a cop sitting in front of the house every day when he'd come home from work. They were watching my brothers, because my brothers were pretty wild. Also, my sister was dating a black guy in Marion in 1969, and that wasn't looked upon real favorably." The Knights family packed up and moved to Worchester County, Massachusetts, around the turn of the decade, when Matthew was five or six years old.

The move north was an enjoyable one for a young boy whose competitive inclinations and angry countenance were quickly put to use on local skating rinks. Matthew was good at hockey, a skill which proved to be of little use upon his return to South Carolina as a fourteen-year-old. His parents now separated, Knights found himself in Spartanburg, though he was never at one address for long. Matthew remembers moving often, and within a three-year period he attended Evans Junior High, McCracken Junior High, Boiling Springs Junior High, Dorman High School, and Spartanburg High. Knights also drifted in and out of family supervision, and many of his friends refer to his being "on his own" or "raising himself" from the time he was about fifteen.

In describing himself as a student, Knights chooses the word "trouble." A ninth-grade expulsion caused him to repeat that grade, and it was by then apparent that Matthew wasn't going to do much of anything in the realms of conduct or schoolwork that he didn't want to do: he soon dropped school completely. What he wanted to do, then as now, was play rock and roll music. "I liked to read books back then," he says. "I mean, I started reading before I was in kindergarten, but I only liked to read if

it was something that I picked up myself. Really, school wasn't anything that was important to me. Music was important."

At first, "music" meant "drumming." It was as a percussionist that Knights first began to make his mark on the Spartanburg music scene. His initial gig was as a drummer for a hard-rock band called The Emeralds. Matthew played drums for various Spartanburg acts until he was about eighteen, when he decided to take up the guitar. "I didn't like the music I was playing as a drummer," he says. "I wanted to play my own music, and I started writing songs. My friend Will Starnes and I started a little group, The Darlings of Naked Philosophy. We played at the Spartanburg Arts Center and at my sister's Jungle Party, which was a pretty famous wild party in Spartanburg." Starnes and Knights then joined forces with bass player Ted Luctenberg in a new group. Matthew led the band and played guitar.

Spartanburg singer/songwriter David Ezell met Knights at the time of the inception of The Daze. Matthew calls Ezell "the first established musician to give me some encouragement." "I ran into Matthew in 1981 or '82," says Ezell. "I'd just started a band called The Driveways at that time. Matthew was sitting at the counter of The Skillet restaurant on Pine Street, and already, at about nineteen years old, he had that interesting look in his eye. He was familiar with my band, and he was very cordial and charming, as Matthew can be when he wants to. He told me that he had started a band that was going to be playing at a club called Arthur's. He said, 'It'll be our debut night, and we'd love for you to come out.'

"Well, I came out and it was infectious. It was substantive and charismatic and full of attitude. Some people, like Keith Richards, are born to strap on an electric guitar: you can see it in the way they move on stage, the way they grip the guitar and lean into it. Matthew Knights was definitely like that. It was real, and anyone would have had to be a fool not to understand that. I think Matthew had more raw talent than any one person I've ever known."

Immediately, Knights became the talk of young Spartanburg. "There were already some infamous stories going around," says Ezell. "There was one story about him going to play some party at the house of some high school girl, some nice house, probably in Converse Heights, and Matthew's on the microphone spewing profanities. They told him to leave, and he walked all the way home, just as angry as an angry young man ever was. Matthew was always repressed, bitter, and too smart for his own good. He's brilliant, and that can sometimes be a hard thing."

To the town's rock and roll fans, Matthew represented something different from popular 1970s acts such as Marshall Tucker, Garfeel Ruff, and Lightwood. Those bands had specialized in Southern Rock, while Knights' songs were informed by the punk sounds of The Clash and the surf-rock of The Trashmen. Unlike a vast majority of bar band guitarists in Spartanburg, Matthew was not aspiring to become another Toy Caldwell, a truly special guitar player who by 1980 spawned a stultifying contingent of painfully derivative imitators. The newness of Knights' sound was not lost on Spartanburg's high school students, who were looking for a new kind of rock and roll hero. "There wasn't a scene among people my age in Spartanburg before he started playing," says Knights' longtime friend Sander Morrison. "For a long time, Matthew was the only original game going that actually said something to people. He was the only local musician that I found interesting."

After the first Arthur's gig, Sander Morrison's high school buddies made it a point to go out and see Matthew Knights. "The second night he played at Arthur's, there were a lot of high schoolers there that were part of the debutante crowd that had not treated Matthew so well in school," says David Ezell. "Some of them went out of curiosity: they wanted to see what was going on with this *outcast*. Somewhere in the middle of the first set, Matthew got upset with his band. Things started not working out musically, and Matthew took his Fender Mustang guitar, raised it over his head, smashed it on the floor, and stormed out the back door, leaving everyone with their mouths dropped. One could theorize that throughout the years, Matthew has been trying to recover from that moment. He had the whole town right there in his grip and then just lost it."

"Yeah, I smashed that guitar," says Knights of that evening at Arthur's. "The tempo was speeding up and slowing down, and I kept getting madder and madder. There were two or three hundred people there that night, and I could just feel myself going down in flames. For people to come and see me and the music not be good, I just couldn't stand it. It just

killed me, and I smashed the guitar. I didn't even own another guitar at the time. I don't know if that show set me back or not, as far as people in this town are concerned. Probably the performance would have set me back more than the guitar-smashing."

In some ways, Knights' passion and temper worked *for* him back then. "One of the things that I initially liked about Matthew was his fire," says Knights' ex-manager Dick Hodgin. "He burned bright and he had 'attitude,' but I liked it. The first time I ever saw him was at Arthur's. David Ezell got me out to see him, and I remember this young punker in a band called Matthew Knights and the Daze, which I thought was the stupidest name in the world. Matthew was only twenty years old or so, but I knew in the first ten seconds I saw him that he

Matthew at a house party (1981)

had it. It was reckless rock and roll, balls to the wall."

Matthew halted his solo career for a time so that he could take a job as drummer for David Ezell's band, The Rage of Europe. It would be the only time in Knights' life that he was able to live solely on money that he made from playing music. A good

tially marketable blend of British-influenced post-punk rock and Southern neurotic paranoia, but the band split after several years together.

"Matthew was playing drums behind two older guys," says Ezell, "and he knew that he should have been up front doing his own thing. We knew how good he was, too, and his

John Gillespie

The Rage of Europe: David Ezell, Matthew Knights, and Jim Orr

draw on the regional club circuit, The Rage could certainly have garnered a record contract had things rolled its way. Each member of the trio, which included bass player Jim Orr, was a songwriter, though Ezell was the band's prime writer and frontman. Songs such as "She's On Vacation," "All You'll See of Me," and "What If (It Drives Me Crazy)" were a poten-

wanting to do his own thing got the better of all of us." The break-up was not amicable: the group's last gig almost ended in blows between Ezell and Knights.

With the dissipation of The Rage of Europe, Matthew lived in Augusta, Georgia, for a few months, spent time with his brother in Massachusetts, came back to Spartanburg (living first with his mother and then with Ted Luctenberg), and then hitch-hiked to Los Angeles. "I wanted to get out of Spartanburg," Matthew says. "California was as far away as you could get, and I liked that. I had a little job working in an upscale super-market at the tip of Beverly Hills in West Hollywood. Liberace would come in the store to buy groceries. I stayed with a guy named Tom Byars, and played music with him at little clubs out there. In 1984, I got lovesick and came home to Spartanburg."

Upon his return, Knights joined forces with Don McGraw, who has played bass for Matthew since that time, and also with manager Dick Hodgin. Hodgin was at the time best known for his work with The Accelerators, a phenomenal rock band based in Raleigh, North Caro-lina, that eventually signed with Profile Records, released two strong but commercially unsuccessful albums, and broke up. The Accelerators were going strong in the mid-eighties, and Hodgin's association with the band gave him the clout to pursue other clients. Enamored with Knights since the first night he saw Matthew at Arthur's, Hodgin signed Matthew to a management contract.

"Matthew is a star," Hodgin says today. "Let's define what a star is: a star is a guy who, when he's up there on that stage, every man in the room wants to be him and every woman in the room wants to go home with him. Matthew is a fucking star, and that actually may have been some of his undoing. But he had that down-home, Americana, red-hot, 'Johnny B. Goode' rock-and-roll sound. He also had a razor wit, a real twist, in his lyrics. He had a skewed vision, and I loved the way he picked things to say and then added the right music to go with it."

Hodgin and his client decided to alter Matthew's last name from Knights to 'Knight,' and, with Hod-gin's encouragement, 'Matthew Knight' began actively seeking a record deal. "That was around 1984, and I was concentrating on writing and on tightening up the band," says Knights. "I hooked up with Dick, and the record companies started coming out to gigs and writing letters. Some of the major companies were interested."

"We had Matthew touring regionally," says Hodgin. "Then we recorded some demos together, and I think to this day that those are the best recordings he's ever done. They captured the natural essence of what Matthew was about, instead of trying to match up to someone else's expec-tations. We just went in and recorded, and there was a tremendous amount of fire in those early sessions. We had a lot of the pieces in place for Matthew to get where he wanted to be, but just because you have one record company guy, or even twenty guys, interested doesn't mean you're gonna get signed. The rest of the pieces didn't happen to fall in place before Matthew started being his own worst enemy."

"You wanted to love the guy, but he wouldn't let you," says David Ezell. "The music was his salvation, but the attention it gave him was a curse. There's nothing like giving a brash, cocky kid some attention: you're unleashing a monster when you do that."

Hodgin remembers a regrettable run-in with a record executive who had the power to sign Knights to a major-label contract. "This guy, Patrick Clifford from A&M Records, came down to see Matthew at a club in Raleigh," Hodgin says. "Matthew put on an absolutely stunning show, and Clifford was knocked out. We went out to sit in the van and talk, and the guy begins to ask Matthew some questions about his music. Matthew looked at him and said, 'Who are you, and what do you do?' This really put the guy off, but he said, 'I'm Patrick Clifford, and I'm the vice president of A&R (Artist and Repertoire, the division of a record company that identifies talent) for A&M Records.' Matthew took a real sarcastic tone with the guy and said, 'Really? Are you?' From that night on, whenever I spoke to Clifford about Matthew, he would say, 'Well, has he got his head on right yet?'"

"I think Dick was a little quick to dismiss Matt when things would go bad," says Sander Morrison, "but then Matthew was just so volatile at the time. I can imagine being in Dick's shoes. I'm sure Dick was thinking, 'I get you a good gig in a good room in front of these record company people, and you show up all messed up, or you're angry Matthew tonight instead of talented Matthew.'"

"During this same era, I saw another side of Matthew," says Ezell. "I was over at his house one day around Christmas time, and Matthew's father, who he rarely saw, came by. Matthew was so glad to see his father, and it was really touching to be there. His dad gave Matt a Christmas present, and Matthew opened it up and it was two pairs of socks. Matthew said, 'Dad, thank you. I needed socks. I can use these.' Really, this goes to the heart of Matthew Knights. The urgency that's in his music may be there because he didn't have anything to fall back on. His parents weren't even in the same town a lot of the time that he was growing up. He was really on his own, walking everywhere. He wants to be loved as much as anyone, and he treasures it when someone does."

Hodgin, Morrison, and Knights himself speak of the mid-eighties as a time when Matthew's personal problems began to overtake his musical abilities, but surviving recordings from this period reveal an enormously talented and undeniably magnetic performer. "I'd Be A Fool To Turn Back Now," "Judge and the Jury," and "Janie's Not the Same" should have been hit songs. "The music is such a small part of the initial steps of getting an act signed," says Dick Hodgin. "One of the things about a young artist, especially one with the fire of Matthew, is that they think, 'I've gotta do it now.' He felt other people were

under control. My music needed some development, and I basically neglected it. I was doing cocaine, which ruined my voice and really put an end to me for a few years. I don't think anybody really wanted to touch me after that. The great drug scare of the eighties, you know? It really pissed Dick Hodgin off, and he has yet to forgive me."

With many of his local bridges seemingly burnt beyond repair, Knights lit out for California again in

Matthew and friends at Dawg Gone in Spartanburg, S.C. (1989)

getting ahead faster than he was. We were on the right course, but he couldn't see it and he didn't have the patience to stick with it."

"This was the time I started getting in trouble," says Knights. "I was having problems keeping myself

1989, leaving a trail of rumor and innuendo behind that would still be waiting for him when he returned. "Matthew felt like he was spinning his wheels, and he took off for Los Angeles," says Hodgin. "He was under the impression that all he had to do was move out there and be a good musician and everybody would notice him. Well, he *was* good, but that doesn't mean anything. He got out there and realized, 'Oh, God, I'm out here on the street with these other 10,000 people from all over the country that think they've got a good band, too.'"

"I was playing out in Los Angeles, and this guy Spike was going to take me into the studio," says Matthew. "He was friends with Mike Curb at Curb Records and we were going to do something, but I just came home. I had a problem with substance abuse, and I realized that going out there to avoid my problem wasn't going to help. I didn't need to be out there in a fuckin' zoo, and I wanted to come home."

> *This is a small town*
> *No need to write the facts down*
> *You'll hear all the gossip*
> *It's worn into the ground*
> *That's no place to be*
>
> —from "When A Hero Dies"
> Matthew Knights

Upon Knights' reemergence in Spartanburg, his relationship with Dick Hodgin went from battered to broken. Matthew quickly formed a new band, Fluffy, and played most every week in the Greenville-Spartanburg area, but he claims that Hodgin was misrepresenting him to club owners as unfit to perform. "My management agreement with Dick was in effect all through my drug thing," Knights says. "He told me he was waiting for me to clean up, and he said when I was ready we'd go back to work. Well, I was ready to go back to work and he was still telling people that I *couldn't* work. I finally demanded that he send me a termination of contract, and he did."

Hodgin disputes the assertion that he attempted to dissuade clubs from booking Knights, saying, "Relations between us were really strained, and I needed certain things to happen before I was going to work with Matthew. Those things never transpired. To this day, though, I've given him the greatest of references to every person in the world: clubs, A&R, and other musicians who are interested in playing with him. Anything I could do for Matthew, I would do it. But I don't like being fired, especially for the reasons Matthew fired me, which were no good reasons at all."

After dissolving his partnership with Hodgin, Knights continued to write songs, make demo tapes, and perform. Fluffy, which featured former Accelerators bass player Mike Johns on guitar, was perhaps Matthew's strongest live band, performing songs such as "The Underdog" with typical power and a typical nuance. Without a manager, though, the band went nowhere. Fluffy was stuck playing local clubs at a time when Knights' reputation around town was not a positive one. As he struggled to climb out of holes that he had admittedly dug for himself, he found very few people who wanted to lend a hand. Most wanted to throw a little dirt themselves.

"Matthew pissed a lot of people off, and he knows it," says Sander Morrison. "He's pissed me off a million times, and I still love him. With Matthew, you forgive a lot. Some people would come up and want to talk to him and he'd be in a mood, and they'd come away going, 'What an asshole.' There was definitely a Matt backlash at some point."

"It's a small town, and when you stand out I think you're up for more attacks," says Knights. "I think the only people who want to see you succeed are your really close friends. Other people want to take what you've already done bad and make it out to be even worse. I didn't do as much dope as people would have you think, but I had a problem with it. My biggest mistake was in admitting it in public, 'cause that just opened up the floodgates. The truth won't get you very far.

"I think in Spartanburg I'm probably considered the biggest asshole that ever was, you know? It comes back to me all the time. Granted, I've had my moments, but I don't think I deserve a title like that. People get from me what they give to me. If they want to be kind and fair, then I'm certainly capable of that. But I can't even walk down Main Street without

somebody screaming something out of their car window at me."

"There were a lot of people that counted Matt out when he was hitting the skids back in 1989," Morrison says. "There were people who thought, 'He'll never pull himself up from this.' I have no idea what was going through his head back then. I think he fooled around with different combinations of drugs and thought, 'I'm Matthew: this isn't going to stick to me. I'll do this and then move on.' He might have just gotten caught up in it. The fact that he finally kicked all that completely, though, shows you something about the strength of this man."

Fluffy folded after drummer Kevin Heuer left the band, and Knights put together the Ex-Presidents, a group that found Knights and bassist Don McGraw playing with Upstate blues guitar legend Alan Heavrin and drummer David "Country" Hollis. The Ex-Presidents' sound was much heavier than Matthew's other bands, with Heavrin's flashy leads providing a counterpoint to Knights' tight, straight-forward rock songs. The group put out two self-released tapes, played a memorable show at a Pacolet, South Carolina, barn party in which Matthew performed an entire set completely naked ("I had to remember to keep the guitar in front of me," says Knights), then folded after a year when Heavrin left. It was during his time with the Ex-

Presidents that Matthew began an association with teenage musical prodigy and future Albert Hill band-leader Aaron Whisnant, a player who today recognizes Knights as a considerable influence.

One major problem during the days of Fluffy and the Ex-Presidents was Knights' inability to sell club owners or record companies on the marketability of his music. Successful bands such as Albert Hill rise to a position of prominence in part by making phone calls and sending out press kits that include biographies, press clippings, and demo tapes or CDs. Putting together a plan to interest others in his act was not something at which Matthew excelled. "Matt

had a burning desire," says Sander Morrison, "but he's not the guy that needs to be handling the phone calls and publicity and all that. He's not the guy that needs to be calling the clubs and making sure that the local paper has a photograph and a tape to review. That was a big bump in the road for him after Dick Hodgin left."

"I guess I always thought somebody was going to find me here in town, and I was pretty wrong about that," says Knights. "I really only sent out about twenty tapes in that whole damn time. We got a letter back from Bar None Records when I was with Fluffy, but we were dumb enough not to put any information on the tape about how to get hold of us. They sent the letter to us in care of X Records in Greenville, but by the time we received it and got back in touch with them, the band was broken up. There's a million more stories like that in my career."

"About three years ago, I sent the Ex-Presidents' tape to Dick Hodgin," says Knights. "He told me, 'Matthew, no one is interested in an aging rocker.' I carried that around with me for awhile. It really got me down until I figured it out. Of course they aren't interested in an aging rocker; dead ones are much more interesting.

"The farce of Dick's statement is that there are only two kinds of people: dead and aging. Sure, I'm an aging rocker, but so is Aaron Whisnant. There's a lot of interest in *him* right now."

Somewhere around the time of his thirtieth birthday, Matthew Knights began to grow up. Free of his drug and alcohol problems, years of accumulated anger and disappointment turned to introspection. "People have talked about Matt's potential since he was nineteen," says Morrison. "I think after he got off the shit, he realized that potential doesn't mean a whole lot. Also, I think he decided that living well is the best revenge. He thought, 'I don't have to be this angst-ridden, pissed-off individual. I'm gonna be happy.' I don't believe he knew before

that he had the capacity for contentment, but it seems to be sitting on him pretty well.

"Matthew has grown a lot. When I first met him, he was twenty years old, and, by his own admission, he was a punk. He's a lot less bitter now. Matthew had it tough: he was on his own as a teenager, living in a shotgun shack on Marion Avenue. Sixteen years old and he was a self-sufficient unit. He's let a lot of that go now. He has a steady girlfriend, Teri, who's been real good for him. He smiles a lot, he's happier, and even his detractors can see these things."

After the dissolution of the Ex-Presidents, Knights formed another trio—this one fell apart when drummer Casey Culbreth left in 1995 to take a job out of town. Matthew then joined an Asheville, North Carolina-

based country/rock group called NC Rail. Knights played electric guitar and contributed backing vocals for the band, which released a CD in 1996 on Middlesex Records, played gigs on the regional club circuit, and broke up before New Year's, leaving Matthew, as he says, "intent on doing my music again."

"The jury's still out on Matt," says Sander Morrison. "I wouldn't be surprised at all to get next month's issue of *Musician* magazine and see a profile in the 'New Faces' section featuring Matthew Knights." If Morrison's statement sounds like wishful thinking on the part of a friend, consider the comments of Knights' ex-manager:

"Matthew's still got the talent, and he's still got plenty of time," says Dick Hodgin. "He's been through a lot, but he's a man now, not a kid. Matthew has made some real turn-arounds. One practical discipline that he's mastered is his guitar playing. When he came back from California, I told him, 'Man, you think you're a lot better than you are. You think you're a really hot guitar player, but you've only got flashes of hot.' By God, he took that to heart. He got blazing good. There's a thing with a musician where they combine the inspiration with the perspiration, and Matthew has really done that now. He's an absolutely incredible guitar player."

It's been a long time since Dick Hodgin has answered questions about Matthew: Hodgin is now the manager of Cravin' Melon, a band whose Mercury Records debut, *Red Clay Harvest*, is a result of three years of the kind of hard work and careful planning that the 1985 version of Matthew Knights so obviously disdained. "Did Matthew have what it takes? Absolutely," says Hodgin. "Does he have what it takes now? Yes. But you can have all the talent in the world and, without the other pieces falling into place, you may never get heard. All of the stories of the bands that got discovered by some weird accident, those are fantasy. One of the biggest parts of the Cravin' Melon story is the work that they've done. They've developed a fan base, they're way ahead of the curve on their web page and their Internet presence, and they've sold over 20,000 copies of their self-produced CDs. This was all calculated."

Of all the things that Matthew has been, "calculated" is nowhere on the list. The passion and inspiration that draw people to his music are a direct contrast to the professional guile needed to make it in the music business. "Matthew is one of those people who was touched by the hand of God," says Hodgin. "He has this inner-fire burning, and there's nothing that he can do about that. It's something he was blessed/cursed with, and he has to deal with that all his life. My dad used to tell me that for every thing you do, you have to pay the price. People like Matthew, Marshall Chapman, the guys in Marshall Tucker: in some way or another, through death, failure, drug addiction, alcoholism or family exile, they all had to fork it over. Look at the price they paid. Look at the price Matthew has paid. Maybe his is a sordid story, but a lot of them are."

Now thirty-four years old, Knights has every bit the ability and opportunity today to become successful in music as he had in 1985. Certainly he is no teen idol, but there are plenty of musicians older than Matthew who are just beginning to see some popular recognition. Knights' failure ever to connect on a national level may also work to his advantage: his name is virtually unknown outside of North and South Carolina, so, as far as club owners and record buyers in other parts of the country know, Matthew is a new artist.

In addition, the national music scene could be infinitely more accepting of Knights than Spartanburg has been. No one at Polygram Records or MTV thinks twice about an artist's past drug habits or questionable decision-making: just ask Eric Clapton, Bob Dylan, Bonnie Raitt or the people who market the music of the late Kurt Cobain.

So the question is not whether Knights could make it out of Spartanburg, it's whether he will. "I feel like

I could've done better," he says. "I could've been on the radio and sold records and all that. Timing has a lot to do with it, and me fucking up has a good bit to do with it, too. A lot of it's my fault, and I've accepted the blame for the whole thing. I think my karma was pretty bad a lot of the way. I guess you end up learning how to be good to other people and to yourself."

"Like Dick Hodgin said, Matthew has been his own worst enemy," says David Ezell. "I think Matt can look at Aaron Whisnant and see how a young man who knows how to handle himself and take on a few compromises here and there to get to a bigger end can succeed. He's still viable as a performer and a songwriter. Through the years, Matthew and I have had a kind of love/hate relationship, but there has never been a lack of understanding on my part for Matthew's talent, or a lack of respect for him as a person. Matthew can still make it: he just needs someone who understands the business to help him along."

So the man who may be Spartanburg's greatest pure rock and roll songwriter waits for a new champion for his music—someone who can finance a demo tape, put together an information package, and get that package in the hands of the right people. "Without that, nothing's going to happen for me," Knights says. "I know I've got the songs, and

I'm still writing good ones. I'm ready to work as soon as somebody wants to help me.

"I used to know that I would be successful at music. I used to say that there was no way around it. Now, I ain't so damn sure. It's such a tough thing, and I've got a lot going against me. It just all depends."

Mark Olenckl

Matthew and the deconstruction of Spartanburg's Dawg Gone (1997)

ALBERT HILL

July 1996 - Nashville, Tennessee

Up to now, it's been aces for Albert Hill. Nashville's Javelina Studios, where the band is recording its debut CD for Universal Records, is a kind of high-tech fun house, complete with a snack room, microphones that cost more than the recording, duplication, and distribution costs of Albert Hill's first two self-released tapes, and an indoor basketball court where the band can blow off steam after a few hours of concentrated music making.

There have been no rookie jitters to this point, and very few rookie mistakes. The project's basic rhythm tracks, which can take weeks to perfect, were played and recorded in a speedy two days. The Big Time is turning out to be as good as advertised, with band members receiving salaries from the record company, plus a *per diem* for food and other living expenses. The five Albert Hillians are musically and financially comfortable, confident that the album that they are now recording will be the enabler through which their most outlandish rock and roll fantasies are made reality.

Suddenly, the bottom drops out of Albert Hill's fantasy world as drummer Kenny Hogan bursts into Javelina's control room.

"We've gotta move rooms!" he says.

"Who says?" asks producer/manager Paul Riddle.

"The hotel."

"Why on Earth would they say that?"

"Because the Doobie Brothers want our rooms!"

Riddle is immediately upset with this development.

Home base for Albert Hill in Nashville

The Doobie Brothers used to chase

Paul's Marshall Tucker Band up and down the Billboard pop charts during the 1970s, and now they have the nerve to chase Albert Hill out of its rooms.

"That pisses me off! We reserved those rooms!" he says.

The storm passes quickly. The Doobie Brothers never actually take Albert Hill's rooms. In a way this is too bad, because Kip, Albert Hill's assistant manager, has by that evening recorded a very funny outgoing message on the answering machine that was to be used by the veteran band. "This is the Doobie Brothers," the message said in part. "We're not here to take your call. We're out dancing, carousing . . . maybe even doing a little disco."

Spartanburg's Albert Hill is a semi-logical progression, the embodiment of the hope that there is an evolved possibility for the albatross that is "Modern Alternative Rock" music. "Alternative" rock is a term that was originally conceived as a means to describe bands such as The Silos, R.E.M., and Sonic Youth: bands that promoted themselves as a direct alternative to the finger-drumming boredom of mass-market rock and roll. By the 1992 release of Nirvana's enormously popular *Nevermind*, though, The Silos had broken up, R.E.M. and Sonic Youth had signed with major recording labels and made

lots of money, and the "alternative" was quickly becoming the mainstream.

Albert Hill's sound purposefully marries the tunefulness of pop music with the standard Alterna-instrumentation and attitude, then takes the whole thing to a different level by adding a sense of dynamic and rhythmic inventiveness and virtuosity that is sorely lacking on modern Alternative radio. Similarities to bands such as Live and The Gin Blossoms may make

Mark Olencki

Albert Hill palatable to the masses, but idiosyncratic instrumental and lyrical subtleties make them interesting to those who care to delve beyond image, strap on a pair of headphones, and listen.

Lead guitarist, lead singer, and chief songwriter Aaron Whisnant has been playing music since his father, a professor at Wofford College, gave then nine-year-old Aaron a $15 Sears guitar and two records by rockabilly guitarist Duanne Eddy. Three years later, Aaron was playing in bands that sounded nothing at all like Duanne Eddy. "My first band was h-h-horrible," he says. Whisnant teamed with bass player Chris Francisco while still in junior high, and the two drifted in and out of a number of forgettable bands through their early high-school years. When singer Robbie Bowen left a local band called Onyx, fifteen-year-old Aaron took his place. Bowen went on to sing for a band called Foxes Zero, a group that also included drummer Kenny Hogan.

Aaron Whisnant

"When Foxes Zero split and I left Onyx, I tried to get Kenny to play drums for this new band I was starting," says Whisnant.

Robbie Bowen remembers the circumstances behind Hogan's initial refusal. "Kenny said, and I quote, 'Aaron's a great guitar player and a great songwriter, but he's just not serious. Ever. I just can't play in a band with him, because he's always messing around.'"

Each future member of Albert Hill knew the others either from Spartanburg High School or from the local band scene. "All of us had played together in one form or another before Albert Hill," says Aaron. "We would run into each other a lot at Dawg

Gone or Delirious."

"Delirious was a bar across from Baskin Robbins on Pine Street," says Kenny. "I used to worship this band called Torn Lace. There was a guy named Ed Johnson who worked the door when Torn Lace played, and I was fourteen years old and wanted to get in: not to drink, just to watch the band. You were supposed to be eighteen to go in, but Ed would slip me in. I'd watch the band and think, 'I want to do *that*.'"

Like almost everyone who grows up in Spartanburg, Aaron, Robbie, and Kenny were aware of The Marshall Tucker Band. They do not, however, claim the Tuckers as an influence, pointing instead to local performers who played Spartanburg clubs in the late 1980s and early 1990s. "I used to go to Dawg Gone a lot when I was in high school and see Matthew Knights," says Whisnant. "And I idolized this band that would play at Dawg Gone called Depo Provera. Three or four years later, I was in a band with the lead singer from Depo. Then, he ended up taking my girlfriend. I've probably written forty songs about that experience.

"I wrote this one song called

'Wood Chipper.' It's about putting his body and her body together through a wood chipper. The whole verse is 'Wop bob bob baddada,' and it's supposed to be the sound of their bodies going through the wood chipper. It's a horrible, horrible song."

"That guy had a rapping style kind of like the Red Hot Chili Peppers," says Bowen. "So when he's going through the wood chipper in the song it sounds just like him rapping: 'Wop bob bob baddada!'"

"Actually," says Aaron, "that breakup was the best thing that ever happened. If that hadn't happened then I wouldn't have met my current girlfriend and I wouldn't have written the Albert Hill songs that will be on this record."

Following high school, Whisnant went on to study audio engineering at

"Current girlfriend" Mary Aldrich (1996)

Mark Olencki

Spartanburg Technical College and opened a small recording studio in his home. He also worked during that time as a soundman at Dawg Gone.

It was at the Dawg that he met back up with Kenny Hogan.

"That was in May of 1994," says Hogan. "I was at the Dawg, and it was Jam Night (a weekly rock and roll open stage). He was running sound that night. He and Chris Francisco were in a different band, and their drummer had just gotten another job somewhere. Aaron's band was real heavy, real loud, and he told me that he wanted to do some songs that were more pop-oriented, that wouldn't fit in with the band he was playing with then. I think Aaron and Chris had been trying for a long time to find some people to play with. Aaron and I knew each other from high school and we'd tried to play in a cover band together when we were in high school. We decided to get together again and see what happened.

"That Monday, he gave me a jam box tape of just guitar riffs. Those riffs turned out to be 'Knocks Down,' 'Dezeray's Hammer,' and three other songs that are going on the disc that we're recording now. We went over to Chris's house to rehearse, and in a week's time we had written seven songs that I thought were good."

The first version of Albert Hill was Whisnant, Francisco, Hogan, and guitarist Joel Cook. They quickly recorded a self-titled demo tape that Kenny took to his drum teacher at Smith Music, Paul Riddle. Paul had been out of the music industry for more than ten years when he heard the tape. "He played it and then played it again, lived with it for a couple of days, and then he said he wanted to get some opinions from the industry on it," says Kenny.

"I was blown away," says Riddle. "I couldn't believe how good the music was."

Riddle began working closely with the band, and Albert Hill worked numerous gigs at the downtown Magnolia's Pub in 1995. As a buzz developed around the band on a local level, Riddle was contacting some of the people he'd come to know back when he was drumming for The Marshall Tucker Band. "I thought about Buck Williams, who owns Progressive Global Agency and handles R.E.M. and did Marshall Tucker years ago," says Paul. "He likes alternative rock, and he's real open about music. I talked to him in Nashville and told him, 'I've got something I want you to hear. If you like it then we'll talk.' He called me back immediately and said, 'I love this.' I said, 'Let me take them back into the studio and we'll take these tracks that we had and do some new ones, mix it, and make a good demo CD.' That's exactly what we did."

That disc, called *Fistunderfinger*, was sold at the band's Magnolia's gigs, placed in local record stores, and sent to industry big-wigs. Says Paul Riddle, "I sent Buck the disc and he called me

from the airport and said, 'This stuff is so great it's ridiculous!' Buck doesn't usually get real excited about stuff, but he was excited about this. We were both excited.

"These guys play louder than Hell, and they're supposed to, but they're also real melodic and real

Albert
Hill

247

dynamic. They can really play. They do some odd-time things, but not to be cute, just because it fits the song. It's very complex, but they make it sound easy.

ALBERT HILL
FISTUNDERFINGER

Also, they're very coachable. With Aaron, I give him just a little idea and he blossoms. He'll not only give me the melody, he'll give me the counter-melody. The musical conversation can get real broad if you're dealing with great players, and that's what we're dealing with here. You start having all this interaction: you start hearing musical questions and answers."

Keyboardist Robbie Bowen was the last to join the band. "Aaron writes a lot of songs on piano," says Kenny Hogan, "and a lot of those songs sounded empty without a piano player. We all knew Robbie, and we knew he was a great singer, so he was the first person that came to mind."

With the band's sound filled out by the addition of Bowen on keys, Riddle

Mark Olencki

Robbie Bowen and guitarist
Joel Cook

and Williams showcased Albert Hill at Magnolia's. Representatives from record companies Universal, Warner Brothers, Mercury, and Sony were in attendance. "There was a lot of interest, but Universal banged

our door down from Day One," says Riddle. "Tom Lewis, their A&R head, has been to Spartanburg three times. He's been to my home and had burgers in the back yard with the band. When he came down the second time, he knew the lyrics better than Aaron. He just loved the stuff. I really leveled with him and said, 'Look, I want these guys to have a great career: don't handcuff us musically. Give me a great engineer, let me produce, and let us go to work.' That's basically what they did. Musically, they gave us free rein."

There are lots of CDs on the market, and only a small minority of them are making a profit. The ones that sell big, like Hootie and the Blowfish's *Cracked Rear View* or Alanis Morissette's *Jagged Little Pill*, make enough money to keep record companies well in the black, more than compensating for the majority of releases, the ones that fall squarely into the "failure" category. The money is made not by sustaining the careers of artists already signed to the label, but by introducing the "Next Big Thing." Hootie's unbelievable debut album sales and quick trip from beloved phenom to popular ridicule is a record company president's idea of the perfect project: build 'em up, clear 'em out, and get ready for the next ones.

Four self-described "regular guys" who attended school in Columbia, South Carolina, Hootie turned mediocre guitar rock into a brief national obsession. Music critics screamed and spat and bar-band veterans yelled, "I coulda done that!" through 1995 and much of 1996 as cash registers across the nation became bloated with greenbacks spent on *Cracked Rear View*.

Record companies began searching almost immediately for a new Hootie (Did anyone ever search for a new Hank Williams or a new Louis Armstrong?), and South Carolina pseudo-rockers such as Edwin McCain raised their hands to volunteer. Somewhere near the mid-point of Hootie-mania, the members of Albert Hill must have looked at one another and thought, "Should *we* do that?" Aaron Whisnant's voice is radio-ready, and the band's guitar-oriented sound is hooky and memorable. The only thing left to meet the requirements would be to dumb the mix down a little, take out some of the odd time signatures and remove any remaining lyrical ambiguities. For whatever reason, the moment of questioning passed quickly and Albert Hill continued playing its own music its own way.

By the summer of '96, Hootie was yesterday's fad (though the band's members were all millionaires), the groups that had made concessions to sound like the Blowfish were scrambling for a new direction, and an equally mediocre but doubly passion-

ate screecher named Alanis Morissette ruled the charts. Morissette's *Jagged Little Pill* became the top album of 1996, selling even more CDs than did *Cracked Rear View*. Ironically, the same fickle fans who had been attracted to Hootie's nice guy image now applauded Morissette's "honesty" in singing about the titillating what and where of her romantic exploits. Hootie's 1996 follow-up, the musically improved *Fairweather Johnson*, sold big for a couple of weeks and then tailed off dramatically.

The rock world of old supported lengthy careers for bands such as The Rolling Stones, Journey, The Doobie Brothers, The Allman Brothers, and The Marshall Tucker Band,

Albert
Hill

249

but the rock and roll landscape into which Albert Hill is seeking admittance is an ever-shifting terrain. One month, Hootie is hip. Three months later, Hootie is passé and Alanis is queen of the charts. Big money is now made or lost in a terrible hurry, and hit songs, not band names, sell records. As "here today, forgotten tomorrow" groups such as The Gin Blossoms and the Spin Doctors can attest, fan loyalty is *so* 1980s.

It is just this reality that Paul Riddle and Albert Hill seek to disrupt. "We don't want just a hit, we want a career," Riddle says. The band's members agree, citing The Dave Matthews Band as an example of an Alternative Rock group that built a large and loyal following before breaking a hit song, "What Would You Say?" on rock radio. After the hit's long commercial run was over, Dave Matthews still had a fan base that would support the band by buying records and concert tickets.

The success of Dave Matthews is very much in mind as Riddle and Buck Williams gauge the proper route to a lasting career for Albert Hill. Part of the master plan is to promote the

Paul T. Riddle   Mark Olencki

debut CD to college and Alternative radio before attempting to get airplay on mainstream pop stations. Riddle also wants to hold off on the release of potential monster hits such as the mid-tempo "Better Steak" until the public has heard at least two other songs from the album, songs that are more indicative of Albert Hill's faster, louder overall sound. "I wouldn't put out 'Better Steak' as the first single for anything in the world," he says. "That song might sell a million copies, but we don't want to set up the wrong image to the public. We want to come out with something that represents the band. They're young, they're rockers, they're energetic: that picture is what we want to show to people first. Then we can worry about the 'money' single. We want to build a career here, and we have to be very methodical and very patient."

It may be that Albert Hill's Spartanburg roots will become a selling point for the group. "It'll be interesting to see how the band's image shapes up as we go," says

Riddle. "I'm not trying to make these guys into the next Hootie. They like the fact that they're from South Carolina and that they're rockin' hard, no disrespect to Hootie. I hope that their being from Spartanburg will be something that we can let people in on. I'm a big fan of what's been going on in South Carolina and in Spartanburg, and it's time people knew. Musicians have known for years."

The rookies are at work. Paul Riddle, not the veteran drummer now but a virgin producer, sits at the mixing board. Aaron Whisnant, who is not a well-known local guitar hero but a complete unknown, sits next to Paul, playing a Gibson Les Paul guitar. Seeing a visitor in the doorway, Aaron smiles, nods, and says, "Come on in, have a seat. We're just fooling around."

They're not just fooling around. Aaron is in the middle of recording a lead guitar track as he speaks. Most people don't like to be interrupted while reading the newspaper or paying bills. Whisnant looks up from the fretboard and addresses his guest even while the tape is rolling on what is either to be a path-

way to rock and roll stardom or a bargain-bin reminder of the fleeting nature of life's possibilities.

Javelina Studio is extremely large, and most people who record here (the list includes Elvis Presley, Chet Atkins, and even Spartanburg's Marshall Chapman) like to set up on the main room's hardwood floor, put on headphones through which each musician can adjust the mix of sounds to his or her own liking, and let 'er rip. Likewise, most producers and engineers prefer to sit together in the glassed-off comfort of the control room, without the presence of musi-

Mark Olencki

cians. Asked why he's playing guitar leads in the control room, Aaron says, "It's way too loud out there."

"Yeah, those guitar amps in the main room are louder than God," explains Paul. "We've got a cable plugged into Aaron's guitar that runs under the control room door and out to the speaker stack. You can stand out there and hear for yourself, but I wouldn't advise it."

Just then, Kenny Hogan enters the back door that leads from the parking lot to the main floor of the studio. "Watch this," says Aaron, as Kenny walks the hardwood toward the control room.

With that, Aaron speaks into the electronic "pick-up" situated under the strings of his guitar. He says, "Kenny, Kenny," but guitar pick-ups are not made to reproduce the human voice. The sound that screams from the amplifier sounds more like "Krucknef, Krucknef." Kenny jumps into the air, clamps his hands over his ears, and screams, "Don't do that!"

The reason for the inhuman volume coming from the amplifier is that a guitar sounds differently played wide-open (at maximum loudness) than played at mid-level. Just in front of the speaker stack is a $100 Shure SM-57 microphone. A couple of feet behind it is what's called a "tube" microphone worth in excess of $3,000. The incredible noise generated by the amps is picked up by the two mics,

passed through the mixing board, blended by engineer Chuck Ainley, and recorded on a reel-to-reel tape deck. Later, various effects (reverb, echo, compression, etc.) will be added to the recorded sound during the "mixdown" stage of the process, which will take place at nearby Starstruck Studios.

As Whisnant records his guitar solos, the comparisons that Paul Riddle makes between Aaron and The Marshall Tucker Band's Toy Caldwell begin to make sense. Caldwell, like Whisnant, was his band's chief songwriter, lead guitarist, and musical leader. Aaron's bandmates also seem to hold him in the kind of awe in which Riddle held Toy. "Aaron walks on stage and it's like *Instant Star*," says Kenny. "He's really a kind of musical genius. It just comes out of him and it's great. This is a band, though. Aaron writes most of the songs, and he comes into rehearsals with the framework, then we build the sound together."

"You know," says Paul Riddle, "the record company is concerned because Aaron isn't in the middle of the picture on the back cover of the CD; he's in the back of the shot. I told them, 'That's the way he likes it.' Aaron's the primary songwriter, he's the lead singer, and he's the lead guitar player, but this is the Albert Hill Band. Aaron and Chris went through a lot of people when they were trying to put the band together, so they know that this music works because of the combination of people who are playing it. Aaron is brilliant, but it takes a band to make these songs come alive."

August 1996 - Nashville, Tennessee

"Music Row" is a romantic name for a place that is quite devoid of romance. It's actually just a bunch of buildings located on 16th or 17th Avenue, about five minutes driving time from the downtown Ryman Auditorium, former home of the Grand Ole Opry.

It is late afternoon when two grunged-up kids riding mountain bikes come rolling down the alley that runs just behind the legendary RCA Studio B, where Elvis Presley cut "Heartbreak Hotel." The kids turn out to be Aaron Whisnant and Robbie Bowen, who are returning from the studio to their rooms at the now Doobie Brothers-less Spence Manor. For the past two months, Aaron and Robbie have cycled all over Nashville, to newsstands, dinners, recording sessions, and strip clubs. In a town whose biggest female star recently attempted to have a helicopter pad put on the roof of her recording studio so that she could come and go with minimum personal exertion, the Albert Hillians are unafraid

to pedal.

Reba McEntire's helicopter pad never materialized, but the building is otherwise totally state-of-the-art. Inside are two large recording studios, and Albert Hill has chosen to mix their CD in one of these. The Spartanburg quintet is the first act not named McEntire to use the glistening new studio called Starstruck. The notion of the bicycle-riding, baseball cap-wearing Albert Hill gang holing up in the cavernous-yet-pristine building they call "RebaWorld" is a bit hard to grasp, and Robbie says that he and Chris Francisco have already been tossed out

Mark Olencki

Robbie, Aaron, and Starstruck Studios (1996)

Inside, Star*struck* is like Star *Trek*. There are no window shades: instead, the push of a button activates L.E.D. circuits inside the glass that fog or defog the giant studio windows within a quarter-second. The automated recording console, a much more reasonable thing on which to spend money, is unmatched in this country. The main studio room is huge, and there is even a "drum porch" situated twenty feet up in the middle of the room (to give the drummer that top of the diving board feeling). Outside the building, life-sized bronzed horses—the millionaire's equivalent of pink flamingos—graze on the lawn and drink from a man-made creek.

Starstruck has none of the soulful vibes of Javelina, but they are no longer needed. The band is through tracking the music: it's all on tape now. The problem is deciding

of the building once.

"Chris and I tried to go in there last week," he says. "This is a couple of days before we were scheduled to go in there for the mixdown. We were still recording next door at Javelina, and we decided to go over and see the Starstruck building. They were conducting a big press tour, taking all these reporters through the new building. Chris and I went in the door and the guy who was leading the tour turned around, looked at us, pointed to the door and said, 'Guys? Uh uh!' He threw us out! I said, 'We'll see *you* next week, pal,' and we left. But now we're mixing our album in the same building where we were just thrown out."

what to do with it, how to mix the separate guitar, vocal, bass, keyboard, and drum tracks into something commercially and artistically viable. That task requires an acoustically perfect listening environment and high-tech equipment that will not add unwanted noise to the tracks.

Mark Olencki

Inside the studio, Chuck Ainley is working on the mix for "Better Steak," the song that Paul Riddle was so excited about before the project even began. Aaron and Robbie have cycled over to observe and put in their two cents. Ainley, who is regarded as one of the top five engineers in Nashville, plays portions of the song and then plays them again, changing a couple of reverb settings or shifting a fader up or down every few seconds. Ainley has left the verses of the song sounding fairly crisp, with the choruses sounding much richer, deeper, and more layered.

"Do you think it's a little effect-heavy on the chorus?" Aaron asks. Ainley grimaces a bit, then says, "Yeah, okay. I can change that."

Aaron's heavy involvement with the mixdown of the record is fairly unusual. Often the mixdown is considered the sole domain of

the engineer and the producer. In Nashville especially, artists are usually not in the studio during mixing. Whisnant has run his own recording studio for years, though, recording and mixing tapes not only for Albert Hill but also for a number of other local bands. He is fully aware of his rookie status, and takes care to remain polite and deferential when voicing his opinions, but he wants the finished product to sound something like the band sound that has rattled around his head since Albert Hill's inception.

When Ainley plays "Better Steak" all the way through, Aaron and Robbie visibly perk up. "Could you put it on the big speakers?" asks Whisnant.

To call them "the big speakers"

Record engineer Chuck Ainley (1996)

Mark Olencki

does not in any way do justice to the monstrous audio components that adorn the walls of the studio. They are the speaker version of monster-truck tires. Chuck runs the playback as Aaron has requested, sliding the volume faders way, way up. The room shakes with the song, and Whisnant and Bowen jump around in a silly, Beavis and Butthead meet John Travolta dance. Even as they mock their own handiwork, it is apparent just how excited the two are by this high-decibel proof that they have recorded an honest-to-God, big-budget rock and roll record. The merriment ends suddenly, however, as Chicago-style pizza is delivered.

Ainley is not pleased with the lunch set-up. "We need forks and knives for this pizza," he says to his assistant engineer. "It's too fat. You can't eat this with your hands."

"I eat it with my hands," says the slight apprentice.

"You eat that with your hands?" Chuck is incredulous. "You're an

animal."

As lunch draws to a close, Paul Riddle arrives at the studio, looking a little worse for the wear of his first major record production. He took the day off yesterday and listened to some pre-mixes for several of the album's songs. Paul appears somewhat pleased with the overall sound of the mixes, but he expresses concern with the snare drum sound on the songs. "The snare needs to be much more up-front in the mix," he says.

Ainley fiddles with the faders and plays "Better Steak" through the big speakers but with the volume turned appreciably down. Again, the snare is not mixed to Riddle's satisfaction. Chuck and Paul spend the next hour listening to the song, discussing the mix, and fiddling with the drum sound. The engineer is concerned that a loud snare sound will rob the song of its radio-ready sheen, while the producer (who, remember, is a drummer) wants the snare to be full of bite

and snarl. "I want it right there in the listener's lap," says Paul. The day draws to a close with the issue still not settled to anyone's satisfaction.

Albert Hill has only recently completed tracking, a process that did not prove as trouble free as had been originally hoped. "The vocals were real difficult for me," says Aaron. "Also, learning to put my ego in my pocket was tough. Chuck and Paul made us change things, and there were a few things they made me change that sort of hurt my feelings. That's what producers and engineers are for, though, and most of the time, three or four opinions are better than one."

"I've learned to say, 'I don't know everything,'" says Robbie Bowen. "I went into the studio the first day and I got real frustrated and real down. See, I've only been playing the keyboard for a short time. I'm really still learning to play, in a way. So Chuck and Paul might say, 'Try this,' and I didn't know how to do what they wanted. They'll change what you've got, take parts out, and tell you to add different things in places. It's hard to play that way, but I'm really happy with what I've got on tape now."

"The first day, it seemed like Chuck and I slapped Robbie's hand every time he turned around," says Riddle. "He went home, came back the next day, and it was the same

thing. Finally, at the end of the second day, we started getting things done and he started seeing how good it was going to sound. That's where the trust is built. The next morning, Robbie came in and said, 'You know, I go home every night and say, "Fuck Paul and Chuck! They don't know a damn thing!" Then I wake up in the morning and realize they were right.' Robbie said that right in front of all the people in the studio, and we all just fell out laughing.

"As it turned out, Robbie was really the Most Valuable Player for the sessions, 'cause that boy is a singing fool. He can sing harmony with Aaron note for note, and it's just uncanny. It sounds like Aaron singing with himself, but there's just a little difference in texture. Also, listen to the break-down on 'So The Row.' Robbie's playing piano almost like Miles Davis played the horn: it's so simple, but so *out*."

"It's not like Paul is some dictator," says Whisnant. "He's real supportive, and he looks out for how we're feeling as well as how we're playing. It's just that recording something like this is a lot different than recording a demo."

"I told the guys, 'I'm not going to be the most popular guy in town a lot,'" says Riddle. "I told them to please be patient with me, that it's not personal. I know from my experience with Marshall Tucker exactly how it feels to have something in your mind musically, to want to contribute something to a song, and then have a producer say, 'That's not gonna work. We can't use that.' It sounds almost silly, but it's not. Those things can be real painful."

Riddle points to the recording of "Better Steak" as one of the more difficult production decisions of the tracking sessions. "Joel Cook co-wrote that song with Aaron. In fact, I think Joel came up with the guitar riff that the whole song is based around. In recording the song, though, there is a guitar part that Joel normally plays on stage, but that Aaron had already played in the studio. Live, it needs the part doubled, but on record it doesn't."

Riddle ended up having to drop Cook's contribution to a song that never would have existed had Joel not developed the guitar riff around which the song is built. "I felt for Joel, and I wanted to make it right, and I wanted him to understand," says Paul. "I think he did. I know that the guys know that my heart's in the right place, and that I'd never do anything to hurt them."

A far brighter side to the sessions centered on meetings with three notable musicians. Bowen stood in line for hours at a Nashville bookstore to meet legendary country singer George Jones, and Whisnant was able to sit and talk music with guitarist Duanne Eddy, Aaron's first guitar influence. The most unlikely star-crossing,

though, was with Tiffany, the former teen queen of 1980s pop.

"I was riding my bike around, and I rode over to this newsstand," says Robbie. "I went in and started reading some magazines, and the guy behind the counter started up a conversation and asked what was going on. I told him that I was with a band that was down here recording. He said, 'I've got a friend, Tiffany. Remember Tiffany from the eighties?' I said, 'Yeah!' I played him some Albert Hill demos, and he seemed to like them, so I said, 'Man, why don't you bring Tiffany by the studio?' I thought it'd be a gas.

"So sure enough, that guy came by the studio and he brought Tiffany. There she was, right in front of us! And what was funny was that Kenny didn't figure out who she was until thirty minutes after she'd been there."

"I didn't know who it was, either," says Aaron. "We were all just going about our business. When Chuck and the assistant engineer found out, they were like, 'Gah, man, if I'd known, I would have been turning knobs and being cool.'"

The worst part of Albert Hill's Nashville experience seems to have revolved around the photo shoots for the album. "Having make-up put on you," says Bowen, "that's the worst."

"Yeah, it was horrible," says Aaron. "We had this lady come in and do up my hair. I looked like I was on

Saturday Night Fever."

"She'd do his hair and turn around, and Aaron would rub his hands through his hair to where it was all standing up," says Robbie.

"Towards the end, it'd be like *this*." Aaron holds up his hair in an approximation of Lyle Lovett. "I figured, if I'm gonna look ridiculous, I'm gonna look really ridiculous. She walks away and says, 'Aaron, what am I gonna do with you?' She started fixing it again and I went *'poot'* (makes sound as if passing gas). She walked off and let the smell wear down, and then came back and fixed it back."

"Yeah," Robbie says. "She was really lovin' us."

Aaron and Robbie are extraordinarily talented Generation Xers, but they are Generation Xers nonetheless, both drawn to and repelled by the forces of commercialism that shaped their teen years. It is fully in character for them to go on like this, making their unique kind of racket, fawning in the presence of bubblegum heroes and farting in the face of glamour.

September 1996 - Spartanburg

Paul Riddle holds a cassette tape labeled *Albert Hill Volume 1*. "This is it," he says. "This is what we did in Nashville."

When the bicycle rides, Doobie Brothers controversies, and snare drum discussions that took place in

Music City are forgotten, the thirteen songs on *Albert Hi'l Volume 1* will be the legacy of summer 1996 for Albert Hill. People in automobiles, living rooms, and libraries will be able to put those songs into a cassette or CD player, turn up the volume, sneer, grimace or smile, and say, "So *this* is what those boys were up to."

By September of 1997, Riddle will be a genius or a fool for thinking that he could go in with next to no previous production experience, and a greener-than-green bunch of kids, and come out with a career-starting record. As he now admits, "I was way out there on a skinny little limb. I was under the gun, because I hadn't produced anything at that level before."

Record production, while overlooked by most listeners, is a complex and often maddening experience. Separate musical parts can be recorded on hundreds of different instruments with hundreds of different microphones in hundreds of different placements at hundreds of different equalization and effects settings, then mixed in an unsettling number of ways. Each decision along the way can add or detract from the finished product. It's like piecing a jigsaw puzzle together, except the pieces interlock in millions of different ways and form an infinite number of finished pictures. You don't get to look at the box for a model, either: it was thrown out years ago.

"The whole experience in

Nashville was an incredible combination of emotions," says Riddle. "It was so easy, difficult, nerve-wracking, and relaxed. I had no idea what I had gone into spiritually when I started, but I can tell you now that it was somewhere that I needed to go."

Often, the spiritual place to which Paul traveled was Capricorn Studios in Macon, Georgia, almost twenty-five years ago when he and five other Spartanburg musicians made an album called *The Marshall Tucker Band*. It is an experience Riddle remembers vividly to this day, recalling especially the excitement that greeted the project, the feeling that what happened in that Georgia studio would change the lives of each person involved. Recording the Albert Hill project gave Riddle a chance to relive that time of innocence and expectation, and he's hardly to blame if he sought to project his emotions onto his young charges:

"I think I'm guilty of that," he says. "It's like you want your wife to feel what you feel sometimes. The trip up to Nashville, Kenny and I were listening to the original demo tapes, checking up on how far we've grown and talking about how much fun we were going to have recording. It took me back to the excitement of being at Capricorn for the first time. In that regard, it was very emotional. I probably wanted the Albert Hill guys to feel the way I was feeling: it just stirred

those emotions for me so much. I loved recording, and I want the guys to be excited about it, to make a great record, and to have a good time."

If the goals were to have a good time and to make a great record, then those goals were at times incompatible. Aaron Whisnant and Robbie Bowen spoke in Nashville about hurt feelings and bruised egos, and their experiences in those areas did not go unnoticed by Riddle. "It was hard for me to cause those things to happen, but I had to produce the band," he says.

Making Paul's job tougher was the fact that he not only produces the band, he is also their manager. "Whatever happens in the studio, we still have to work together," he says. "Other producers can just get on a plane, go back to Los Angeles and never have to see the band again if they don't want to. With this band, we *all* come home to Spartanburg. That can be a very big positive, but it can also make things difficult."

The actual playing and record-

ing of musical parts—the tracking—was the easiest part of Riddle's production job, and he proved adept at altering normal studio procedures when necessary. "I knew that getting Aaron's vocals was going to be a little different," he says. "Aaron wouldn't sing in front of anyone but me and Mark (the assistant engineer). We sent Chuck Ainley home, and put up baffles in front of and in back of Aaron. We had a lamp in there, too. I said to Aaron, 'Listen, we've done this on *Fistunderfinger*, and it's gonna be fun this time, too.'"

The most difficult choices were made during mixdown at Starstruck. Most vocal and instrumental levels were easy to set, but the problem was Kenny's snare drum. Paul wanted it up in the mix, and Chuck Ainley wanted it down. "That situation got a little testy," says Riddle, in an uncharacteristic understatement.

Though it came close to an impasse, the snare drum controversy finally worked itself out. Riddle held a private meeting with the band in which the mixdown problems were discussed, along with the various

Mark Olencki

solutions to those problems (including demanding that the snare level be raised, leaving the snare low in the mix, or leaving Tennessee and flying to Los Angeles to mix the record with another engineer). "I also reminded them in that meeting of Chuck's situation," Paul says. "He was trying to mix the best record he could—that's what we hired him for—and he's a *very* well-respected engineer." At the very time that the band meeting was taking place, Ainley was re-thinking his position. "The next day," says Paul, "Chuck came in and said, 'You know, I heard it in the car and I think I can turn the snare drum up.'"

Only a minimal proportion of the hopefully hundreds of thousands of people who hear *Albert Hill Volume 1* will think for even a split second

Kenny Hogan

Mark Olencki

about the prominence of the snare drum attack in the musical mix, yet the Nashville recording sessions nearly ground to a halt over just that problem. Music is not a universal language; it is a highly subjective experience that is different for every person who hears it or takes a part in its making. Riddle's strong stand over what many producers and musicians would consider a small matter is an indicator of just how importantly he views the notion of artistic autonomy for Albert Hill and of how hard he is willing to fight for that autonomy. A musician such as Marshall Chapman, who today considers her 1978 sophomore album virtually unlistenable because of the producer-inflicted drum sounds, would certainly understand. There are

places for compromise—photo shoots, Monday morning newspaper interviews, and backstage meet-and-greets —but Albert Hill is a young band whose musical output is willfully of their own making.

Asked whether he is happy about the finished album, Paul is quick to answer. "Absolutely," he says. "I think we got exactly what we wanted to get. I'm also real pleased by the way Aaron plays guitar on this record. That was one of my goals going into the studio: to get Aaron to really show what he can do on guitar. And, whether he likes it or not, Aaron plays a lot of guitar licks that are just Southern. He can't help it, 'cause he's heard it all his life. You can't grow up in Spartanburg and not be affected by that Southern music."

In autumn of 1996, the band released a self-titled five-song EP/CD featuring home studio recordings of four songs on *Albert Hill Volume 1* plus a song called "Cisco Kid." The EP is financially backed by Universal, produced by Aaron Whisnant and mixed in part by Universal's head of A&R, Tom Lewis, but it is distributed by Chicago's tiny Fuse Records. "That EP is really just about business," says Riddle. "It was done in the bedroom, and it's not supposed to sound like a finished record. It's just to create momentum and get us in some markets where we haven't been heard before.

"You have to remember that no

one knows who we are. We're really just getting started, and this EP is a tool to give clubs or get played on college radio stations. This is something we can use to build momentum for when the real record comes out. There's no huge promotional push by Universal on the EP, and that's where we had to be careful. If it was on Universal and it didn't sell but a few copies, it would look bad. So this will be in stores, and it will be distributed through Fuse, and it will be out of the way by the time the real record is released. This is just like Dave Matthews did. That's a real good example, and you better bet your butt that was very carefully planned out."

Planning things out is how Riddle spends most of his time in the interim between the finishing and release of *Volume 1.* "Today, a Saturday in late September, I need to talk to Tom Lewis, the head of A&R, I need to talk to the head of marketing, I need to talk to Buck Williams at the talent agency, and I have to talk to the band's attorney about some things

Mark Olencki

that have happened in the past two days. Buck and I talk daily, and often several times a day. I talk to Tom Durr, head of marketing, at least once a day."

Riddle is still teaching drum lessons at Smith Music, though the lessons are often interrupted by the aforementioned business conversations. "It's a daily struggle to keep up with all of this, and it really takes up every spare moment I have. I'm learning about merchandising, budgeting for tours, and a whole lot of other stuff. My main job is keeping everything cool for the band. I want them to be able to just walk on stage and play music. It's difficult for them now. They've been good sports, but it's hard to go out and open in clubs for no money."

To expand its fan base outside of South Carolina, Albert Hill has been playing regional clubs, usually opening shows for bands such as Spider Monkey and Jump, Little Children.

It's a "take the music directly to the people" concept that is decidedly unglamorous and often unprofitable, but the group is slowly making a name for itself outside of Spartanburg. "I feel good about the way things are shaping up," says Paul. "We just have to be patient. It's a lot like when Marshall Tucker was starting out. I can see that Kenny is going to end up playing a role similar to what Tommy Caldwell played with the Tuckers: he's going to be the unspoken leader and the mediator.

Chris Francisco   Mark Olencki

"You know what Kenny asks when he gets home from these little tours? My phone rings and he wants to know when he can come take a drum lesson. I love that. To me, that pretty well sums it up. It's not, 'I just signed a big ol' record deal,' it's 'When can I take a drum lesson?' We've got a lot of integrity in this crowd. These are good boys."

And so the story either ends happily or it doesn't. "Better Steak" will hit or miss, and Albert Hill will be famous or forgotten or stuck in the murky in-between. Five young musicians from Spartanburg are about to slam head-first into a corporate record industry that is concerned not with Albert Hill's integrity or Southern

influences or snare drum sound or even musical virtuosity. Universal Records wants Albert Hill to make it in a musical climate where less than one percent of all acts that released albums in 1995 were able to sell over 250,000 copies of their product. Only one of ten record projects actually turns a profit. In order to make a real impact, music and image must be packaged together into something that masses of people will feel compelled to purchase.

"I don't even know how to define the group's image," says Paul. "They are what they are. Marshall Tucker was what we were—we just went out every night and played music we liked. There's that parallel again. These guys don't think about how it looks or even what it is: they just do what they do.

"I'm proud of them," Riddle says, considering for a moment exactly what it is that his band is up against. "I feel like they've got a shot." MM

Mark Olencki

Mark Olencki

16 EPILOGUE

When I began writing *Hub City Music Makers*, I set out to learn why this Piedmont mill town has produced such a staggering array of musical talent. More than a year later, I'm still puzzled. The *who*, *what*, *when*, and *where* of Spartanburg popular music are covered within these pages in some depth. The *why* remains a mystery.

There are good reasons why music is an important part of life in Spartanburg: the front-porch society prevalent in the mill villages lends itself to playing and singing; the city's location in a spot where highways and railways converge brings outside influences and personalities into the city; the upper class's acceptance and financial support of classical music adds a dose of culture; and the success of earlier generations of musicians is inspirational to younger players. These factors make it more likely for Spartanburg to produce musicians of conse-

quence, but not this many. (There are circumstances that make pregnancy a likely occurrence, but no sane obstetrician goes around predicting quintuplets for couples who conceive under those conditions).

Writer/producer Jim Rooney called attention to Spartanburg's unusual output of music makers in his role as master of ceremonies at the tribute concert to Walter Hyatt that took place at Nashville's Ryman Auditorium in June 1996. Calling Hub City native Marshall Chapman up on stage to be part of a show that had already featured Spartans Champ Hood and David Ball, Rooney said, "I don't know what it is about that town . . . must be something in the water." The comment was made in jest, but it may have contained more truth than Rooney would have known. Irene Hicks, an eighty-one-year-old retiree from Clifton Mill #1, reports that she and other workers in the mill's spinning room witnessed an eight-year-old Hank Garland out the workroom window stripping naked and diving off a bridge into the waters of the Pacolet River.

There are a number of cities—Nashville, Austin, New York, Los Angeles, and Detroit among them—to which top singers and players are drawn, and Spartanburg's most exemplary musicians have often found it necessary to migrate to one of these music industry centers in order to forge a career, expand an audience, or make a record. Spartanburg is different: musicians aren't drawn to this place, they are made in this place. For the Hub City music makers, Spartanburg is, as Walter Hyatt and I surmised one spring day over a long lunch, both a cradle and a trampoline.

ACKNOWLEDGMENTS

Peter Cooper extends thanks to: my family for their love and encouragement; Charlotte At The Beep for time and understanding, transcription help, and all the other stuff; friends Baker Maultsby, Mike Shapiro, Scott Martin, and Harris King; Gene, Barbara, Lewis, and Russ at Horizon Records (Greenville's one-stop store for Spartanburg music); Dean Dan and Kit Maultsby for dinners, ball games, pillows, and other kindnesses small and large; Kathy and John at The Handlebar; Anna Ballard for research assistance and general good humor; Eric Taylor, Jim Lauderdale, and Jason Ringenberg, fine artists and finer people; Norman Love and Larry Turner; the dynamic duo of Pat Jones and Debbie Knebel; Rick Lee; Mike Johnson; Chip Smith; Steve Stinson; Steve Clark; Allen McDavid Stoddard; John Wilson; Gary Henderson; Frye Gaillard, who showed me how it should be done; Jerry Zolton; Kristi York, Gina Webb, Danielle Truscott and the lovely and talented Frank Rabey for running my articles; my pals at Sullivan and at Irmo Middle, students past and present; George and Tammy Hyatt for mint tea, spaghetti, insight, laughter, and song; Ashley Fly for flashlights upside the head; Harrison Kisner for finding Alvin; Joe McConnell; Don McGraw for the tapes; Tim at Papa Jazz; Deno Trakas for teaching me to write, John Bullard, John Cobb, and Beth Ely for reading the final text; all those who set aside time to be interviewed for this book; the musicians of Spartanburg.

Words won't begin to express sufficient appreciation to Hub City editors Betsy Teter and John Lane and book designer/photographer Mark Olencki. A tip of the hat to David Ezell, who has made invaluable contributions to this project through his roles as informant, sounding board, inspiration, and friend.

The Hub City Writers Project wishes to thank Doyle Boggs at Wofford College; Beth Broadwell, our Pagemaker guru; Charlotte Huskey at the Spartanburg County Historical Association; Steve Parris and Jim Harrison at Converse College; Nancy Dickson at WSPA; the *Spartanburg Herald-Journal*; George McCorkle; Paul T. Riddle; Albert Hill; Andre Kerr; Matthew Knights; Ace Rickenbacker; Daryle Ryce; Joe Bennett; Marshall Chapman; Fats Kaplin; Trix Records; the Hyatt family; the Hood family; Don Bramblett; Fayssoux McLean; Kenny Gates; Bob Beatty; Ross Holmes; Dorothy Chapman; the Inman-Riverdale Foundation; Lloyd Yearwood; Christian Steiner; Steve Canaday; Fabry of Nashville; Edward Silverman; the Arts Partnership of Greater Spartanburg;

the late Alfred Willis; John Gillespie; Steve Rey; Karen Huff; Erick P. Byrd; Les Duggins; Rick Back; Greg Savalin; Jim Knox; and Thomas McCarver.

A hoist of the fork goes out to Ike's Korner Grill, the Nu-Way Lounge, and The Skillet for good food, good drink, and meeting spots. All are Spartanburg traditions with decades of service. Two notes of lost traditions: Joe Wynn of Smokey Joe's Bar-B-Q, who knew that barbecue is not just a sauce but a way of cooking, and The Piedmont Steak House (1918-1997), former site of the legendary jelly omelet and the Elvis chair.

Every effort has been made to trace the copyright holders of visual material and we apologize in advance for any unintentional omissions. We would be pleased to insert the appropriate acknowledgment in any subsequent edition of this publication.

Publication of *Hub City Music Makers* has been made possible through the generous contributions of the following:

The Arts Partnership of Greater Spartanburg
The Inman-Riverdale Foundation

Ms. Anne Bain
Mr. and Mrs. William Ball
Ms. Anna Ballard
Mr. and Mrs. Bill Barnet
The Beacon
Mr. and Mrs. Vic Bilanchone
Mr. and Mrs. Glen B. Boggs II
Mr. H. Leland Bomar
Ms. Susan Bridges
Capital Ideas Advertising & Public Relations
Mrs. Lou Cecil
Ms. Marshall Chapman
Mr. and Mrs. Arthur Cleveland
Mr. John Wiley Cooper
Mr. and Mrs. Wiley Cooper
Mr. and Mrs. Duncan Ely
Express Music
First South Bank
Mr. David Forrester
Mr. and Mrs. Sam Galloway
Mrs. Jeri Greene
Mr. and Mrs. Ralph Hilsman
Mr. and Mrs. John Bell Hines
Mrs. Ruth S. Hughes
Mr. Vince Hughes
Ms. Wallace E. Johnson

Dr. and Mrs. Julian Josey
Mr. Charles W. Jones
Mr. John Lane
Mr. and Mrs. Paul Lehner
Mr. Norman Love
Mrs. Billie McConnell
Mr. and Mrs. Les McMillan
Mr. and Mrs. E. Lewis Miller
Ms. Edna Morris
Olencki Graphics, Inc.
Mr. and Mrs. Stephen Parks
Mr. and Mrs. Dwight Patterson Jr.
Dr. Michael Patton
Ms. Cindy A. Pugh
Pulliam Investment Co.
Ms. Karen Randall
Mr. and Mrs. Jon Emmett Shuler
Mrs. Pamela Smuzynski
Spartanburg Dance Theatre (1980)
Mr. Chris Story
Ms. Betsy Teter
Mr. Larry Turner
Mrs. Sarah Miller van Rens
Mr. and Mrs. Jay Wakefield
Wofford College
Mr. and Mrs. Donald Yates

Publication of this book is supported in part by the Arts Partnership of Greater Spartanburg, the Spartanburg Friends of the Arts and other private donors, the South Carolina Arts Commission, the National Endowment for the Arts, and the City and County of Spartanburg.

All the proceeds from the sale of this book go to the Hub City Fund of the Spartanburg County Foundation.

T he Hub City Writers Project is a diverse group of local authors whose purpose is to foster community and awareness through the literary arts. Our metaphor of organization purposefully looks backward toward the nineteenth century when Spartanburg was known as the "hub city," a place where railroads converged and departed.

As we approach the twenty-first century, Spartanburg is fast becoming the literary hub of South Carolina with an active and nationally celebrated core group of poets, fiction writers and essayists. We celebrate these writers—and the ones yet born—as one of our community's greatest assets. William R. Ferris, director of the Center for the Study of Southern Culture, says of the emerging South, "Our culture is our greatest resource. We can shape an economic base . . . And it won't be an investment that will disappear."

Mark Olencki

A graduate of Wofford College in Spartanburg, South Carolina, Peter Cooper is a freelance music writer whose articles appear in such publications as *Creative Loafing*, *Mountain Xpress*, and *The State* newspaper. He currently resides in Rock Hill, South Carolina, where he teaches school and lives with his guitar, his computer, his fax machine, and his CD collection. This is his first book.

Cook, mulcher, good neighbor, connoisseur of brew pubs, Lyle Lovett and B-grade science fiction thrillers, Mark Olencki is also a graduate of Wofford College. He and his wife, Diana, have one son, Weston. They are residents of the downtown Hampton Heights neighborhood. Mark has exhibited his photography in competitions and shows throughout the Southeast. His photographs are included in

Diana Olencki

the permanent collection of the State of South Carolina, the Spartanburg County Museum, and the private collections of many businesses and individuals. He is president of Olencki Graphics inc., a photo/graphics design firm in Spartanburg.

Colophon

Hub City Music Makers was designed
using Adobe® PageMaker® 5.0a on a "well-seasoned"
Power Macintosh® 7100/80 packing quad drives (totaling
4.3 gigs of storage), 132 meg of ram, a Polariod SprintScan
35 Plus®, an HP ScanJet IIcx®, and various peripheral devices
in a first edition of 5000 soft-bound and a limited edition
of 150 case-bound copies. The display typefaces are Birch,
Schmutz ICG Clean and Corroded. The body typefaces are
all members of the Italian Garamond family. This book is a
dual 750ml Cragganmore® and Glenkinchie® production
with a little help from Guinness®.